Hypnotic Relaxation Therapy

Gary R. Elkins, PhD, ABPP, ABPH, is a professor and director of the doctoral program in clinical psychology at Baylor University, Department of Psychology and Neuroscience. He is also the director of the Mind–Body Medicine Research Laboratory at Baylor University, where he leads a team of postdoctoral fellows, graduate and undergraduate students, and clinical research staff. Dr. Elkins also serves as an adjunct professor of psychiatry and behavioral science in the Texas A&M University College of Medicine. In addition, he maintains a private practice in the areas of clinical health psychology, hypnotic relaxation therapy, and cognitive–behavioral psychotherapy

Dr. Elkins has served as vice-chair of the Texas State Board of Examiners of Psychologists, as well as president of the American Society of Clinical Hypnosis, president of the American Board of Psychological Hypnosis, vice-chair of the Council of Representatives of the International Society of Hypnosis, and chair of the Fellows Committee of the Society for Psychological Hypnosis. Dr. Elkins is also a fellow of the American Psychological Association.

Dr. Elkins's areas of research are hypnotic relaxation therapy in the treatment of hot flashes, psycho-oncology, pain management, and mind–body interventions in behavioral medicine. He has presented over 100 workshops in clinical hypnotherapy nationally and internationally, has over 60 publications in the area of hypnosis and psychotherapy, and is the co-author of the groundbreaking publication, *Standards of Training in Clinical Hypnosis*, which has set the standard for professional education in clinical hypnosis.

Dr. Elkins has received numerous honors including: the Morton Prince Award from the American Board of Psychological Hypnosis, the Presidential Award from the American Board of Psychological Hypnosis, the Excellence in Teaching Award from the Department of Psychiatry and Behavioral Sciences at Texas A&M University College of Medicine, the Presidential Citation Award from the Texas Psychological Association for public service, and an Award of Merit from the American Society of Clinical Hypnosis. In 2012 he received the complementary and alternative medicine research investigator award from the Society of Behavioral Medicine.

Dr. Elkins earned his doctoral degree from Texas A&M University and served his clinical internship at Wilford Hall USAF Medical Center in San Antonio. He holds board certification in Clinical Health Psychology from the American Board of Professional Psychology and diplomate status from the American Board of Psychological Hypnosis.

Hypnotic Relaxation Therapy

Principles and Applications

Gary Elkins, PhD, ABPP, ABPH

SPRINGER PUBLISHING COMPANY
NEW YORK

Springer Publishing Company, LLC

11 West 42nd Street
New York, NY 10036
www.springerpub.com

Acquisitions Editor: Stephanie Drew
Production Editor: Michael O'Connor
Composition: S4Carlisle Publishing Services

ISBN: 978-0-8261-9939-3
e-book ISBN: 978-0-8261-9941-6

13 14 15 16 17 / 5 4 3 2 1

The author and the publisher of this Work have made every effort to use sources believed to be reliable to provide information that is accurate and compatible with the standards generally accepted at the time of publication. The author and publisher shall not be liable for any special, consequential, or exemplary damages resulting, in whole or in part, from the readers' use of, or reliance on, the information contained in this book. The publisher has no responsibility for the persistence or accuracy of URLs for external or third-party Internet websites referred to in this publication and does not guarantee that any content on such websites is, or will remain, accurate or appropriate.

Library of Congress Cataloging-in-Publication Data

Elkins, Gary Ray, 1952-
Hypnotic relaxation therapy : principles and applications / Gary Elkins.
p. ; cm.
Includes bibliographical references and index.
ISBN-13: 978-0-8261-9939-3 — ISBN-10: 0-8261-9939-9 — ISBN-13: 978-0-8261-9941-6 (e-book)
I. Title.
[DNLM: 1. Hypnosis—methods. 2. Relaxation Therapy—methods. WM 415]
RC497
615.8'512—dc23 2013008751

Printed in the United States of America by Courier Printing.

To my lovely wife, Guillerma Gamez Elkins, for her unending love and encouragement that have given me the support needed to write this book. It is as much her work as mine that made this possible.

Contents

Foreword Cassie Kendrick, PsyD *ix*

Preface *xiii*

Acknowledgments *xvii*

1. **Historical Foundations** ***1***
2. **Principles of Hypnotic Relaxation Therapy** ***7***
3. **Theoretical Basis for Hypnotic Relaxation Therapy** ***17***
4. **Hypnotic Induction and Formulation of Suggestions** ***27***
5. **Case Conceptualization and Treatment Planning** ***47***
6. **The First Hypnotic Relaxation Therapy Session** ***57***
7. **The Second Hypnotic Relaxation Therapy Session** ***67***
8. **The Third Hypnotic Relaxation Therapy Session** ***77***
9. **Session Four and Beyond** ***87***
10. **Assessment of Hypnotizability** ***99***

11. Dealing With Resistance *125*

12. Refining Hypnotic Inductions and Interventions *137*

13. Pain Management *147*

14. Smoking Cessation *161*

15. Post-Menopausal and Hot Flash Symptoms *169*

16. Anxiety Management *183*

17. Insomnia *195*

18. Hypnotic Relaxation Therapy to Facilitate Insight *205*

19. Ethical Considerations in the Practice of Hypnotic Relaxation Therapy *221*

Appendix: Hypnotherapy and Hypnotic Relaxation Therapy: What You Need to Know 227

References 231

Index 245

Foreword

When my mentor—and the author of this text—Dr. Gary Elkins, initially approached me about writing the foreword to this book, I wondered why he would ask me, a mere postdoctoral fellow with absolutely no name recognition, to take on such a task. It seemed obvious that he would ask another renowned scholar, clinician, or "big name" in the field, rather than a recent doctoral graduate. But, as I read the text, I began to understand his purpose. He knew the journey I had recently traversed to learn hypnosis. He knew how I had struggled, as a beginner, to incorporate hypnotic relaxation therapy into my work with patients. In other words, he knew that I would fully understand the value of the text before you.

While I am one of the fortunate few who received individual supervision and instruction from one of the field's most prominent scholars and clinical practitioners, the path I journeyed to learn hypnotherapy was by no means easy, and understandably so. Though I studied with one of the greats, hypnotherapy involves much more than can be communicated through weekly, individual instruction, even from the most skilled of teachers. So, my journey, much like that of others before me, involved piecing together a hodgepodge of personal instruction, clinical and research work, and virtual mountains of reading in a somewhat disorganized, haphazard, and often confusing manner. I knew that hypnotherapy was a powerful addition to my therapist's toolbox, and I knew I wanted to learn the skillful art of its effective delivery. But, like many others beginning their journey, I often found myself feeling lost and drowning in a sea of information meant for practitioners who were well beyond my skill level. Like others trying to incorporate hypnotherapy into their practice, I found myself struggling with the question, "Where do I begin?" This book provides that answer.

What you hold in your hand is a manual designed to guide psychological and medical professionals in the process of integrating hypnotherapy into their professional practice. While a number of such books have been written, the distinctive features of this text set it apart as most desirable for practicing clinicians. In this foreword, I highlight the unique features of the book that I—keeping in mind the labor of my own learning experience in its beginning, and considering it now that I am more developed but still have ample room to grow—find most valuable.

When I initially set out on my journey to learn hypnotherapy, and began the long process of amassing articles, studies, clinical descriptions, and research on hypnosis and its applications, I longed for a framework in which I could encapsulate my newly found knowledge. Chapter 2 does exactly that, and imparts the basic principles of hypnotic relaxation therapy. This book offers the first complete presentation of these fundamentals in a manner that is not only supported by empirical research, but is also consistent with the author's 30 years of experience as a clinical practitioner. This section provides a detailed description of the foundations of hypnotherapy and its incorporation into clinical practice.

Once I had a few successful clinical cases under my belt, I became anxious to use hypnotherapy with other patients who I was confident could benefit from the therapy. However, I struggled to understand how to adapt what I had learned to the nuances of each new case. I wondered, "Is it okay if I . . . ?" Like any other practitioner new to a therapy or treatment, I was eager to use my new skill, but I didn't want to mess up what I knew could be a profound experience for my patients. This text offers the guidance that I sought, and continue to seek, when working with new cases. In contrast to a "one-size-fits-all approach," this book provides specific, easy-to-follow guidelines for developing hypnotic suggestions in a flexible manner that will enable the clinician to effectively address individual patients' unique needs.

Additionally, this text lays out clear guidelines for case conceptualization, how to assess hypnotizability, and presents the concepts of hypnotic relaxation therapy in a session-by-session approach that professionals will find especially useful when wondering, "Well, the last session went really well, but where do I go from there?" Further, case examples and transcripts of specific hypnotic inductions drawn from the author's wealth of clinical and research experience will provide the clinician with clear illustrations of how to effectively integrate hypnotherapy into his or her practice. These features give the reader a bird's-eye view into actual sessions with a master in the field. Thus, practitioners learning to use or refining their skills in hypnotherapy don't have to wonder, "Am I doing this right?"

Practitioners, students, and clinicians will want to have a copy of this comprehensive book, not only to use as a training manual, but also to have as a "go-to guide" to troubleshoot typical problems. For example, the entirety of Chapter 11 is devoted to dealing with resistance. In reading the chapter, I found myself remembering my work with specific clients, wishing I had the book in hand when I questioned how to handle tough cases, and thinking about how the specific skills in the text would be helpful in my clinical work now. The thoughtful details laid out in this chapter will provide clinicians with a better understanding of resistance, its precipitants, and factors involving its maintenance, and they will gain the skills to assess and manage resistance and craft hypnotic suggestions accordingly. As practitioners develop the ability to effectively provide hypnotic relaxation therapy, they will find themselves returning to this book time and time again when asking, "But what do I do when . . .?"

Finally, this book presents foundational principles of how to address common problems such as chronic pain, anxiety, insomnia, and hot flashes, and clinicians searching for an effective and safe way to address these issues will find the practical guidance of these chapters indispensible. The complete, well-thought-out guides to treating these common disorders will lead the clinician through each step of the entire treatment process, from assessment and case conceptualization to completion of the hypnotic induction. The transcripts and case examples in each chapter provide clear illustrations of how to apply the techniques presented. This is the type of reference guide clinicians seek out when learning or honing their skills in a therapy. It is the reference guide I wish had existed just a few short years ago. Though Dr. Elkins does not suggest this text be used as the authoritative end for persons seeking to learn hypnotherapy, but rightfully recommends additional training and mentorship, the clinician who utilizes this text will find growing confidence in his or her ability to successfully incorporate hypnotherapy into everyday practice.

Dr. Elkins brings to this book his extensive experience in research, teaching, and professional practice with scholars and practitioners in psychology and medicine. The breadth and depth of his professional experience make him uniquely equipped to train the novice and skilled practitioner alike. His deep understanding of hypnotherapy and its applications are clearly reflected in this text, and clinicians will find this easy-to-use manual a welcome companion in their quest to develop new skills in hypnothearpy.

Cassie Kendrick, PsyD
Postdoctoral Fellow in Clinical Health Psychology
Mind–Body Medicine Research Laboratory
Baylor University

Preface

This book is a basic training manual for the practice of hypnotic relaxation therapy (HRT). While hypnotherapy in various forms has existed for many years, it is only more recently that clinical research has begun to provide greater clarity on the effectiveness of hypnotic interventions in clinical practice. I have identified the term "hypnotic relaxation therapy (HRT)" to signify the particular theoretical basis for hypnotherapy that will be presented in this book, and to emphasize the use of hypnosis within an evidence-based approach to professional practice. In this book the terms "hypnotic relaxation therapy" or HRT and "hypnotherapy" will be used interchangeably with the explanation that HRT represents an integration of hypnosis and a cognitive–behavioral approach to treatment.

Hypnosis has a wide range of applications in psychotherapy and medicine. In spite of this, hypnosis is presently underutilized. This may be due, in part, to misconceptions about hypnosis or lack of training in current hypnotherapy methods. Perhaps an even greater reason is that training and approaches to hypnosis have varied a great deal and there is a lack of consensus on what "hypnosis" involves as a therapy. In teaching numerous workshops, I have been impressed with the need for a well-grounded clinical conceptualization and a systematic approach so that professionals can learn to provide hypnotherapy in a consistent manner.

This book begins with the principles of HRT, and the theoretical basis for conceptualizing this approach to hypnotherapy is introduced. The process for structuring sessions, treatment planning, assessment of hypnotic ability, dealing with resistance, and applications of hypnosis are also discussed. The basics of how to provide hypnotic relaxation therapy in clinical practice are illustrated throughout the book and various applications are presented. Transcripts of interactions in presenting HRT and interventions are described and provide guidance for wording of hypnotic relaxation therapy interventions.

A basic assumption of HRT is that individual differences in hypnotic abilities exist. There is a wealth of research to support this contention and this book introduces a new instrument to assess hypnotizability in the clinical context, the Elkins Hypnotizabilty Scale (EHS). The EHS was developed for ease of administration, time efficiency, and clinical relevance. The normative, reliability, and validity data on the instrument are presented along with scoring criteria and information.

In the second part of the book, some of the most relevant applications of HRT are presented. While the applications of hypnotherapy are quite varied, I discuss HRT in the treatment of pain, anxiety, insomnia, hot flashes, smoking cessation, and facilitating insight because these are among the most recognized applications.

This book has several unique features:

1. It is the first presentation of the principles of HRT.
2. It presents a new theoretical conceptualization for HRT and hypnosis. This is the first book to integrate cognitive–experiential self theory with understanding the process of HRT and intervention.
3. It provides guidelines for case conceptualization of HRT as either a primary or adjunctive intervention.
4. A new scale to measure hypnotizability, or a person's ability to experience a hypnotic trance, is introduced. The clinical utility of assessment of hypnotizability is explained as a component of case conceptualizations.
5. A session-by-session approach to HRT is presented that will lend itself to future clinical research and will be useful in patient care.
6. Guidelines for formulating hypnotic suggestions are described within a flexible approach to achieve individualization of hypnotic interventions.
7. Case examples drawn from the author's 30 years of experience as a clinician, researcher, and professor at a major university are presented. The book provides transcripts of hypnotic relaxation interventions and explanations of how to integrate HRT with other interventions.
8. It is the first book presentation of the author's extensive research into HRT as an effective, nonhormonal intervention for hot flashes among breast cancer survivors and postmenopausal women.
9. It provides a brochure for use in educating patients about hypnotic relaxation therapy.
10. The book is designed to be utilized as a reference guide and much-needed training manual for clinicians interested in hypnotic relaxation therapy.

HOW TO USE THIS BOOK

Hypnotic Relaxation Therapy: Principles and Applications is designed to provide foundational knowledge, clear guidance, and clinical examples of sufficient detail to enable readers to use HRT in their practice. It is recommended that this book be read initially through in its entirety, in order to best follow the guiding principles and theoretical foundations of clinical interventions. The book is also designed to serve as a reference for the practicing clinician. Guidance and transcripts for completing hypnotic inductions to achieve relaxation and goal-directed suggestions are provided. The use of standard inductions with individualization can be very beneficial for many patients. In later chapters, guidance on treatment of specific disorders is provided. The clinician should become skillful in completing hypnotic inductions and individualizing hypnotic suggestions before moving on to developing these more specialized skills.

The clinician should also become familiar with the principles of HRT and its theoretical basis as outlined in Chapter 3. Guidelines for hypnotic inductions and formulation of hypnotic suggestions are provided in Chapter 4. These guidelines should be frequently referenced until the clinician can identify how to develop hypnotic relaxation–based suggestions that are consistent with the laws and principles of hypnotic suggestion.

The book also outlines the content of HRT interventions on a session-by-session basis. Transcripts of hypnotic relaxation inductions should be utilized in a flexible manner that considers patients' individual differences and preferences. Skill in providing HRT is developed through practice. It is recommended that readers identify a mentor to review their hypnotic inductions and give feedback on their style and understanding of HRT. This book also provides some resources that may be beneficial in the practice of HRT, including a discussion of ethics and an informational handout for patients.

In addition, the reader will learn how to assess hypnotizability with the EHS. Assessment of hypnotizability is an excellent way to develop skills in hypnotic induction and to learn about hypnotic responses. Conducting at least 12 competent administrations of the EHS is necessary to become minimally skilled.

Additionally, this book provides the essentials for application of HRT in treatment of particular issues such as chronic pain, smoking, hot flashes, anxiety, insomnia, and facilitating insight. The clinician should strive to become familiar with both the broader literature in each area as well as the methods and applications of HRT. In this regard, the careful assessment of patients and problem areas is discussed in Chapter 5. Assessment and case formulation are essential in treatment planning that integrates HRT. The clinician should use this book as a frequent reference for assessment and treatment planning, as well as a resource for skill development.

HRT is an evidence-based approach that integrates existing knowledge of research with respect for each patient's values, religious beliefs, world views, goals, and preferences for treatment. These are very important considerations to keep in mind, as each patient is unique. I believe that the integration of research with a deep respect of the individual ultimately results in the best professional practice of hypnotherapy. The goals of relieving suffering and promoting health are best served when research, ethics, and professional skills are well integrated.

Acknowledgments

I have been blessed with the finest colleagues, mentors, students, and friends that I could ever imagine, all of whom directly or indirectly helped me in writing this book. In fact, it would be impossible to write a book of this kind without the dedicated help of others and the existence of foundational theories, research, and practice methods developed over time.

First, I wish to express my thanks to the many colleagues that have all taught me a great deal about hypnotherapy. I am grateful for the previous work by several outstanding clinicians, in particular Dr. Harold Crasilneck, who taught me the basics of hypnotherapy and the many uses of hypnotic relaxation intervention. Harold was a great mentor and friend.

I am also especially grateful for Dr. Seymour Epstein, for his teaching and guidance regarding cognitive–experiential self theory and his many discoveries regarding the process of personality and the functioning of the unconscious mind. In addition, I wish to thank the researchers who have brought the study of hypnosis into modern science, in particular, Dr. Ernest Hilgard, who established the hypnosis research laboratory at Stanford University, and whose research advanced the understanding of hypnotizability and hypnotic phenomena.

In the Mind–Body Medicine Research Laboratory I have been privileged to work with and teach the finest students and postdoctoral fellows in the country, including: Cassie Kendrick, PsyD, Lauren Koep, PsyD, Ashley Gartner, PsyD, Jeff Bates, MD, Jacqueline Dove, PhD, Jennifer Bunn, PhD, Aimee Johnson, MA, William Fisher, MA, Jim Slwinski, MA, Kimberly Hickman, BA, Amelia Yu, BA, Derek Ramsey, BA, Nik Olendski, BA, Juliette Bowers, MA, and Xuan-Shi Lim, MSCP.

I have been blessed with a dedicated staff that includes Vicki Patterson, BA, and Cassie Kendrick, PsyD, to whom I am eternally grateful for their many readings, suggestions, and numerous edits to this work. In addition, I am especially grateful for two past postdoctoral fellows who contributed to this work: Joel Marcus, PsyD, who is now director of psychosocial oncology at Oschner Clinic in New Orleans, LA, and Michelle Perfect, PhD, now an assistant professor at the University of Arizona, Tucson, AZ.

I am deeply grateful to Stephanie Drew and Kathryn Corasaniti, of Springer Publishing, for believing in me and for their invaluable advice and guidance in preparation of this manuscript.

Finally, I want to thank my patients, who have taught me so much over the years. Working with patients is essential to developing skill in providing hypnotic relaxation therapy.

Gary Elkins, PhD, ABPP, ABPH

CHAPTER 1

Historical Foundations

Methods associated with hypnotic relaxation such as focusing one's attention, mental imagery, and suggestions for physical and emotional relaxation and health and healing have been practiced for hundreds, perhaps thousands, of years. Musês (1972) identified that hypnosis-like sessions may have been practiced over 3,000 years ago in ancient Egypt during the reign of Ramses XII. Also, MacHovec (1979) found that hypnotic methods were likely used more than a thousand years ago in the "sleep temples" of ancient Greece. Certainly, the methods of hypnotic suggestion, relaxation, and mental imagery existed long before the word hypnosis *came into being.*

In this chapter, the history of hypnosis will be reviewed. This is an important starting place because knowledge of hypnosis's historical foundations is essential to understanding the development of hypnotic relaxation therapy (HRT). In addition, knowledge of the history of hypnosis is very beneficial for understanding the origins of myths and misconceptions about hypnosis.

Knowledge of the history of hypnosis is very beneficial for understanding the origins of myths and misconceptions about hypnosis.

MESMERISM

The history of modern hypnosis began with Franz Anton Mesmer (1734–1815). Mesmer was an Austrian physician who practiced in Vienna and later in Paris. His work, beginning in the late 18th century, introduced the terms *animal magnetism* and *mesmerism*. Mesmer passed magnets over his patients while providing suggestions for healing their ailments, but he later found the magnets were unnecessary to achieve the desired results. After moving to Paris in 1778, his methods became controversial and King Louis XVI of France commissioned Benjamin Franklin and others to investigate his practices. The Franklin Commission conducted a number of tests and concluded that the therapeutic effects of mesmerism were in fact due to "imagination, imitation, and touch" and that there was no such thing as the purported animal magnetism. As a result, Mesmer and his practice were discredited (McConkey & Perry, 2002; Forrest, 1999) and moved to obscurity.

EARLY HISTORICAL EVENTS IN THE DEVELOPMENT OF HYPNOTIC INTERVENTIONS

As a result of Mesmerism being discredited, the ancient methods associated with relaxation, mental imagery, and suggestions were largely abandoned by the medical community until the early 1800s. It was during this period that a Scottish physician, James Braid (1785–1860), began using methods in which patients were instructed in eye fixation techniques to achieve a trance state. He initially thought the process was similar to sleep, and he coined the term *hypnotism* from the Greek word for sleep. However, he later realized that, during hypnosis, the patient was not asleep, and he began to favor the term *monoideism* to note the concentrated attention and prolonged absorption that were involved in the hypnotic process (Spiegel, Greenleaf, & Spiegel, 2000). During the 19th century, the English physician James Esdaile (1808–1859) performed over 100 surgical procedures using hypnosis as the sole anesthesia while on assignment in India. Later, as chloroform became available, the use of hypnosis during surgery became rare.

During the 19th century, the English physician James Esdaile (1808–1859) performed over 100 surgical procedures using hypnosis as the sole anesthesia while on assignment in India.

In France, hypnosis was increasingly used by the neurologist Jean Martin Charcot (1825–1893) to treat patients with hysterical disorders. Charcot believed that hypnosis was related to hysteria and had a neurological basis. Around the same time, Ambroise-Auguste Liebeault (1823–1904) and Hippolyte Bernheim (1837–1919) published research on their work using hypnosis with medical and psychiatric patients. In contrast to Charcot's pathological/neurological theories of hypnosis, they emphasized psychological factors, such as suggestibility, as the underlying mechanisms of therapeutic effects. Sigmund Freud studied with both Charcot and Liebeault, and before developing his theories of psychoanalysis, practiced hypnosis. In 1880, Freud collaborated with Josef Breuer (1842–1925) in the famous case of Anna O. In this case, hypnosis was used for direct symptom removal and to explore underlying unconscious issues. At the time, it was assumed that memories recovered during hypnosis could be resolved through abreaction, the expression and emotional discharge of unconscious ideas, which provided a cathartic release of pent-up emotions.

Sigmund Freud, before developing his theories of psychoanalysis, practiced hypnosis.

Interest in hypnosis began to decline as Freud went on to develop his theories of psychoanalysis and technique of free association. However, in later years, Freud appeared to show greater acknowledgment of the benefits of hypnosis as he spoke of the need to blend "the pure gold of analysis plentifully with the copper of direct suggestion" (Jones, 1959). A contemporary of Freud's, Pierre Janet (1859–1947), developed additional theories that emphasized dissociation as a primary psychological defense and mechanism of hypnosis. However, following Charcot's death in 1893, the scientific study of hypnosis declined.

Later, hypnosis was used in pain relief and in the treatment of traumatic stress during World Wars I and II; however, research continued to be limited during this time. An exception was the work of Clark L. Hull (1884–1952), who began research into hypnosis and investigated the role of hypnotizability.

RISE OF THE SCIENTIFIC STUDY OF HYPNOSIS

Following World War II, interest in research and the clinical applications of hypnosis grew. In 1949, the Society for Clinical and Experimental Hypnosis was founded in the United States. The American Society of Clinical Hypnosis was founded in 1957, and in 1959, the International Society of Hypnosis was established with affiliates around the world. Additionally, in 1969, the American Psychological Association (APA) formed a division of Psychological Hypnosis (now called the Society for Psychological Hypnosis [SPH], Division 30 of the APA).

> In the 1950s, the development of the Laboratory of Hypnosis Research by Ernest Hilgard (1904–2001) at Stanford University was particularly instrumental in transforming research in the field of hypnosis.

Along with these developments, hypnosis increasingly became a subject of rigorous research. In the 1950s, the development of the Laboratory of Hypnosis Research by Ernest Hilgard (1904–2001) at Stanford University was particularly instrumental in transforming research in the field of hypnosis. Significantly, Hilgard and his colleague, Andre Weitzenhoffer (1921–2004), contended that, in order to fully evaluate its therapeutic value, there must be a standard measure of hypnosis. As a result, the Stanford laboratory not only focused on understanding hypnosis, but also sought to create a standardized instrument for assessment of hypnotizability (Hilgard, 1979). This work resulted in the development of the Stanford Hypnotic Susceptibility Scales (SHSS; Weitzenhoffer & Hilgard, 1959).

> The introduction of the Stanford Scales to measure hypnotic susceptibility and the increasing scientific rigor in clinical studies marked the beginning of a new era in the advancement of understanding hypnosis in health care.

In 1959, Martin Orne (1927–2000) established the Hypnosis Research Project at the Massachusetts Mental Health Center, and in 1964, he moved his laboratory, The Unit for Experimental Psychiatry, to the University of Pennsylvania. Like the researchers at the Stanford lab, Orne and his colleagues acknowledged the importance of measuring hypnotizability in conducting research and in evaluating the therapeutic value of hypnosis. The development of the SHSS provided a reliable and valid measure of hypnotizability and a means to advance the empirical evaluation of hypnotic responsiveness (Morgan, Johnson, & Hilgard, 1974). Further, the advent of the SHSS was important because it finally afforded investigators the means to empirically investigate variability related to individual responsiveness in the clinical use of hypnosis (Butler et al., 2009). The introduction of the SHSS to measure hypnotic susceptibility and the increasing scientific rigor in clinical studies marked the beginning of a new era in the advancement of understanding hypnosis in health care.

MILTON ERICKSON AND INDIVIDUALIZED APPROACHES

Erickson emphasized that hypnotic suggestions are likely to be most effective when taking into account the patient's unique preferences, interests, and motivations.

While Hilgard and others focused on scientific investigation of hypnosis, interest in the clinical applications of hypnosis grew as well. Milton Erickson (1901–1980) was a psychiatrist and leading practitioner of clinical hypnosis. He was a founding member of the American Society for Clinical Hypnosis and served as the society's first president. Erickson became known for his innovative and artistic uses of hypnotic phenomena in psychotherapy. During his lifetime, he published over 100 articles and developed a number of induction and clinical methods, including the use of indirect and permissive suggestions and metaphors. His approach was characterized by an emphasis on individualizing interventions to the needs of each patient and creatively interweaving direct and indirect suggestions, metaphors, and informal hypnotic inductions (Erickson, Rossi, and Rossi, 1976; Haley, 1973; Erickson, 1977a, b). Erickson emphasized that hypnotic suggestions are likely to be most effective when taking into account the patient's unique preferences, interests, and motivations (Erickson, 1977b). His creativity and innovations, which continue to influence the field, established that hypnotic suggestions may be delivered in a variety of ways.

Hammond (1983) identified a number of myths about Erickson and "Ericksonian Hypnosis," such as the idea that indirect and permissive suggestions are in some way superior to direct suggestions. While this is a common myth, it has been established that some individuals respond better to direct suggestions and some better to indirectly worded suggestions (Alman, 1983; McConkey, 1984). For an extensive bibliography of Erickson's publications on hypnosis, see Gravitz and Gravitz, 1977.

INTEGRATION OF CLINICAL RESEARCH AND HYPNOTHERAPY

During the latter half of the 20th century and leading up to the present time, there has been an increasing amount of empirical research to test the effectiveness of hypnotic interventions. This new development in the history of hypnosis represents a unique integration of clinical research in the area of hypnotherapy. Although details of hypnotic procedures and suggestions differ depending on the goals of the intervention or the research endeavor, most contemporary hypnosis research involves suggestions for relaxation, mental imagery, and hypnotic phenomena. The evolving research literature on clinical hypnosis includes randomized clinical trials as well as single group designs and case studies. The quality of these studies supports the use of hypnosis in the treatment of a wide variety of psychological and medical disorders. In 1996, the National Institutes of Health (NIH) released a report from a study panel that recognized hypnosis and mind–body interventions that use relaxation as having significant benefit in the treatment of chronic pain, insomnia, and other disorders.

In 1996, the National Institutes of Health released a report from a study panel that recognized hypnosis and mind–body interventions that use relaxation as having significant benefit in the treatment of chronic pain, insomnia, and other disorders.

The vast majority of empirical studies involve the application of hypnotic relaxation-based inductions in combination with suggestions for mental imagery and symptom reduction. Hypnotic relaxation inductions and suggestions have been used extensively in the reduction of anxiety and in the treatment of stress-related problems because hypnotherapy often involves suggestions for relaxation and increased control (Barabasz & Watkins, 2005). In addition to experiencing hypnosis within a therapeutic relationship, patients are usually taught self-hypnosis in order to better manage symptoms that may be related to stress.

In addition to stress-related conditions, hypnosis has a broad range of other applications as well. Studies have documented the use of hypnosis for general pain management (Brown & Hammond, 2007; Hawkins, 2001; Montgomery, DuHamel, & Redd, 2000), which includes: (a) decreasing the intensity of pain; (b) reducing suffering from pain and pain-related negative affect; (c) decreasing use of pain medications; and (d) improving recovery from pain-related procedures (Montgomery, David, Winkel, Silverstein & Bovbjerg, 2002; Patterson and Ptacek, 1997). Hypnotic relaxation-based interventions have also been studied in cancer-related pain (Elkins, Cheung, Marcus, Palamara & Rajab, 2004; Neron & Stephenson, 2007), tension and migraine headaches (Olness, MacDonald, & Uden, 1987), labor length and labor pain (Brown & Hammond, 2007), and procedural pain and anxiety (Elkins et al., 2006; Enqvist, Bjorklund, Engman, & Jakobsson, 1997). Recent comprehensive reviews (Patterson & Jenson, 2003; Elkins, Jensen, & Patterson, 2007) have found that hypnosis

Patients are usually taught self-hypnosis in order to manage symptoms that may be related to stress, but hypnosis has found a broad range of other applications as well.

Hypnosis has also been used with favorable results in the treatment of several mental health conditions, including chronic depressive syndromes and post-traumatic stress disorder.

can provide a significant analgesic effect for many types of pain and meets the criteria for "well-established treatments." In these studies, hypnotic relaxation-based interventions for pain relief were found to be superior to placebos for both acute and chronic pain.

Further, hypnotic relaxation and suggestion has been used in the treatment of gastroenterological disorders such as irritable bowel syndrome (Galovski & Blanchard, 1998; Palsson, Turner, & Whitehead, 2006; Prior, Colgan, & Whorwell, 1990), as well as vasomotor events (e.g., hot flashes; Elkins et al., 2008), and dermatological disorders (Spanos, Stenstrom, & Johnson, 1988; Spanos, Williams, & Gwynn, 1990), Moreover, hypnosis may moderate the effects of stress on immunity (Keicolt-Glaser, Marucha, Atkinson, & Glaser, 2001). It has also been used with favorable results in the treatment of several mental health conditions, including chronic depressive syndromes and post-traumatic stress disorder (Bryant, Creamer, O'Donnell, Silove, & McFarlane, 2008; Gruzelier, 2006).

This trend toward clinical research is likely to continue as the most effective components of hypnotherapy and its applications become better known and there is greater acknowledgment of hypnotic relaxation interventions. The emphasis on research is directed toward influencing the practice of hypnotherapy based upon empirical findings. The concept that high-quality clinical research can contribute to best practices in hypnosis is likely to have the positive effect of expanding knowledge and improving clinical practice.

CHAPTER 2

Principles of Hypnotic Relaxation Therapy

The accumulated historical evidence supporting hypnosis provides validation for relaxation-based hypnotic interventions. In fact, most empirical research studies of hypnosis have utilized relaxation induction and suggestions. The term hypnotic relaxation therapy *(HRT), rather than the term* hypnosis, *more accurately describes the approach used in clinical practice and research. It is relatively free from the negative historical connotations of the term* hypnosis, *and also maintains a distinction from other forms of the word, which may suggest some form of entertainment, such as a magic show. I have found that some patients prefer the term* hypnotic relaxation therapy *because they feel it is more descriptive of the actual intervention.*

In the practice of HRT, it is recognized that individual differences in hypnotic ability exist, and these differences should be viewed as an important consideration in treatment.

In the practice of HRT, it is recognized that individual differences in hypnotic ability exist, and these differences should be viewed as an important consideration in treatment. The process of HRT has several characteristics, beginning with a hypnotic induction for relaxation (phenomenological and physical). Suggestions are given for deepening the hypnotic state, during which the patient may achieve deeper relaxation and involvement in imaginative experiences. Once the hypnotic state, or trance, is achieved, appropriate hypnotic suggestions are given within a cooperative therapeutic relationship between therapist and patient. Therapeutic suggestions are generally presented in a positive manner aimed toward achieving the patient's goals (Crasilneck & Hall, 1985). Response to hypnotic suggestion is characterized by a shift in consciousness, such that the subconscious mind is more available while the conscious mind is distracted or dissociated, to some degree, from the control of behavior.

The patient experiences a sense of involuntariness or effortlessness in responding to hypnotic suggestions. Patients can also be taught self-hypnosis (Lynn, Kirsch, & Rhue, 1996) in order to achieve greater control and symptom relief. Patients who have a higher degree of hypnotizability may benefit more quickly or achieve more control of symptoms (Hilgard & Hilgard, 1975); however, even patients in the lower range of hypnotizability may be able to achieve considerable gains with appropriate intervention.

Therapeutic suggestions are generally presented in a positive manner toward achieving the patient's goals.

In this chapter, the principles of HRT are introduced and described. The methods described here are based upon many years of clinical work with hypnosis as well as the increasing body of empirical research on the application of hypnosis in therapy. The principles of HRT are illustrated through a single case example of "Linda," a 38-year-old Caucasian woman, who was referred by her family physician for treatment of anxiety and stress-related tension headaches. Organic causes of her headaches were ruled out through a neurological consultation, and hypnotherapy was recommended. Linda was a very good candidate for HRT because she was in the mid-range of hypnotizability, she was motivated for treatment, and she had some insight into the relationship between stress and her symptoms before she began hypnotherapy. She had not had any previous experience with HRT, but she was open to a mind–body intervention.

PRINCIPLES OF HRT

Principle #1: HRT is most effective within a positive therapeutic relationship

It is essential that a positive, trusting relationship be established between the therapist and patient before proceeding with a hypnotic induction. Without trust, the effectiveness of hypnotherapy is limited, and if a relationship of trust is not established, the patient may experience resistance, have difficulty achieving a trance state, have a negative experience with the process, or experience only limited benefit. Trust is particularly important because, during an induction, the patient is asked to set aside critical judgment, accept hypnotic suggestions uncritically, and respond without conscious interference.

In Linda's case, the therapeutic relationship was established by first providing attentive listening and seeking to understand her perception of her symptoms. Any misconceptions about HRT were discussed, and she

During an induction the patient is asked to set aside critical judgment, accept hypnotic suggestions uncritically, and respond without conscious interference.

was given an opportunity to ask questions. The process of hypnotic induction was described, and the therapist was careful to ensure that Linda's questions were answered and the process was well-described and acceptable to her.

If questions or hesitancy remain once the relationship is established, it may be better to delay the hypnotic induction until the patient is reassured and feels positive about the intervention. Rushing into the first hypnotic induction, without attending to the therapeutic relationship, can result in a less-than-optimal experience for the patient and negatively affect the process of HRT.

Principle #2: HRT is directed toward empowering the patient

The goal of HRT is to provide the patient with both relief and a greater sense of symptom control. In the initial session, patients experience response to hypnotic suggestions and learn how to make hypnotic relaxation work best for them. The patient's experience with HRT provides increasing confidence that symptoms can improve with experience and practice. With Linda, this involved teaching her self-hypnosis to reduce the stress and tension that were associated with her headaches. During hypnosis sessions she was able to experience a calm and relaxed state, and her headaches were virtually eliminated during the hypnotic state. Linda was given a CD recording of a HRT session so that she would be able to practice the therapy at home. Daily practice was recommended, and, as with many patients, Linda found the practice to be both pleasant and empowering. She was learning how to use hypnosis on her own. In later sessions, Linda was given specific instructions on how to practice self-hypnosis without relying on the CD recording. These instructions were written out and she was given the opportunity to practice during the session. Linda was not only learning how to gain greater control of her headaches; she was also learning hypnotic relaxation, a method that she could use to manage stress and sleep better, as well as in other situations.

> Patient's experience with the use of HRT gives them increasing confidence that symptoms can improve with experience and practice.

Principle #3: HRT recognizes that there are individual differences in hypnotizability

Hypnotizability refers to the degree to which an individual has the ability to experience a response to hypnotic suggestion. It is possible to identify a person's hypnotic ability as being in the low, moderate, high, or very high range. For example, easy hypnotic suggestions (such as instructions to close your eyes) do not require a high degree of hypnotic ability, while response to more difficult suggestions (such as being able to hallucinate "seeing" an object during a hypnotic induction) may only be within the ability of the highly hypnotizable. At the heart of the hypnotic experience is dissociation

(Orne, 1959; Bowers, 1976; Frankel, 1976; Hilgard, 1986; Hilgard & Hilgard, 1983)—the ability to achieve a split in consciousness so that response to hypnotic suggestion is involuntarily experienced and more difficult suggestions can be achieved. Therefore, the term a *trance* or *hypnotic state* during HRT refers to a degree of therapeutic dissociation. Dissociation occurs on a continuum rather than in a dichotomous manner; therefore, the higher the hypnotizability, the greater the individual's ability to achieve a psychological dissociation or trance state. About 10% of the adult population is highly hypnotizable (Hilgard, 1965), and a slightly lower percentage is in the low range. Most of us are in the midrange of hypnotizability. Additionally, research has demonstrated that hypnotizability is a relatively stable trait that can be accurately measured over time. In one study, the correlation between baseline and reassessment of hypnotizability over a 20-year period was found to be .71 (Piccione, Hilgard, & Zimbardo, 1989). Recognizing that people vary in their hypnotic abilities can give useful information to the therapist in determining how to best work with an individual in providing hypnotherapy.

The higher the hypnotizability, the greater the individual's ability to achieve a psychological dissociation or trance state.

There are a number of scales that have been developed to measure hypnotizability (Weitzenhoffer & Hilgard, 1959; Weitzenhoffer & Hilgard, 1962; Weitzenhoffer & Hilgard 1963; Morgan & Hilgard, 1978–1979). Each has advantages and disadvantages in regard to the time involved and structure of the scales. The *Elkins Hypnotizability Scale* (EHS), which is presented in detail in Chapter 10, was developed during research with clinical populations. This measure is a brief assessment (about 20 minutes) that provides a range of scores from 0 to 12 and can be administered at any time during the course of HRT. Linda obtained a score of 8, indicating that she was in the moderate (mid) range of hypnotizability and had at least a moderate ability to experience dissociation. This bolstered confidence that, in the absence of resistance, she would be able to benefit from hypnotherapy within a relatively brief period of time and that she could likely achieve a sufficient depth of hypnotic experience.

Principle #4: HRT assumes all communication is processed, to varying degrees, within both conscious and unconscious awareness

Humans have a divided mind that involves both conscious and unconscious processing of information (Epstein, 1994). During everyday waking consciousness, information is processed by a hierarchy of cognitive operations both within, and outside of, conscious awareness (Hilgard, 1974; Hilgard, 1977). During normal, alert wakefulness, these processes are relatively well integrated, and our experience and awareness is primarily directed by the conscious mind. This has several implications for the practice of hypnotherapy. First, it is understood that the unconscious mind is processing information even during the awake, alert state. Hypnotherapy involves therapeutic communication, and that communication occurs on multiple levels of awareness. Therefore, the therapist should be mindful of *all* communication, not just that which takes place during a hypnotic induction. The unconscious mind operates in regard to feelings, impressions, and beliefs that may, or may not, be consistent with that of the conscious mind. Second, as previously noted, a hypnotic induction is directed toward achieving a shift in consciousness such that the subconscious mind is more available to respond to suggestion. During a hypnotic induction, suggestions are given for the patient to "let go" of conscious effort and allow the unconscious mind to respond. As the patient becomes absorbed in his internal world and achieves dissociation, it becomes possible to allow the unconscious mind to respond.

Hypnotherapy involves therapeutic communication and that communication occurs on multiple levels of awareness.

During the first session, the therapist sought to foster positive expectancy for Linda's experience of HRT. Further, the process of a hypnotic induction was explained: "The hypnotic state involves a process of letting go—letting go of conscious effort, letting go of resistance, and letting go of defenses. During hypnosis, there is nothing you have to do and nothing you have to try to do consciously. Just allow yourself to become absorbed in your own experience and allow your unconscious mind to respond to the suggestions. The deeper the relaxation, the better the response you will be able to achieve."

Principle #5: HRT sessions are goal directed

HRT and hypnotic suggestions are most effective when directed toward a specific goal. Specific suggestions can have specific effects. For example, if the goal is for the patient to experience feelings of coolness (as would be the case in treatment of post-menopausal hot flashes), then images of walking down a mountain path on a cool or snowy day may be most effective. On the other hand, if the goal is for the patient to experience warmth in her back (as might be the case in treatment of chronic back pain), then images of sitting before a warm fireplace might be most appropriate. This requires planning on the part of the therapist so that the intervention is consistent with both the goal for the session and for the overall therapy. This gives a focus to hypnotherapy sessions and defines when the therapy goals have been accomplished. In Linda's case, the overall goal was for her to achieve control and relief of her headaches. However, the goal of the initial session was for her to gain experience with hypnotic relaxation. She came for her first hypnotherapy session while experiencing a headache after a stressful day. The therapist set the goal for the session by asking, "Would it be alright with you if you were to be able to reduce the headache during today's session? Would it be acceptable to experience a cool, calm feeling across your forehead as the pain becomes less and less?" Her positive answers to these questions set the goal for her session and established specific hypnotic suggestions for her treatment. By the

Hypnotic suggestions are most effective when directed toward a specific goal.

third session Linda had already gained some insight into her headaches and had begun practicing hypnotic relaxation with the CD.

Principle #6: HRT uses a biopsychosocial formulation in treatment planning

In planning hypnotherapy, it is important to consider the whole person: physical and medical history, psychological factors, and social environment. It is helpful to conduct a detailed history and construct a list of problems and strengths. It is also important to identify an accurate diagnosis. If the diagnosis is wrong or neglected, then the treatment may be wrong as well. Before beginning hypnotherapy with Linda, a diagnostic interview was completed. This included a review of the history of her headaches, past medical or psychiatric treatment, current medications, social and family history, and mental status examination. She had diagnoses of tension headaches and depression. Linda's strengths included her level of insight, intelligence, and hypnotizability. Primary problems included her work environment and tendency to experience pain during times of stress. While the depth of the diagnostic interview can vary depending on the patient's complaint, it is crucial to understand the patient's symptoms within the context of his or her environment and history.

It is crucial to understand the patient's symptoms within the context of his or her environment and history.

Principle # 7: HRT is integrative

HRT may be utilized as either the primary treatment modality or as an adjunctive therapy. It is most often integrated with cognitive–behavioral interventions, and evidence-based interventions are preferred. For example, in the treatment of a patient with social phobia, HRT might be integrated with social skills training and systematic desensitization or exploration of unconscious issues. In the case of Linda, HRT was the primary intervention, but it was integrated with cognitive–behavioral therapy approaches to stress management.

HRT is most often integrated with cognitive–behavioral interventions.

Principle #8: HRT uses a variety of methods for hypnotic induction, suggestion, and facilitating therapeutic experiences

Understanding the theoretical foundations of hypnotherapy allows the therapist to be flexible and creative in devising hypnotic inductions and suggestions. Hypnotic suggestions may be formulated in a directive manner,

Hypnotic suggestions may be formulated in a directive manner, through permissive suggestions, or through implication and nonverbal communication.

through permissive suggestions, or through implication and nonverbal communication. Many patients prefer a more directive approach in which the intent of the suggestion is easy to identify. Examples of directive and nondirective approaches are provided in Chapter 8. Linda had a preference for focusing on her breathing to begin the process of hypnotic induction, followed by directive suggestions for calm feelings and comfort to achieve greater control of her anxiety and headaches.

Principle #9: HRT is both structured and individualized

HRT sessions are structured to complete a hypnotic induction and to achieve the goals of the session. In addition, a course of HRT generally ranges from 6 to 12 sessions depending on the individual and his or her presenting problem. The initial session is devoted to an assessment and preparation of the patient for treatment. In this regard, the first session is structured as a clinical interview and in a manner similar to cognitive–behavioral therapy. The second session involves a hypnotic induction and instructing the patient in the use of HRT. Subsequent sessions are also focused upon specific goals and toward greater individualization of the specific hypnotic suggestions, post-hypnotic suggestions, and teaching self-hypnosis.

The individualization of hypnotic suggestion makes the intervention more powerful and relevant to the patient.

Hypnosis may also involve a process of dissociation in which one is able to detach from external stimuli and become even more aware of experiencing the effects that are suggested and imagined.

The structure of a hypnotic induction generally begins with instructing an individual to focus attention on a spot or area. This is followed by suggestions for relaxation and eye closure, and then for deepening the involvement in the experience of hypnosis. Suggestions for mental imagery are also given, and the patient is asked to experience the suggestions in an intense manner. In this regard, hypnosis may also involve a process of dissociation in which one is able to detach from external stimuli and become even more aware of experiencing the effects that are suggested and imagined.

As the goals of the session are accomplished, suggestions for alerting to conscious awareness are given. While there can be considerable variation and complexity in how this structure is achieved, the basic outline is familiar in HRT. At the same time, there is considerable individualization in the specific suggestions and imagery that are utilized with a particular patient. The individualization of hypnotic suggestion makes the intervention more powerful and relevant to the patient. Transcripts for hypnotic interventions can be very useful; however, interventions should be sufficiently individualized based upon the patient's preferences, past experience, and personal responses. Linda had a preference for nature and the experience of being outside near a particular beach on the ocean. This was a memory from her childhood that she was able to identify as her "safe place" where she could "relax and find comfort."

Principle #10: HRT may be directed toward developing coping skills, relieving symptoms, facilitating insight, or preventing relapse

It is important to recognize that hypnotherapy can be used to achieve much more than simply a relaxed state. Achieving deep physical and/or emotional relaxation can be therapeutically useful in achieving a range of goals. However, there are four broadly defined uses of hypnotherapy:

- First is the development of coping skills. Patients may learn how to use self-hypnosis to reduce anxiety, remain calm in difficult circumstances, or to mentally rehearse a task. A person who is having difficulty with anger might learn how to use hypnotic relaxation to reduce anger and cope with feelings.
- Second, HRT can be used for symptom relief. For example, suggestions for hypnotic analgesia could be given to a patient with chronic pain due to an injury.
- Third, during a hypnotic induction, conscious defenses are lowered and unconscious material is more available. Suggestions may be given for the patient to gain greater understanding of the cause, underlying dynamics of, or emotional associations with symptoms. In a later session, Linda became aware of underlying feelings toward a coworker that she had previously not recognized. While imagining that she was in her "safe place," suggestions were given that she "would . . . become aware of any feelings that are associated with her headaches . . . an underlying cause." She then became aware of increased tension in her head and shoulders, and she recognized the stress associated with the way a coworker was acting toward her. This insight was of significant benefit in focusing coping skills introduced in future sessions and in confronting the situation.
- Fourth, HRT can be integrated and focused on relapse prevention. Regular practice of hypnotic relaxation techniques in combination with follow-up and individualized post-hypnotic suggestions can help maintain gains previously achieved in therapy.

During a hypnotic induction, conscious defenses are lowered and unconscious material is more available.

The practice of hypnotherapy is a continual process of learning and growing through knowledge and experience.

BECOMING A CLINICIAN SKILLED IN HRT

When utilized by a skilled clinician, HRT is a powerful tool that can bring about many positive benefits. However, in the hands of the untrained, it can lead to failure or negative outcomes. As a clinician, a basic rule to follow is that you should only use hypnotherapy to treat a condition that you would be competent to treat without hypnosis. In becoming skilled at hypnotherapy, it is first necessary to have a sufficient background in establishing a therapeutic relationship with patients, clinical interviewing, psycho-diagnosis, and knowledge of the types of disorders your patients may experience. As an example, treating patients with chronic pain requires that the clinician be knowledgeable about various types of pain (cancer, neuropathic, benign) and consult with colleagues as necessary.

The methods of hypnotherapy can be learned through reading and attending lectures. However, the most important aspect of developing skill in hypnotherapy is practice. Just as surgery cannot be learned through reading alone, hypnotherapy requires observation and practice. It is especially beneficial to identify a mentor and have an opportunity to receive feedback regarding specific patients and sessions. Also, some clinicians may want to pursue certification in clinical hypnosis as a way of advancing knowledge. The American Society of Clinical Hypnosis and the Society for Clinical and Experimental Hypnosis have certification programs and continuing education seminars. It is important to always seek out professional organizations or individuals with the highest level of credentials. The practice of hypnotherapy is a continual process of learning and growing through knowledge and experience.

CHAPTER 3

Theoretical Basis for Hypnotic Relaxation Therapy

This chapter presents a theoretical model for understanding hypnotic relaxation therapy (HRT). Hypnotherapy is a complex process, and effective therapy often requires individualized interventions that address a particular patient's personal experience and dynamics. However, it is possible to identify the basic underlying principles that contribute to our understanding of hypnotherapy. HRT proposes three key components that interact in a synergistic manner: (1) the conscious and unconscious minds; (2) social/cognitive factors; and (3) adaptive dissociation. Although suggestions for relaxation are not required to achieve a hypnotic state, the clinical relevance of therapeutic relaxation during hypnotic inductions is addressed.

A basic principle of HRT is that all information is processed at both conscious and unconscious levels of awareness.

THE CONSCIOUS AND UNCONSCIOUS MINDS

A basic principle of HRT is that all information is processed at both conscious and unconscious levels of awareness. HRT provides a method to achieve greater access to the unconscious and to empower the patient to produce changes within both the conscious and the unconscious mind. This being said, what exactly is the unconscious mind and how does it work differently from the conscious mind?

Conceptualizations of the unconscious mind have come in three great waves of theoretical formulations (Epstein, 1994). The first wave was Sigmund Freud's identification of the unconscious mind over 100 years ago. This was the first dual-process theory of personality (involving both the conscious and unconscious minds) and represented the "discovery" of the unconscious mind. The importance of the unconscious was further emphasized as Freud hypothesized that much of human experience and behavior is actually the result of the influence of the *unconscious mind* rather than deliberate, conscious thought processes. Freud proposed that the unconscious mind is more primitive and operates according to *primary process* thinking in which fantasy, wish fulfillment, displacement, condensation, symbolic representation, and association are primary mechanisms (Epstein, 1994). In contrast, the conscious mind operates using *secondary process* thinking (i.e., the rules of logic and rationality). As Freud proposed, the concept of dual processing of information outside conscious awareness is widely accepted. However, Freud's description of the unconscious mind as the source of motivation has been questioned, and additional explanations of how the unconscious mind operates have been advanced.

The second wave of understanding of the unconscious was developed from a cognitive, rather than a psychoanalytic, position (Epstein, 1994). From this perspective, the unconscious is conceptualized as the *cognitive unconscious* and is not associated with psychoanalysis. Rather, this model of unconscious cognition states that information is automatically processed without voluntary effort and outside of conscious awareness as a natural mode of operation. Kihlstrom (1990) described this conceptualization of the unconscious as a "kinder and gentler" unconscious in comparison to the psychoanalytic conceptualization. However, a limitation of the cognitive unconscious is that it does not account very well for emotionally driven perceptions and behavior. While it correctly identifies that cognition occurs outside of conscious awareness, it fails to fully explain how the unconscious mind operates or processes information. Therefore, with regard to hypnotherapy, the concept of the cognitive unconscious has not been fully satisfactory.

> HRT supports the theoretical formulation proposed by Epstein (1973) that we have a divided mind: the rational system and the experiential system.

The third wave of understanding of the unconscious mind is Epstein's Cognitive-Experiential Self Theory (CEST; Epstein, 1973; 1994; 2003). This theory introduces a new and more comprehensive understanding of the unconscious mind. It uniquely identifies that the unconscious mind operates as an *experiential system* that is emotionally driven and processes information automatically, rapidly, and effortlessly. Events are primarily represented concretely and imagistically (Epstein, 1994), and through the use of thought, metaphors, narratives, scripts, prototypes, and images the experiential/unconscious mind achieves generalization and responds to information. In contrast, the conscious/rational system is a deliberative, effortful, and logical system that operates primarily through the use of language. For this reason, we are most aware of the rational system during everyday waking consciousness. The experiential/unconscious integrates elements of primary process thinking with the cognitive unconscious to create a new conceptualization of the unconscious that is consistent with the principles of HRT.

> While the conscious and unconscious minds interact in a synergistic manner, the two systems greatly differ in their features and ways they operate.

HRT supports the theoretical formulation proposed by Epstein (1973) that we have a divided mind: the rational system and the experiential system. All information is processed by these two independent but interactive systems. While the conscious and unconscious minds interact in a synergistic manner, the two systems greatly differ in their features and ways they operate. The rational/conscious system acts according to a set of analytical principles and is influenced by reason and logic. It operates in line with a person's understanding of the rules of reasoning and evidence as well as ideas that may be culturally transmitted. Its actions are conscious, analytical, effortful, relatively slow, affect-free, and highly demanding of cognitive resources. In contrast, the rapid, unconscious action of the experiential system is holistic, associative, and emotionally driven. The experiential/unconscious system encodes reality in images, metaphors, and narratives, and it is slow to change except through repetition or intense emotional experience (Epstein, 1994). A comparison of the two systems is presented in Table 3.1.

Table 3.1

Comparison of the Unconscious/Experiential and Conscious/ Rational Systems (adapted from Epstein, 1991).

Experiential System	*Rational System*
1. Holistic	1. Analytic
2. Emotionally driven	2. Logically driven
3. Outcome oriented	3. Process oriented
4. Influenced by "vibes"/gut feelings	4. Influenced by conscious appraisals
5. Perception is influenced by concrete images, metaphors, and narratives	5. Perception is influenced by abstract symbols, words, and numbers
6. Rapid information processing	6. Slow information processing
7. Slower to change	7. Changes more rapidly
8. Operates automatically, effortless	8. Operates through conscious effort
9. Understanding comes through experience	9. Understanding comes through logic and evidence

In HRT, the patient is able to enter an altered state in which the dominance of these two systems shifts. There is greater access to the experiential/ unconscious system, and behavior more directly reflects the action of this system. As a result, the response to hypnotic suggestion is characterized as feeling automatic, involuntary, or effortless, which indicates that the response is achieved with decreased effort from the rational/conscious system. In other words, there is decreased conscious effort in responding, and behavior reflects the work of the experiential/unconscious system.

SOCIAL–PSYCHOLOGICAL COMPONENTS OF HRT

There is considerable evidence that social–psychological factors play a role in hypnotic responding. Social–cognitive theories posit that social and psychological factors, such as expectancy and the hypnotic context, contribute to hyponotic responsiveness. (Braffman & Kirsch, 1999; Kirsch & Lynn, 1998). These factors are certainly important and may be most relevant to consciously driven behavior and response to "easier" hypnotic suggestions, such as arm levitation or heaviness.

Social–cognitive theories posit that social and psychological factors such as attitudes, expectancies, and motivations all contribute to response to suggestion during a hypnotic induction.

The effects of response expectancy, or a person's belief that he or she will respond to a particular treatment or therapy, have been demonstrated widely in medical and psychological research (Kirsch & Lynn, 1998). Research has demonstrated that the effects of expectancy are so powerful that a person's response to placebo will be congruent with his or her expectation, even if what is expected is opposite of the supposed effects of a pharmacological treatment (Bridell et al., 1978, as cited in Kirsch, 1985). Response expectancies have the ability to influence perception and tolerance of pain, pulse, and mood (Kirsch, 1991), and expectancy has been cited as a relevant factor in hypnotic responding (Kirsch & Council 1989). In fact, Kirsch (1985, 1991) proposed that the effects of hypnosis can be attributed to heightened expectancies (Kirsch, 1990, as cited by Kirsch, 1991, p. 440). Further, research has shown that using environmental cues to enhance expectancy has been shown to produce greater responsiveness to suggestion (Wilson, 1967), alter hypnotizability scores, and affect perception of nonvolition (Wickless and Kirsch, 1989).

HRT occurs within the context of a social interaction in which one individual is identified as the therapist and the other as the patient or client. Positive expectancy is enhanced by the patient's perception that the therapist possesses knowledge and the expertise needed for the intervention. Expectancy is further created by identifying the intervention as hypnotic in nature. This means that the patient's understanding of hypnosis should be addressed and further refined before beginning a hypnotic induction. Negative expectations can lead to negative results, and it is important to attend to the patient's perception of the hypnotic intervention.

HRT occurs within the context of a social interaction in which one individual is identified as the therapist and the other as the patient or client.

These roles and expectations can be initiated by both direct communication and by subtle cues, such as diplomas on the wall and interpersonal interactions, beginning with the first contact and scheduling appointments. All of these contextual factors contribute to expectations and can be a powerful source of indirect hypnotic suggestion. It is really a matter of whether or not the hypnotherapist is aware of these factors and utilizes them toward therapeutic benefit for the patient.

There are actually many factors that contribute to the hypnotic context and thereby influence expectancy. Some of the prototypical aspects to consider in providing a positive context for hypnotherapy are:

- *Office location:* Is the office located in a setting such as a private office or clinic that communicates a therapeutic environment?
- *Furnishings:* Is the office furnished in a manner that is conducive to relaxation (i.e., with a recliner, chairs)?
- *Therapist characteristics:* Does the therapist present him- or herself in a professional manner, conveying confidence and knowledge?
- *Decorations:* Is the office environment pleasant? Does it convey professionalism and expertise? Are there degrees and certificates displayed?
- *Expectations:* Is hypnotic relaxation explained to the patient in a manner that fosters a positive expectation for outcome? What is conveyed in terms of expected roles of the therapist and patient?
- *Motivation:* Is the patient motivated to engage in the process? Is resistance low?

The importance of the hypnotic context cannot be overstated. Among other things, this defines the process as therapeutic, and conveys a level of expertise on the part of the health care provider. In HRT it is assumed that when the roles of the therapist and the patient are identified, and a context for a positive expectancy is created, the therapeutic process is enhanced.

ADAPTIVE DISSOCIATION

Another dimension of HRT is the concept of a trance state. This involves an altered state of consciousness in which there is greater availability of the unconscious/experiential system. The process by which this is achieved is dissociation. During everyday waking consciousness, individuals are most aware of the functioning of the rational/conscious system. Our behavior seems to be primarily directed by our conscious thoughts and awareness. However, during a hypnotic induction, responses should arise from the experiential/unconscious system, and the rational/conscious system should become secondary. When this happens, responses to hypnotic suggestion are often experienced as involuntary by the patient. While dissociation can be conceptualized in a pathological manner, the process of achieving a degree of dissociation during hypnotic relaxation is intentional and adaptive, as it provides a means to communicate with and influence the experiential/unconscious system. Therefore, the trance, or hypnotic state, is considered to be an adaptive, therapeutic form of dissociation.

The importance of the hypnotic context cannot be overstated. Among other things, this defines the process as therapeutic.

To better understand what is meant by "adaptive dissociation," it may be helpful to first discuss the hypnotic state and review prior theories of dissociation as related to hypnosis.

The reality of the hypnotic state has been validated by several studies.

THE HYPNOTIC STATE

The process of achieving the initial hypnotic response is characterized by an "attentive, receptive, focal concentration."

The reality of the hypnotic state has been validated by several studies. At Stanford University, Kosslyn, Thompson, Costantini-Ferrando, Alpert, and Spiegel (2000) used positron emission tomography (PET) to investigate the hypnotic state. Participants underwent a hypnotic induction and were then evaluated by PET scan to determine how areas of the brain responded to suggestion during the hypnotic state. When participants were given the suggestion to see a particular color, the color perception areas of their cerebral hemispheres were activated. This occurred even when the participants were looking at a black-and-white (noncolor) pattern. Further, when participants were given the suggestion to actually see the black-and-white pattern, activity in the color perception area of the brain decreased. While contextual and social–psychological factors can play a role in hypnosis, this clearly demonstrates that perceptual alterations during hypnosis involve a change in brain activity. In another study using PET during a hypnotic induction, participants were given suggestions to "hear" a particular sound. Highly hypnotizable subjects demonstrated activation in the right anterior cingulate cortex area of the brain, an area activated when sound is heard (or in this case, when sound is suggested in a hypnotic state) but not when the sound is simply imagined (Szechtman, Woody, Bowers, & Nahmias, 1998).

During hypnosis, patients may experience an alteration in sensations or a decreased awareness of time and orientation to place (Rainville, et al., 2002). The process of achieving the initial hypnotic response is characterized by an "attentive, receptive, focal concentration." It is important to conceptualize the hypnotic state as "a normal activity" that can occur outside of a hypnotic induction. Examples include being absorbed in reading a book, suspending critical judgment while watching a movie, daydreaming, or other similar activities (Spiegel, Greenleaf, & Spiegel, 2000). In some ways, this aspect of hypnosis may be similar to that of other mind–body therapies such as relaxation, guided imagery, mindfulness, and meditation in that they all can involve some aspects of an altered state of consciousness.

Dissociative Theories of Hypnotic Response

Theories of dissociation originated with Pierre Janet (1907), who theorized that hypnotic responding reflected a process of dissociation during which some mental processes become separated from consciousness. Janet believed that hypnotic responses reflected the patients' restricted awareness of usually accessible material and openness to suggestion. Following Janet's ideas, Ernest Hilgard (1973; 1977; 1991) introduced the "neodissociation" theory of hypnotic responding. Hilgard theorized that hypnotic responses reflect executive control of cognitive subsystems becoming briefly suspended, and control shifts such that responses are experienced as involuntarily occurring. Hilgard noted that, "If dissociation is conceived broadly to imply an interference with or a loss of familiar associative processes, most phenomena of hypnosis could be conceived as dissociative" (1991, p. 84). Kenneth Bowers' (1990; 1992) model, Dissociated Control Theory, also identified dissociation as an underlying aspect of hypnotic responding. Dissociated control theory states that during a hypnotic experience there is a shift in pathways of behavioral control. The individual achieves a state, usually of relaxation, in which subsystems of control are activated and a decrease in administrative control results in a decreased perception of effort during hypnotic response. Behavior is dissociated from conscious, executive control, and the patient's experience of nonvolition is viewed as accurate (Bowers, 1992).

Dissociated control theory states that during a hypnotic experience there is a shift in pathways of behavioral control.

It has been noted that dissociative theories share two basic assumptions: that humans possess the innate capacity to discern internally and externally provoked events, and that hypnotic responding involves alteration in this process, precipitating dissociation or an altered state of consciousness (Woody & Sadler, 2008).

The Concept of Adaptive Dissociation

During a hypnotic induction, the patient experiences concentrated attention and absorption in internal experiences, while awareness of external stimuli fades to the background. While in the hypnotic state, the patient's perception and cognitive processing of information are altered. The degree of the patient's dissociation is indicated by his or her ability to experience the feelings, images, and behavioral and physical responses that are suggested. The functioning of the rational/conscious system diminishes and the patient's responses are more directly influenced by the experiential/unconscious system. As the patient achieves a more dissociated state, the responses are experienced as occurring involuntarily without conscious control.

The concept of adaptive dissociation is consistent with the general observation that more difficult hypnotic responses (such as pain control, alteration in sensory perception, suggested positive or negative hallucinations, etc.) may be related to the patient's capacity for dissociation. Essentially, the depth of trance refers to the degree to which the individual is able to shift awareness from the rational/conscious system to the experiential/unconscious system, such that his or her responses arise more from the experiential/unconscious system. The process by which this is achieved is dissociation. The deeper the trance state, the more responses are perceived as occurring involuntarily and

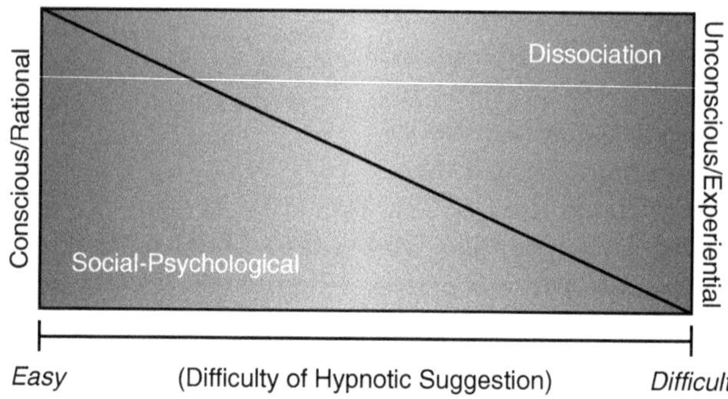

Figure 3.1
Adaptive Dissociation and Hypnotic Response

internal experiences are perceived as reality. In a sense, the person's internal world, or his or her experiential/unconscious system, assumes executive control. In this model, dissociation has a positive function in that it facilitates greater hypnotic responding. This is illustrated in Figure 3.1.

To summarize, adaptive dissociation refers to an individual's ability to achieve a shift in executive control such that there is greater awareness of the responses that arise from the experiential/unconscious system.

THERAPEUTIC RELAXATION

When emotionally relaxed, patients experience deep inner calm. They become "an observer of their own experience."

In addition to the aforementioned factors that influence a person's response to hypnosis, relaxation often plays a role in hypnotic interventions. While suggested relaxation is not essential to hypnotic responding, it is highly useful therapeutically and is integrated into HRT. Relaxation during hypnosis may be physical, emotional, or both. Physical relaxation refers to a reduction in muscle tone and decreased activity of the sympathetic nervous system. In addition to muscular relaxation, the changes associated with deeper physical relaxation include decreasing heart rate and respiration. Breathing becomes slower and perhaps deeper. Blood pressure may decrease and there is an increase in skin conductance and alpha brain waves. These changes are similar to what Benson (1975) refers to as "the relaxation response."

Emotional relaxation refers to the patient's internal experience of peaceful and calm feelings. In the process of psychotherapy, it is very likely that the achievement of emotional relaxation is the most helpful and therapeutic. When emotionally relaxed, patients experience deep inner calm. They become "an observer of their own experience" and begin to notice thoughts, feelings, and images as the experiential/unconscious system becomes more available.

Relaxation is not the same as a trance state, but it can be a step toward achieving a shift in consciousness.

Most hypnotic inductions involve suggestions for relaxation. The suggested relaxation may be direct, such as, "You can begin to experience a deeper and more relaxed state as you begin to drift into hypnosis." Alternatively, relaxation may be implied by the therapist speaking softly and suggesting relaxing images, such as being at a beach or a place where the patient has felt calm in the past. Relaxation is not the same as a trance state, but it can be a step toward achieving a shift in consciousness. As the patient becomes more deeply relaxed there are alterations in bodily sensations and awareness. For example, the patient may experience a "drifting and floating feeling," a "feeling of heaviness," or awareness of unimportant external sounds may dim.

While relaxation is not ultimately necessary to achieve a hypnotic state, it is therapeutically useful. Suggestions for muscular relaxation can provide a pathway to achieving emotional relaxation, and emotional relaxation provides a base for an inner sense of control to access the unconscious mind, which is essential for some aspects of hypnotherapy.

Hypnotic response involves a process of adaptive dissociation and an increased availability of the experiential system.

SUMMARIZING HRT

Hypnotic response involves a process of adaptive dissociation and an increased availability of the experiential/unconscious system. Social and psychological factors, such as motivation, expectancy, and social influence, are integrally involved in the process. The rational system (conscious control and effort) plays a primary role in response to easy hypnotic suggestions, such as eye closure or lowering an arm. However, in order for individuals to respond to more difficult suggestions (such as pain control, or visual or auditory alterations), the rational/conscious system must become secondary so that the individual's experience arises primarily from the experiential/unconscious system.

HRT is a psychotherapeutic intervention that uses this process to gain greater access to, and influence of, the experiential/unconscious system and achieve physical and emotional relaxation.

Each person is unique and will have various associations within his or her individual experiential/unconscious system. In clinical practice, consideration should be given to creating interventions that influence the rational/conscious system by capitalizing on social–psychological factors and accessing the experiential/unconscious system. The clinician can utilize the theoretical model of HRT in the development of hypnotic interventions and to understand patients' varied experience of HRT.

CHAPTER 4

Hypnotic Induction and Formulation of Suggestions

Success in conducting hypnotic inductions and formulating hypnotic suggestions is dependent on a number of factors, including the hypnotherapeutic relationship, which is the establishment of trust and a cooperative relationship between therapist and patient. It is also important to understand the laws of hypnotic suggestion. With these foundations in place, the clinician can begin the process of developing hypnotic suggestions and integrating hypnotic phenomena into clinical practice.

THE HYPNOTHERAPEUTIC RELATIONSHIP

Before beginning a hypnotic induction, it is essential to first establish rapport and a positive, therapeutic relationship. In preparing the patient for a hypnotic induction, it is important to discuss the patient's perception of hypnosis and his or her goals for treatment. It is also useful to discuss the process of the hypnotic induction. This may involve providing the patient with a description of the induction that will be used, establishing assurance that the induction is acceptable, and gaining the patient's acceptance of the process. In addition, goals of both therapy as a whole and the individual intervention may be reviewed to assure that they are consistent with the patient's desire. The nature of a hypnotic induction requires that there is a collaborative, though unequal, relationship between the therapist and patient. The therapist guides the patient toward relaxation and a trance state. As a patient responds to hypnotic suggestion, conscious defenses are lowered, and the patient has an internal experience of "letting go" of conscious control in order to be guided by the hypnotherapist. The patient will most likely achieve this state within a positive and trusting therapeutic relationship. The vulnerability experienced by the patient should be respected prior to, during, and following the hypnotic induction. This is done by providing the patient with a safe environment and promoting confidence,

> It is important to discuss the patient's perception of hypnosis and his or her goals for treatment.

reassurance, and attention to the patient's emotional reactions and concerns. The importance of the hypnotherapeutic relationship cannot be overemphasized and should be considered at all times when providing hypnotherapy.

LAWS OF HYPNOTIC SUGGESTION

The development of hypnotic suggestions is complex and should be individualized to meet each patient's experience and goals. In addition, it should be kept in mind that suggestions can be given directly or indirectly. Suggestions in hypnosis are not commands; rather, they provide guidance and opportunities for learning and responding. The guidelines that follow explain the laws of suggestion and how to formulate hypnotic suggestions.

Law of Concentrated Attention

The law of concentrated attention states that, when attention is focused on an idea or a set of ideas, it tends to become realized, and we are more likely to notice and experience the suggested "idea." For example, an individual may not be aware of any sensations in her hands. However, as a suggestion is given to, "Notice your hands, notice the weight of your hands" and then to, "Notice that your hands can become heavier and heavier . . . as if you are holding a heavy bucket of wet sand," the awareness of the hands becomes more apparent and the experience of heaviness more likely. One implication of the law of concentrated attention is that suggestions may be repeated to help the patient move toward the desired effect. This is especially true for important suggestions that are directly related to the goal of the hypnotherapy session. With repetition, the suggested effect is more likely to occur to a greater degree.

> The law of concentrated attention states that, when attention is focused on an idea or a set of ideas, it tends to become realized, and we are more likely to notice and experience the suggested "idea."

Law of Reversed Effect

The law of reversed effect states that the harder one tries, the more one fails. This means that the harder one *consciously* tries to respond to hypnotic suggestion, the less likely one is to succeed. As previously discussed, an essential feature of a hypnotic response is the experience of *involuntariness*. Ideally, the response to hypnotic suggestion is effortless. Rather than *trying* to imagine or respond, the patient should adopt an attitude of *allowing* a response to occur. In fact, if the patient tries to respond through conscious effort, it tends to interfere with an actual hypnotic response. One way in which the law of reversed effect is integrated into hypnotic suggestion is through directing the patient toward *letting go* with wording such as, "During your experience of hypnosis today there is

> The harder one consciously tries to respond to hypnotic suggestion, the less likely he or she is to succeed.

nothing that you have to do, and nothing that you have to try to do . . . just noticing and allowing response in whatever way it occurs. . . ." In this regard, the patient cannot "fail," as her experience is valued as personal and individual. Using the law of reversed effect encourages the patient to experience hypnosis as a unique process in which she becomes more of an observer of her own responses and feelings.

Law of Dominant Affect

The law of dominant affect (sometimes spelled "effect") states that a stronger emotion replaces a weaker emotion. One way to think of this is that the wording of hypnotic suggestion provides a kind of road map for responding; however, it is the inclusion of affect or emotion within the suggestion that gives the suggestion energy. It should be kept in mind that the intention of hypnotic suggestion is to influence the unconscious/experiential system. Because the unconscious mind functions in an associative manner and uses the language of emotion and metaphor, suggestions are more powerful if they include emotional content that is personally relevant to the patient. For example, an unemotional suggestion for the patient to experience being at a beach might be, "Now you can experience that you are at a beach. Notice the sand on the beach . . . you can see everything at the beach today." This same suggestion can be made more powerful by the addition of emotional content, such as:

It should be kept in mind that the intention of hypnotic suggestion is to influence the unconscious/experiential system.

> "Now you can experience that you are at a beautiful beach where you can feel calm and peaceful; it is a wonderful place to be . . . as you feel the sand on the beach you can feel the warmth of the sand and it can remind you of other times when you have felt warm and safe . . . you can see everything on the beach today, feeling secure and happy . . . perhaps you are there with someone you love."

Further, if the patient has actually been to a beach, she is more likely to make unconscious associations with the suggested experience. One characteristic of the trance state is that suggestions may be accepted in a literal manner, such that unconscious associations lead to a literal experience of suggestions. If suggestions are given for going to a beach, and the suggestions are delivered in a manner that is powerful for the patient, the patient is more likely to feel that she is actually at a beach and "experiencing everything that is there."

HYPNOTIC SUGGESTION AS A THREE-STEP PROCESS

The process of delivering a hypnotic suggestion can be conceptualized as involving three progressive steps. The first step involves communicating what is going to happen. This directs the patient's experience and builds anticipation and expectancy for a particular response within a particular timeframe. For example, to suggest an arm levitation, it would be appropriate to suggest:

> "In a few moments, you may begin to experience a change in sensation in your left arm . . . this arm can become lighter and lighter . . . almost weightless . . . and as it does it can float upward."

The second step in the process of hypnotic suggestion involves communicating that what has just been anticipated is now happening. For example:

> "Now, as you become aware that the arm has become lighter, as I touch this arm . . . it floats up, that's right . . . letting it float up higher and higher . . . very good."

Once the patient has responded to the suggestion, the third step is to communicate a sense of completion and validation, such as:

> "Very good. Now this feeling passes and you are able to go on to an even deeper state of hypnosis and relaxation as your arm returns to the chair."

The positive and validating suggestions that are given provide a basis to go on to the next suggestions to help the patient achieve his or her goals for the hypnotherapy session.

PACING AND LEADING

Learning to carefully observe the patient and to pace suggestions to match the patient's experience is a crucial part of the skill involved in providing hypnotherapy. Careful observation on the part of the clinician allows for: (1) detecting subtle cues to indicate the patient's responses: (2) being sensitive to the patient's emotional state (positive or negative) in response to suggestions; and (3) varying the pace of suggestions with appropriate pauses.

Learning to carefully observe the patient and to pace suggestions to match the patient's experience is a crucial part of the skill involved in providing hypnotherapy.

For example, in providing suggestions for relaxation, it may be effective to pace suggestions with the patient's breathing and signs of reduced muscular tension. As the patient achieves a more relaxed state, breathing may become slower and deeper. This is fairly easy to detect and provides a means to begin pacing. An example of pacing suggestions for relaxation with the patient's breathing would be:

> "As you become more relaxed, *(pause for breath)* letting all of the tension go *(pause for breath)* from your forehead, *(pause for breath)* neck *(pause for breath),* and shoulders."

Suggestions should be formulated to communicate a positive, rather than a negative, idea.

Pauses serve an important role in the process of hypnotherapy and in pacing and leading. Pauses . . . act as . . . bookends for important suggestions. Along with pauses, pacing and leading involve utilization of the patient's present experience. As the patient becomes aware of a particular feeling or response, his experience can be integrated into the overall process of the hypnotic induction. For example:

> "As you become aware of the feelings associated with your breathing, you may notice that your breathing becomes a little slower or deeper . . . and as you do, this can serve as a cue to become even more relaxed . . . the more comfortable the breathing . . . the deeper the relaxation."

In this way, the patient's own behavior, awareness, and responses serve as a basis for pacing and then leading into the hypnotic experience. Leading refers to providing suggestions that guide the patient into the next experience toward the present goal. For example:

> "As the tension becomes less . . . you find that soon there is a change in sensations in your arms . . . they become heavier . . . more relaxed and calm."

The process of pacing and leading is repeated throughout a hypnotherapy session and can be learned with practice.

POSITIVELY WORDED SUGGESTIONS

Suggestions should be formulated to communicate a positive, rather than a negative, idea. For example, in utilizing hypnotic relaxation therapy (HRT) in pain management, suggestions such as, "You can notice more and more comfort across your forehead," would be preferred over, "You should ignore the burning, searing pain across your forehead . . . pay no attention to the pain." Positively worded suggestions are consistent with both the law of concentrated attention and the law of reversed effect. By focusing attention on a positive outcome, it is more likely to occur. The law of reversed effect would predict that the more the patient tries to ignore pain, the more difficult it would become over time. For example, the suggestion to, "Try not to think of pink elephants," is more likely to increase, rather than decrease, the likelihood that the individual will begin thinking about pink elephants!

It is important to follow the patient's progress and to provide positive reinforcement throughout a hypnotherapy session.

REINFORCEMENT

Reinforcement is useful both within and outside of trance. It can be given by noticing the patient's progress and providing acknowledgment of those responses. Such acknowledgment can be as simple as, "That's right . . . you are doing very well." It is important to follow the patient's progress and to provide positive reinforcement throughout a hypnotherapy session.

CREATE POSITIVE EXPECTANCY

Suggestions can be directed toward creating positive expectancy for specific suggestions or the overall treatment goals. This is achieved through both verbal and nonverbal communication. As noted above, in the hypnotherapeutic relationship, there is communication of genuineness, trust, cooperation, and confidence. The hypnotherapist can best communicate a positive expectancy when he or she has confidence. Such confidence can be communicated directly. For example, "I am confident you will be able to achieve a measure of pain control with the practice of self-hypnosis." Another way to set a positive expectancy is through asking questions prior to the hypnotic induction, such as, "Would it be alright with you if your pain were to decrease by 50% during today's session?" Knowledge of the patient's prior experience, hypnotic ability, and motivation can contribute to the hypnotherapist's confidence and communication of positive expectancy.

The hypnotherapist can best communicate a positive expectancy when he or she has confidence.

UTILIZATION OF HYPNOTIC PHENOMENA

The term hypnotic phenomena refers to suggested effects that can be subjectively experienced and/or objectively observed during the hypnotic relaxation session. Examples of hypnotic phenomena include responses to suggestions for arm levitation, glove analgesia, arm heaviness, or hallucinated sensations such as sights, sounds, or smells. A key characteristic of hypnotic phenomena is that the patient experiences them as *involuntary,* or automatic. Suggestions are given, and the therapist observes the response. Hypnotic phenomena are not the result of conscious effort or "trying" to imagine or comply with suggestions. Rather, in addition to other factors, they result from an attitude of allowing a response.

A key characteristic of hypnotic phenomena is that the patient experiences them as involuntary, or automatic.

Hypnotic phenomena can be very useful to validate the trance experience, assess hypnotic abilities, gauge resistance, and help the patient move toward specific therapeutic goals. For example, a patient who has a fear of needles and needs to have blood drawn for a medical examination may benefit from a hypnotic relaxation session that includes suggestions for "numbness" in the area of the blood draw. Suggestions can first be given for a glove analgesia. For example:

> "Now your left hand can become more and more numb . . . less sensitive to discomfort . . . as if an analgesic feeling were coming into that

> hand . . . more and more numb, thick, and rubbery . . . able to feel pressure, but no pain . . . numb . . ."

As the patient responds to these suggestions, he might verify the resulting change in sensation by touching the left hand with the right.

> "Good. Now, as you are aware of that numbness, go ahead and touch your left hand with your right hand . . . Notice how numb, thick, and rubbery it is . . ."

Suggestions can then be given for the patient to experience that same feeling of numbness when undergoing a blood draw. Such a suggestion might be,

> "Now you can feel comfortable and relaxed, no concerns . . . the deeper the relaxation, the greater the numbness . . . the greater the comfort . . ."

It is always important to provide suggestions to remove any suggested hypnotic phenomena prior to ending the session. The only exception to this would be if the experienced hypnotic phenomena are intentionally suggested as a post-hypnotic response (discussed later in this chapter).

The process of individualization involves gaining knowledge of the patient's past experience, preferences, and responses.

Hypnotic suggestions may be general or more individualized. General suggestions are ones that are generally applicable to everyone, such as, "Day by day, you will be able to notice some positive feelings." General suggestions may also be suggestions that are somewhat generic, such as, "As you imagine walking along a path, each step can seem to take you to a deeper level of relaxation." While general suggestions are very useful and often provide an initial basis for hypnotherapy, the principles of HRT indicate that more individualized suggestions are likely to lead to greater success. The process of individualization involves gaining knowledge of the patient's past experience, preferences, and responses. Individualization is more easily achieved with knowledge of the patient's prior experience with hypnotic inductions and self-hypnosis. Some information regarding individualization may be gained from discussion of the patient's past experiences, conscious preferences, and ideas. However, the only way to gain knowledge of the patient's best response at the experiential level is through practice and observation. Therefore, the post-hypnotic inquiry, during which the patient is asked about his subjective experience with hypnosis, is most helpful in individualization of future hypnotic inductions. It is often difficult to achieve a great deal of individualization in the first HRT session; however, through inquiry and gaining information regarding the patient's responses and reactions to the induction, it is possible to modify and individualize

Hypnotic suggestions may be presented in a directive or permissive manner.

future inductions to reflect a greater degree of personal preference and to provide for the best outcome and acceptability. Hypnotic suggestions are very detailed, and the specifics of the patient's experience in a trance state are necessary in order to "enter into the patient's experience" and truly achieve meaningful individualization in future sessions.

DIRECT VS. PERMISSIVE SUGGESTION

Hypnotic suggestions may be presented in a directive or permissive manner. Directive suggestions are characterized by direct wording, such as, "I now suggest that you experience a greater degree of relaxation in your right arm. . . ." The statement is unambiguous, clear, and to the point. Direct suggestions are preferred in many instances, especially when working with patients who are reasonably hypnotizable and in whom resistance is low. In contrast, permissive suggestions are very useful in increasing the patient's sense of control and choice. From a permissive suggestive approach, suggestions are considered more as invitations within several alternatives. In fact, permissive suggestions are primarily characterized by the concept of choice. For example, in suggesting relaxation using permissive suggestions, one can suggest:

> "Perhaps you can begin to notice some change in sensation in your right arm; perhaps you can notice a lightness or a heaviness . . . lighter or heavier . . . or perhaps you notice that as one arm; the left one or the right one, becomes lighter . . . the other one becomes heavier."

INDIRECT SUGGESTIONS

Indirect suggestions are somewhat similar to permissive suggestions. They are integrated with direct and permissive suggestions and characterized by some degree of ambiguity in the desired response. Advantages of an indirect approach are that it is useful in bypassing resistance and in presenting suggestions in a way that minimizes defensiveness. The primary disadvantage of indirect suggestions is that the ambiguity may be such that the intended response fails to be well communicated (even at an unconscious level). Examples of indirect suggestions are: implication of response, suggestions that are truisms, questions as suggestions, suggesting all possible responses, and use of past experiences.

Advantages of an indirect approach are that it is useful in bypassing resistance and in presenting suggestions in a way that minimizes defensiveness.

- Implication of response refers to providing suggestions in which the desired response is only implied, but not directly suggested. For example, "I don't know in what way you will experience hypnosis; however, you can notice what happens . . . " This type of suggestion *implies* that something will happen; that there will be some noticeable experience, and that the noticeable experience will be a part of hypnosis.

- Suggestions that are truisms are especially useful in setting expectancies and in providing a basis for an initial response. For example, the suggestion, "It is possible to become more relaxed" is a truism. It does not directly suggest a response, but simply states a fact. As this suggestion is accepted (pacing), it is possible to go on to another suggestion phrased as a truism, such as:

Suggestions that are truisms are statements of fact. They are very general, and provide a means for indirect suggestion.

> "Relaxation can be quite pleasant and there have been times when you have experienced a greater or lesser degree of relaxation in your right arm . . ."

  Again, suggestions that are truisms are statements of fact. They are very general, and provide a means for indirect suggestion.
- Questions as suggestions represent another way to introduce suggestions while minimizing defenses. This is especially useful when there are defenses related to control issues. The suggestions are presented as a series of questions. For example, in facilitating a relaxed state, questions as suggestions could be phrased as:

> "Can you notice your shoulders? Can you notice a degree of tension in the shoulders? Would it be acceptable for the shoulders to become more relaxed? Can you imagine relaxation spreading from your shoulders into your arms? Is it possible to go into a deeper level of hypnosis?"

  As with all suggestions, the principles of pacing and leading are utilized in presenting indirect suggestions, including suggestions as questions. It is important to note the patient's response and then phrase suggestions to facilitate a positive experience toward achievement of goals. In this way, the methods are integrated rather than being a choppy combination of simple techniques.
- Suggesting all possible responses provides suggestions in which failure is impossible. For example, in suggesting a motor response in a patient's right arm, suggestions could include:

> "As you go into a deeper level of hypnosis you may or may not notice your left arm . . . the arm may become lighter or heavier . . . it may have another sensation . . . or lessening of sensation . . . that arm may just seem to rest there without changing . . . it's possible to notice what happens . . ."

  This approach to suggestion can be useful in dealing with conscious or unconscious resistance and can provide some insight into the patient's responses.
- Use of past experiences can also be a basis for indirect suggestions. The hypnotherapist must have sufficient knowledge of the patient's past experiences to assure that these suggestions are acceptable and to bring about memories that are consistent with the goal for the session. If the patient's past

experiences are not well known, then suggestions should be more general and "safe." An example of suggestions that elicit past experiences might be,

> ". . . and you have had a lot of experience with closing your eyes . . . You might recall a time when you were sitting and listening to a speaker, perhaps as a student in a classroom . . . or during a church service . . . and you might have noticed that your eyelids wanted to close . . . and as you allowed them to close, they did . . . And you might recall that this was a pleasant sensation . . . a pleasant memory . . . allowing your eyelids to close and drifting into a more relaxed state . . . a pleasant hypnotic state."

Evoking memories that are both personal and positively related to the goal can be a very powerful way to formulate hypnotic suggestions, as they can be personally relevant and can be re-experienced in detail.

LANGUAGE OF THE EXPERIENTIAL SYSTEM

Whether suggestions are presented in a direct, indirect, or permissive manner, it is important to consider how the unconscious/experiential system processes suggestions. The experiential system is more feeling-based and responds to suggestions, in part, with emotion, "vibes," and affect. Therefore, the emotional content of suggestions should always be considered when formulating phrasing. In addition, it is important to keep in mind that the experiential system processes suggestions in a holistic, rather than an analytic, manner (as the rational system does). Further, when suggestions are accepted, the experiential system encodes them as concrete images and metaphors. For example, if a suggestion is given for a patient to "sit in a comfortable chair in front of a fireplace," the patient's experience is concrete (involving the feeling of literally being in a chair with a fireplace burning in front of her) and metaphorical (the associations and meaning of such an experience are likely to be positive or negative based upon past experiences). In addition, the unconscious/experiential system is much more associative than the conscious/rational system. When suggestions are presented, they are responded to as they are associated with certain feelings. The experiential system processes information without regard to logic. In fact, the term *trance logic* refers to the ability to easily tolerate logical inconsistencies during hypnosis. This means that illogical ideas (i.e., "you can find that as you are sitting there, somehow you are also at a beautiful beach, experiencing being at the beach . . . or floating over the beach . . . just floating on a cloud"). Additionally, in comparison to the conscious/rational system, the unconscious/experiential system is more crudely differentiated and tends to respond in the immediate context in a more simplistic manner. Responses are more immediate, feeling-based (not necessarily rational or logical), and more likely to be categorical. Therefore, the language used to access the unconscious/experiential system is more holistic, metaphorical, concrete, and feeling-based than that used to access the conscious/rational

As the depth of the hypnotic state deepens, suggestions are more likely directed toward influencing the unconscious/experiential system.

system (which is more logical, analytical, and mediated by conscious appraisal of events). Suggestions during hypnosis can be directed toward both the conscious/rational system and the experiential systems; however, as the depth of the hypnotic state deepens, suggestions are more likely directed toward influencing the unconscious/experiential system.

STRUCTURE OF HYPNOTIC RELAXATION INDUCTION

There is a great variety of hypnotic induction techniques. However, most inductions begin with a focus of attention and then move on to suggestions for relaxation, deepening trance, and therapeutic goals. Although the complexity and integrative nature of a particular session will vary depending on the goal for that session and the patient's individual response, the structure of a standard hypnotic induction can be summarized in the following steps. Note, however, the steps are not necessarily followed in the same order in all inductions.

Step I: Focusing of attention

Asking the patient to begin to focus his or her attention represents the beginning of the process toward achieving a trance state. The patient may be asked to focus her attention on a spot on the wall, the back of her hand, or an object in the room. The specific item to focus on is less relevant than the patient's willingness to engage in the process. Asking the patient to focus on a spot is largely a conscious response by the patient. However, the focus leads to the experience of other things fading into the background and greater access to the experiential system. Suggestions may be given, such as:

> Asking the patient to focus his or her attention represents the beginning of the process toward achieving a trance state.

> "You can begin the process of hypnotic relaxation by sitting back into the chair and allowing your head to be supported by the cushions . . . Now find a spot to focus your attention . . . there is a spot on the wall . . . As you bring your attention to this spot, focus on it intently . . . and as you do . . . other things begin to fade into the background . . . more and more . . . as you focus there."

Step II: Initial suggestions for relaxation

As the patient begins to narrow his focus, initial suggestions for relaxation are given. At the early stage of induction, suggestions to associate relaxation with another response, such as breathing, may be given, as this can present a benefit later in the session. By way of example:

> ". . . and as you focus your attention there, I don't think you would mind taking a deep breath of air . . . and as you exhale, become more deeply relaxed. Take that breath of air now, and as you breathe out,

> let all the tension go . . . Each breath of air takes you into a deeper and more relaxed state . . . a wave of relaxation that begins to come over you . . . muscles relaxing . . ."

Step III: Eye closure

Suggestions are then given for the patient's eyelids to close. These suggestions are given in a way that partly facilitates the process of "letting go" of conscious control and experiencing some degree of "automatic responding." Suggestions toward this goal could include:

> ". . . and as you notice that relaxation, the muscles around your eyelids can begin to relax . . . and as they do, the eyelids begin to feel heavy . . . It would be so pleasant to just let them become heavier and allow them to close . . . and as the eyelids begin to close . . . the relaxation becomes deeper . . . Let them close . . . heavier and heavier . . . more calm and relaxed . . . even deeper now. . . . as they close all the way."

Step IV: Encouraging a fading of the generalized reality orientation

As the patient responds to these suggestions, he becomes more aware of his own internal reality and the processing of suggestions at the level of the experiential system. As this occurs, the patient becomes less aware of the external reality, and there is often an alteration in physical sensations. This alteration is sometimes referred to as a *fading* of the *generalized reality orientation* (GRO). This refers to the patient's subjective experience of changes in sensations. The patient may experience heaviness and greater relaxation, a rocking or floating feeling, or decreased awareness of his body or events around him. In a sense, the patient begins to become more of an observer of his own experience. An example of a suggestion for fading of the GRO follows:

> "As you become aware of a greater degree of relaxation, you may notice other sensations that begin to occur. Your breathing may become a little slower or deeper, your heart rate may become a little slower, and you may notice a heaviness or a floating feeling . . . a feeling as if you are floating in space . . . just drifting and floating . . . deeper and deeper relaxed . . . Other things continue to fade into the background so that you are mainly aware of my voice and deeply absorbed in feelings of relaxation and comfort."

Step V: Deepening suggestions

Following GRO fading, suggestions are then given to deepen the experience of hypnotic relaxation. This includes suggestions for physical, emotional,

> Often, suggestions for physical relaxation provide a beginning to achieve the deeper and more meaningful emotional and mental relaxation.

and mental relaxation. The feeling of calmness is generally more important than physical relaxation. Often, suggestions for physical relaxation provide a beginning to achieve the deeper and more meaningful emotional and mental relaxation. Suggestions may be given to associate absorption, relaxation, and dissociation with counting or another progressive experience. For example:

> "Now, as I begin to count the numbers from 10 to 1, each number that I count will serve as a cue to enter a deeper state of hypnotic relaxation . . . deeper and deeper relaxed . . . 10 . . . Notice that wave of relaxation as it begins to spread across your face, your neck and shoulders . . . 9 . . . your jaw, and all the muscles of your face . . . 8 . . . more deeply calm . . . perhaps noticing shapes or colors before you . . . colors associated with relaxation and calmness . . . as you go deeper relaxed . . . 7 . . . And you may recall sounds associated with relaxation . . . such as the sound of a gentle rain . . . letting your mind drift to such memories . . . and deeper relaxed and more calm . . . 6 . . . letting all the tension go so that the relaxation becomes more complete . . . Your arms relax . . . they become heavy . . . hands so relaxed they can seem to be less a part of you . . . 5 . . . Halfway there . . . twice as relaxed . . . and the relaxation can spread to your upper back and your lower back . . . let all the tension go . . . 4 . . . and then the calmness becomes more apparent to you . . . feeling more calm and more at ease . . . no tension . . . no stress . . . 3 . . . The relaxation becomes more complete as the back . . . the shoulders . . . stomach . . . legs . . . and feet relax . . . and going into an even deeper level of hypnotic relaxation . . . 2 . . . deeper and deeper relaxed . . . Any tension can be released now . . . and, 1 . . . All the way there . . . completely relaxed . . . so calm . . . nothing bothers or disturbs . . ."

Mental imagery forms the vehicle to guide the experience of the experiential system, while the degree of dissociation, in this context, determines the depth of trance.

Step VI: Mental imagery and dissociation

Dissociation refers to a shift in consciousness that increases access to the experiential system and decreases the rational system's role in response to generalization. Mental imagery forms the vehicle to guide the experience of the experiential system, while the degree of dissociation, in this context, determines the depth of trance. That is, the greater the dissociation (the patient's experience is more internal and experiential), the greater the depth of trance. Possibilities for dissociation include direct and indirect suggestions for a split in information processing. For example:

> "As you hear my voice, with one part of your mind . . . you are aware that you are here sitting comfortably . . . and yet with another part of your

> mind you find that you are walking through a flower garden . . . on a beautiful spring day . . . experiencing everything that is there."

Suggestions for mental imagery should be of sufficient detail and richness to foster the patient's experience. Details of sights, sounds, feelings, taste, and so on, should be given as appropriate to the session and the patient's individual preferences.

Step VII: Setting the overall goal

HRT is actively goal directed.

HRT is actively goal directed. Goals in HRT can be thought of in terms of overall goals and goals for a particular session. During the initial assessment, an overall goal is determined. This is the focus of treatment and represents a measureable outcome of therapy. The second consideration for goal setting is the establishment of a goal for a *particular session.* In this regard, each session is focused on a particular goal that is connected to the overall goal for hypnotherapy. For example, if the overall goal is symptom reduction in a patient with tension headaches, the goal for a particular session might be to identify a place where the patient feels calm and comfortable with no headaches, even if temporarily. An example of this is:

> "There has been a concern about headaches . . . headaches related to stress and tension . . . and today, finding a place where you are comfortable . . . safe . . . and calm . . . and as you go to this place . . . finding that the headache hurts less and less . . . It is replaced by a feeling of warmth . . . or a tingly sensation . . . certainly greater comfort . . . and so letting your mind drift . . . letting your unconscious mind take you to a place where you find comfort . . . real comfort . . . the tension . . . the headache fades away."

In this case, the goal for the session is to identify a place where the patient can experience comfort. The specific mental imagery that is suggested should be consistent with the goal and connected to an effect that will reduce symptoms, facilitate insight, or achieve another goal. A variety of hypnotic phenomena may be utilized toward this goal. The use of hypnosis to achieve a particular effect can help to make the patient more confident to use hypnosis in an effective manner. The demonstration of hypnotic phenomena during a session can involve suggestions for deep relaxation, analgesia, arm levitation, or other effects that validate that response to suggestion is, in fact, occurring.

Step VIII: Reinforcement of response

Suggestions to encourage and acknowledge progress are given throughout the session. Additionally, it is especially important to validate the achievement of the goal for that session. Once the goal is achieved, suggestions for reinforcement should follow. For example, in the case of tension headaches noted above, reinforcing suggestions such as the following could be given,

> Suggestions for returning to conscious alertness should be given in a calm and unhurried voice.

> "... and as you do notice the comfort across your forehead ... as you are aware the headache has become less ... faded further and further ... that the comfort is greater ... This is a good, positive feeling ... and just nodding your head yes ... as you notice the comfort across your forehead ... Very good ... you are doing very well ..."

Step IX: Post-hypnotic suggestion

A positive response to suggestion and symptom reduction during the session is very important. It is also typically desired that improvement in symptoms, insight, or other areas continue after the session ends. This is where post-hypnotic suggestions come into play. Post-hypnotic suggestions are suggestions that are given while a person is in a trance state, with the idea that the effects of these particular suggestions will be experienced after the patient returns to a fully awake, alert state. Post-hypnotic suggestions may be given for (1) continued improvement, or (2) response to a suggestion that will occur at a later time. Both may be integrated into the session. For example, a post-hypnotic suggestion to continue improvement could be,

> Post-hypnotic suggestions are suggestions that are given while a person is in a trance state, with the idea that the effects of these particular suggestions will be experienced after the patient returns to a fully awake, alert state.

> "... and this relaxation and comfort across your forehead will continue for a long time ... You will find that the comfort continues even when you return to conscious alertness ... A greater comfort ... a greater control."

An example of a post-hypnotic suggestion for a future response could be,

> "You have done very well ... and in the coming days ... the cause of these headaches will become more apparent to you ... The stress associated with causing these tension headaches will come more into your conscious awareness ... perhaps in your thoughts ... or perhaps in a dream that stands out to you ... in some way ..."

Another way post-hypnotic suggestions can be utilized is to suggest learning self-hypnosis. Self-hypnosis practice is often a part of HRT, so post-hypnotic suggestions could be given, such as,

> "In the future you will find that you will be able to use self-hypnosis to achieve a sufficient depth of trance. You will be able to enter a hypnotic state easily and quickly whenever you wish to use hypnosis and when it is appropriate and helpful to you."

Here, the process of self-hypnosis could also be suggested. Post-hypnotic suggestions can be repeated, depending on their complexity, to emphasize their importance. Following this, suggestions for alerting are usually given.

Step X: Alerting

Suggestions to encourage and acknowledge progress are given throughout the session.

Prior to alerting, any unintended hypnotic effects should be removed through suggestion. Then the patient can be guided into conscious alertness. Suggestions for returning to conscious alertness should be given in a calm and unhurried voice. Abrupt cues for returning to alertness, such as snapping fingers, should be avoided. Suggestions for alerting can be given in a direct manner, such as counting. For example:

> "As I begin to count the numbers from one to four, you are returning to conscious alertness . . . 1 . . . more aware of this room, this time and place . . . 2 . . . returning to conscious alertness . . . And soon your eyelids can begin to open . . . 3 . . . eyelids opening . . . feeling calm . . . refreshed . . . and relaxed . . . and 4 . . . All the way back . . . alert . . . and able to discuss your experience with hypnotherapy today."

As an alternative, suggestions for alerting may be given in a permissive manner, such as:

> "And now in your own time . . . and in your own way . . . returning to conscious alertness . . . in a time and in a way that just feels about right to you . . . and as you do . . . your eyelids can open as you return to conscious alertness . . . in your own time . . . at your own pace. . . . eyelids opening as you come all the way back . . ."

Once the patient opens her eyes, it is important to verify alertness. For example, the therapist might ask, "What are you most aware of now? . . . How do you feel? . . . Are you alert?" Once a positive answer is given, there can be some post-hypnotic discussion to process the session.

HYPNOTIC INDUCTIONS

As noted above, there are a variety of ways to suggest a focus of attention and to initiate a hypnotic relaxation induction. Among the most common hypnotic inductions are: (1) eye-focus induction, (2) breathing-focus induction, (3) coin-drop induction, (4) arm-levitation induction, and (5) arm-lowering induction. These inductions are useful. as they provide for easy observation of a patient's response, which then allows for pacing suggestions. Sample verbalization for each of these inductions is provided below.

(1) *Eye-focus induction:* One approach to eye-focus induction has already been described in the sample verbalization for the steps of a hypnotic

relaxation induction procedure. Another preferred approach to this induction is to begin with a dimly lit room and to have the patient focus on a small light or an object that can be seen with the lights turned down. One way the therapist can guide the patient into an eye-focus induction is,

> "In a moment I will turn down the lights and ask that you find a comfortable position in which to sit . . . Notice the small light in front of you . . . and focus your attention on that light . . . As you focus there . . . other things begin to fade into the background . . . the light may seem to move or become dimmer as you focus there . . . and as you do . . . allow a feeling of relaxation to come to you . . . more and more . . . a feeling of deep relaxation . . . Your forehead relaxes . . . your eyes . . . your jaw . . . your neck and shoulders . . . The eyelids may feel heavy and they may begin to close . . . as you drift deeper and deeper relaxed . . . drifting into a hypnotic state where you can achieve the things you wish to achieve in hypnosis today."

Note that, if the therapist is using a light to complete an eye-focus induction, the light should not be especially bright. A light such as on an electronic clock should suffice.

(2) *Breathing-focus induction*: Awareness of breathing can also be utilized as a focus point for a hypnotic relaxation induction. This is especially useful in both working with patients who have some prior experience with hypnotherapy and teaching self-hypnosis. The patient is guided to begin with her eyes closed and then to bring attention to her breathing. Suggestions are then given for noticing changes in breathing patterns, and this is associated with deepening relaxation, dissociation, and trance. The principles of pacing and leading are utilized, and observation of the patient's responses helps to guide the specific suggestions, timing, and pattern of suggestions. An example of a breathing-focused induction is as follows:

> Awareness of breathing is especially useful in both working with patients who have some prior experience with hypnotherapy and teaching self-hypnosis.

> "In a few moments you can begin the process of entering a deep state of hypnotic relaxation by focusing on your breathing. Just settle back into the comfort of the chair . . . allow your eyelids to close . . . and begin to focus your attention on your breathing . . . Your breathing is always with you . . . sometimes more in your awareness and sometimes less in your awareness . . . Notice the feelings that go along with breathing in and breathing out . . . Notice the coolness of the air in your nostrils as you breathe in, and the feeling of letting go and drifting . . . deeper relaxed . . . as you breathe out . . . allowing a feeling of deeper relaxation to come to you with every breath . . . each time you breathe out . . . thinking the word "relax" . . . and the body and the mind respond to this word . . . relax . . . taking a deep breath of air . . . And as

> you breathe out . . . normally and naturally . . . a wave of relaxation can seem to come to you. Your forehead relaxes . . . your neck and shoulders relax . . . and you notice that your breathing may have already become a little slower . . . a little deeper . . . and as it does, you can drift . . . into an even deeper state of hypnosis . . . deeper relaxed . . . a relaxation that spreads to your back . . . your shoulders . . . your chest . . . and your stomach . . . breathing in and out just takes you to a deeper level of relaxation . . . so that now even your legs and feet relax further . . . calmer . . . And your breathing . . . each time you breathe out . . . takes you into a deeper state of hypnotic relaxation . . . whether you are aware of your breathing . . . consciously . . . or not."

Following the induction, suggestions can then be given for dissociation and mental imagery for deepening trance and achievement of therapeutic goals.

(3) *Coin-drop induction*: The coin-drop induction technique can be used with adults or children. The procedure is first explained to the individual and then demonstrated. It involves asking the patient to hold a coin (such as a quarter or half-dollar) between the thumb and first finger of the dominant hand. The arm should be extended straight out in front of the body. The patient is then instructed to focus attention on the coin and to let other things fade into the background. The patient is given the suggestion that the fingers holding the coin will begin to relax, and that, as the coin drops, it will serve as a cue for the eyelids to close and to begin to enter a state of hypnotic relaxation. The wording for initial induction is:

> "Now, as you are sitting comfortably, take this coin and hold it between your first finger and thumb. Hold your arm straight out in front of you and hold the coin so that it is facing downward, toward the floor . . . Now, begin looking at the coin . . . intently . . . focusing your attention on the coin . . . and letting other things fade into the background . . . You can hear my voice . . . but other things fade into the background . . . you focus on the coin . . . allowing a feeling of relaxation to come to you . . . your forehead relaxing . . . the muscles of your eyes . . . relaxing . . . more and more . . . a spreading relaxation . . . Soon your arm may begin to feel a little tired . . . or heavy . . . the relaxation spreads across your shoulders . . . and as you focus on the coin . . . the fingers around the coin will soon begin to . . . relax . . . and as they do . . . as the coin drops . . . it will serve as a cue for your eyelids to close and you drift into a very deep state of hypnotic relaxation . . . just a very good feeling of deep relaxation . . . in every positive way . . . And drifting, then . . . into a deep hypnotic state . . . in which you can accomplish all of the things in hypnosis that you would like to accomplish today . . . the fingers relax . . . and . . . you allow the coin

An arm levitation induction can be especially validating, as the patient is able to experience a hypnotic phenomenon (arm rising without conscious effort) during the induction procedure.

> to drop . . . now . . . and the eyelids now close . . . good . . . and you are drifting into a deep state of hypnotic relaxation."

At the end of the session, after alerting, it may be useful to give the coin to the patient as a reminder or to facilitate practice of self-hypnosis using the coin-drop technique.

(4) *Arm-levitation induction*: This induction involves providing suggestions for the patient to experience a feeling of lightness or weightlessness in an arm. As the patient experiences a subjective feeling of lightness, her arm can be observed as "floating upward." An arm-levitation induction can be especially validating, as the patient is able to experience a hypnotic phenomenon (arm rising without conscious effort) during the induction procedure. However, this method is most likely to be effective with individuals in the moderate or higher ranges of hypnotizability. If the patient is in the lower range, then the method can be enhanced by the therapist gently lifting the arm if the patient does not readily achieve arm levitation. This may be useful in preventing the patient from experiencing "failure" if this is used as an induction method. Once the arm rises, it can be followed by suggestions for heaviness and eye closure. The following wording can be utilized for an arm-levitation induction:

> "Please allow your hands to rest comfortably on your thighs with your palms facing down, and allow your body to relax. Now, please bring your attention to one of your hands . . . your left hand . . . or your right hand . . . Focus on that hand . . . very intently . . . Notice how the hand rests there . . . comfortably . . . observe the back of the hand . . . the veins . . . the fingers . . . Soon a change in sensation in that hand can occur . . . it can become lighter and lighter . . . and as it does, it begins to float up . . . You will be able to enter a deep state of hypnosis now . . . notice that hand, and it does become lighter . . . the fingers may twitch . . . and begin to lift . . . the arm becomes lighter and lighter . . . it soon begins to float up . . . easily . . . weightless. . . . lighter than air . . . it is floating up . . ."

If the patient's arm does not begin to float up, the therapist may use additional verbalization such as, "Good, now as I touch the wrist . . . the arm begins to float up even more," and gently lift the wrist with as much support as necessary to lift it. If no involuntary lightness occurs, then lower the hand and follow with suggestions for eye closure. For example:

> ". . . that's right . . . very good . . . it floats up higher and higher . . . and you can observe this . . . but it might be even more pleasant to soon allow your eyelids to close and go into an even deeper state of hypnotic relaxation . . . so now, a feeling of heaviness will soon come to the arm . . . And as it begins to become heavy . . . and floats down to your lap . . . allow your eyelids to close . . . As they close you are going into a deeper and more relaxed state . . . that's right . . . your arm becomes heavier now . . . floating downward . . . your eyelids are closing . . . going deeper and deeper relaxed . . . a deeper state of hypnosis."

Remember that suggestions should be paced with the indications that the patient is responding to suggestions (e.g., the hand, wrist, and arm raise in response to suggestions).

(5) *Arm-lowering induction*: An arm-lowering induction is somewhat easier to utilize and achieve, even with individuals in the lower range of hypnotizability. The patient is first instructed to hold an arm out in front of the body, palm facing up, and then suggestions for heaviness are given. As the arm begins to lower, suggestions for relaxation, eye closure, and deepening the hypnotic state are given. This method is one to which most patients can respond, as fatigue and gravity make eventual lowering of the arm almost inevitable. Suggestions for an arm-lowering induction may include:

An arm-lowering induction is somewhat easier to utilize and achieve, even with individuals in the lower range of hypnotizability.

> "Please lean back into the cushions of the chair . . . allow your head to rest . . . and hold your right (or left) arm out in front of you . . . straight out . . . with the palm of the hand facing upward . . . Focus on this hand . . . and soon it will begin to feel very, very heavy . . . and as it begins to feel so very heavy . . . it can lower . . . and your eyelids can close . . . and you can relax . . . And now as you focus on the hand . . . and the arm . . . they become heavier . . . as if you were holding a bucket of heavy wet sand . . . the sand is so heavy . . . And as you feel the heaviness . . . allow it to become even heavier . . . you may want to add some more wet sand to the bucket . . . so that it becomes heavier and heavier . . . Very good . . . As the hand and the arm begin to drift down . . . allowing your eyelids to drift down . . . as the hand comes to rest . . . comfortably in your lap . . . the eyelids close . . . all the way . . . closed . . . and a feeling of deep relaxation . . . drifting into a hypnotic state . . . can begin to come to you . . . as the hand rests there . . . and normal sensations come to the hand . . . you can drift even deeper relaxed . . . deeply hypnotized . . . deeper and deeper . . ."

Again, following the induction, suggestions can then be given to facilitate hypnotic relaxation, mental imagery for calm feelings, and to suggest achievement of therapeutic goals.

ADDITIONAL HYPNOTIC INDUCTIONS AND INDIVIDUALIZATION

It should be noted that hypnotic inductions can also be developed on an individual basis depending on the patient's preferences and circumstances. For example, some patients may prefer to begin the hypnotic induction with their eyes closed and focus upon inner feelings. In other cases, patients may prefer to initially focus on a sound (such as a gong, music, or water sound) or a favorite picture (such as a nature scene). All of these can be effective methods for hypnotic inductions. In all cases each patient's individual preferences should be explored and utilized.

CHAPTER 5

Case Conceptualization and Treatment Planning

Hypnotic relaxation therapy (HRT) utilizes a biopsychosocial approach to case conceptualization and treatment planning. When engaging in treatment planning, it is important to remember that HRT may be the primary intervention, or it may be utilized as an adjunctive therapy in the overall treatment approach for a particular patient and problem.

While assessment is an ongoing process within HRT, the initial assessment, case conceptualization, and hypothesis formulation is usually done in the first few sessions, before initiating the first actual session of HRT. The purpose of the assessment is to determine an overall treatment strategy. As the clinician begins the processes of case conceptualization and treatment planning, there are several key concepts he or she should keep in mind. These concepts and considerations are outlined below and illustrated with the case conceptualization that was developed in planning HRT for "Linda," who presented with stress and tension headaches (this patient was discussed in Chapter 2 and additional information is presented here).

PRESENTING PROBLEMS

During the initial consultation, it is important to identify the patient's primary concern or symptom. This identifies the goal of the intervention and provides a focus for treatment. Determining whether or not hypnotherapy is indicated for the presenting problem is also a part of this process. Hypnotherapy has been shown to be of benefit in the treatment of a wide variety of disorders, ranging from chronic pain to menopausal hot flashes and even to some dermatological symptoms. That being said, in general, symptoms that are involuntarily experienced, such

During the initial consultation, it is important to identify the patient's primary concern or symptom.

as pain, anxiety, stress, depression, psychophysiological disorders, somatization symptoms (including conversion disorder), and habit and behavioral disorders, can be treated with HRT. Additionally, HRT can facilitate cognitive changes and insight into underlying unconscious issues. Despite the broad applications of hypnotherapy, there are some instances in which its use would be contraindicated. For example, patients who present with antisocial behavior, criminal behavior, or who have unrealistic expectations will not benefit from HRT. HRT emphasizes an empirical basis for intervention, and ongoing clinical research is likely to reveal new applications in the future.

HRT emphasizes an empirical basis for intervention, and ongoing clinical research is likely to reveal new applications in the future.

Other relative contraindications include consideration of the patient's intellectual ability. Hypnosis is a complex concept and the patient should have sufficient mental ability to understand the process and utilize hypnotic relaxation in an effective manner. For example, one patient was referred for hypnotherapy for tobacco cessation. However, the patient was profoundly mentally retarded and tobacco had been (inappropriately) used as reinforcement in a mental health program, leading to nicotine dependency. The patient did not have the mental capacity to understand the purpose of the appointment and had no desire to discontinue use of tobacco. In this example, hypnotherapy was not the treatment of choice and the patient was referred for behavioral intervention at the program or system level.

It is important that the therapist emphasize, from the outset, that HRT is a collaborative process with the goal of empowering the patient. It is not something that is "done to the patient." If the patient has the expectation that he or she will be hypnotized and forced to change his or her behavior, then this unrealistic expectation must be addressed before proceeding. For example, one patient was self-referred, requesting hypnotherapy "to make me lose weight." The patient had the expectation that she would be "hypnotized" and that weight loss would occur without any diet changes or engaging in exercise. She offered, "I have already tried those things and they didn't work; now I just want to be hypnotized!" It was explained that HRT is a useful adjunctive intervention that can be combined with a cognitive–behavioral approach to weight loss in order to achieve changes in cognition, lifestyle, and diet.

The presenting problem should be clearly identified and then a judgment made to determine appropriate goals for HRT.

The presenting problem should be clearly identified and then a judgment made to determine appropriate goals for HRT. In addition, at this time, the hypnotherapist should consider appropriate outcome measures to evaluate the patient's progress toward accomplishment. Throughout this process, it is important to remember that HRT is goal-directed and time-limited.

HISTORY OF THE PRESENTING PROBLEM

A thorough review of the history of the patient's presenting concern can be helpful in revealing the onset of symptoms and associated psychological, physiological, or social factors that may need to be addressed.

TIMELINE AND KEY EVENTS

A timeline involves determining a chronological history of the concern. Past diagnostic testing, evaluations (medical or psychological), and previous treatments should be reviewed. It may be helpful to ask, "Why does the patient come for treatment at this time?" If the problem has persisted for several years, the patient may have developed secondary gain or other issues that complicate treatment. Secondary gain refers to any factors that may tend to reinforce the patient's symptoms. Examples of secondary gain include financial compensation, attention for symptom complaints, or avoidance of unpleasant tasks due to symptoms. Also, to a greater or lesser degree, physical, psychological, and environmental factors may be involved in understanding the presenting concern.

It is important to determine if the presenting problem is primarily an organic condition that requires medication or surgical intervention.

PHYSICAL FACTORS

It is important to determine if the presenting problem is primarily an organic condition that requires medication or surgical intervention. Past medical history should be reviewed, and the clinician should determine if an appropriate medical evaluation has been conducted or if a referral is needed. Additionally, it is important to define what physical changes would be consistent with the patient's desire for symptom relief.

PSYCHOLOGICAL FACTORS

Psychological factors contribute to most emotional and medical problems, and the patient's past psychiatric history and current symptoms should always be considered in treatment planning. The patient's emotional well-being, as well as any evidence of depression, chronic anxiety, or stress should be carefully assessed. In addition, because there is considerable evidence that cognition may be involved in the maintenance of many problems, such as depression, anxiety, and chronic pain, the patient's thoughts about his or her problems should be discussed. For example, a patient with low self-esteem may hold maladaptive thoughts about themselves and others. It is especially important to identify if the patient is engaging in catastrophic thinking such as, "The problem is terrible. I can't stand it; it's awful."

The patient's emotional well-being, as well as any evidence of depression, chronic anxiety, or stress should be carefully assessed.

Also, the patient's problem may be related to behavioral reinforcement or classical conditioning. During the initial interview, any sources of reinforcement of the presenting problem, such as attention, financial support, or avoidance of responsibilities, should be reviewed. Also, the clinician should explore any history of classical conditioning of symptoms.

SOCIAL ENVIRONMENT

Discussion of the patient's social environment includes a review of any social support, interpersonal stress, and family dynamics. For example, asking the patient questions such as, "Who is the most supportive person in your life? Tell me about your family. What events are most stressful in your life right now?" can facilitate greater understanding of the presenting concern.

EXPERIENTIAL REPRESENTATIONS

Identification of how the presenting problem is represented within the unconscious/experiential system is perhaps the most subjective and complex aspect of the case conceptualization. It is an ongoing process, and the fullness and individual nature of the patient's experiential representation is likely to come more to the surface as hypnotherapy proceeds over time. However, it is possible to gain some insight and understanding within the first few sessions. Since the experiential system processes information differently from the rational system, it is likely that the patient's symptoms are represented in some symbolic or narrative form, or as an image. Symptoms may represent positive or negative aspects of the self and serve some protective function, of which the patient is not consciously aware. The idea of the experiential system should be introduced to the patient as,

Symptoms may represent positive or negative aspects of the self and serve some protective function, of which the patient is not consciously aware.

> "We all have a conscious and an unconscious mind. The unconscious is primarily experiential and operates in terms of feelings, symbolism, associations, memories, and *stories* or narratives. I am interested in finding out how you understand the symptom or problem within your unconscious. For example, can you think of your symptom or problem as being represented symbolically?"

This discussion can then be followed by additional questions to explore possible representations. For example, the following questions have been used productively in exploration symptoms:

- "How would you describe your experience of the symptom?"
- "Have you ever had a dream about the symptom; what happened in the dream?"

- "When the symptom is at its worst, can it seem to have its own emotion? Does it feel angry, fearful, or calm?"
- "Can you imagine being without the symptom? Where can you imagine it could go?"

The information is used in the overall case conceptualization and can provide very useful guidance in forming specific hypnotic suggestions.

MENTAL STATUS

In considering a patient for hypnotherapy, a brief mental status examination should be conducted as a part of the interview. The patient's emotional well-being as well as any evidence of depression, chronic anxiety, or stress should be carefully assessed. It is also important to make inquiries regarding any suicidal or homicidal ideation or intention. Additionally, if the patient has a relevant psychiatric history, the clinician should determine if he or she is experiencing psychosis or other symptoms of thought disorder, for example, "Do you ever hear or see things that others cannot see or hear?" This is important in order to rule out any serious psychopathology, assure that hypnotherapy is appropriate for the patient, or provide a referral if necessary.

In considering a patient for hypnotherapy, a brief mental status examination should be conducted as a part of the interview.

HYPNOTIC EXPERIENCE AND ABILITY

The interview should also include a discussion to determine if the patient has had any previous experience with hypnosis. The clinician should determine whether the experience was positive, and if the patient has any particular expectations. It may also be helpful to gain an estimate of the patient's hypnotic ability. This is ideally done by administration of a hypnotizability measure, such as the *Elkins Hypnotizability Scale,* which is described in Chapter 10.

DIAGNOSIS

A formal diagnosis is developed based upon the presenting symptoms, past history, and mental status examination. The diagnosis can be helpful in determining treatment interventions and planning.

The interview should also include a discussion to determine if the patient has had any previous experience with hypnosis.

SUMMARY STATEMENT AND GOALS

A brief summary of the case conceptualization is then provided and specific goals are identified.

STRENGTHS AND WEAKNESSES

After treatment goals have been established, the clinician should identify any particular strengths that may help the patient progress toward his or her goals. Also, any weakness or anticipated factors that may lead to resistance or interfere with progress should be identified.

MANAGEMENT PLAN

The management plan should include a list of interventions, including those involved in HRT as well as other, nonhypnotic interventions that are recommended. I prefer to list these in bullet form for easy reference in the future.

DISCUSSION OF HRT

It is important that the clinician and patient share a mutual understanding of the problem and fully agree upon the treatment plan.

The overall case conceptualization should be reviewed with the patient and modified according to the patient's feedback. It is important that the clinician and patient share a mutual understanding of the problem and fully agree upon the treatment plan. This typically involves a discussion of the HRT process during the first or second session, as time allows. An example case conceptualization based upon the patient "Linda," who was first identified in Chapter 2, follows. This case will also be further elaborated upon in Chapters 6 through 9, in which the details of each session are discussed.

Case Conceptualization and Planning Hypnotherapy: The Case of Linda

Identifying information

Date: 01/23/2012
Name: Linda
Age: 38 years old
Referral from: Family Medicine Clinic

Presenting problems

The patient is a 38-year-old married Caucasian woman with a history of stress and stress-related headaches. She was referred for HRT by her family physician.

History of concerns

Timeline: *The patient states that she first began experiencing headaches about six years ago after the birth of her daughter. She initially was having headaches about every 3 to 4 weeks. She states that she began taking over-the-counter medications for pain. However, her headaches have become progressively worse, and she is now having headaches almost every day.*

Physical Factors: *The patient relates that, about 4 months ago, she was referred to a neurologist. The neurological examination ruled out any potential organic causes of her symptoms. The patient's medical history is significant for migraine and tension headaches, as well as for sinus problems. She also complains of difficulty with going to sleep at night. Her current medications include: Tizanadine, magnesium, Imipramine, Tramadol, Citalopram, and multivitamins.*

Psychological Factors: *Linda recognizes that she is experiencing considerable stress. She gives an example of her 79-year-old mother, who has a number of significant medical problems, and who had been living with her. Because of her own increased headaches and her mother's declining health, Linda was not able to continue taking care of her mother, and she had to move in with Linda's sibling. In addition, Linda reports that she works part-time as a substitute teacher, and she finds the combination of all of these issues contribute to her stress. She states that she believes her headaches are related to stress. She also notes that she often has thoughts such as: "I am overwhelmed, I can't cope, etc." She reports that, when her headaches are especially bad, she will spend most of the day in bed. She has no prior history of counseling.*

Social Environment: *Linda and her husband have been married for the past eight years. Her husband is 40 years old and is employed with an electrical construction company. The patient is currently a stay-at-home mother. Her daughter is 6 years old. She describes a close and supportive relationship with her husband. Family-related stresses are noted above.*

Experiential representations

Linda described her headaches as being associated with feeling "tense from head to toe." She states that her head throbs "as if a block of ice was on my head." She states that she "worries" and that the headaches are most severe when she "feels the burden of all the responsibilities." She states that sometimes the feelings of guilt and sadness are "like a dark cloud."

Mental status

The patient came for today's visit neatly and appropriately dressed and well oriented. She was cooperative, and it was possible to establish a good level of rapport with her. She readily admits to feelings of depression, anxiety, and stress. She states that her appetite varies but that she commonly skips breakfast. Her energy level has decreased and she is concerned about her weight increasing. She states that she has been worried about her sleep and that she often does not go to sleep quickly even when she is sleepy. She denies any suicidal or homicidal thought or intention. Her thought processes are logical and goal directed, and there is no evidence of any thought disorder.

Hypnotic experience and ability

The patient completed the Elkins Hypnotizability Scale and received a score of 8, consistent with a moderate degree of hypnotic ability. It is noteworthy that she was able to respond to suggestions for heaviness, arm levitation, and mental imagery and dissociation. She reported the experience to be positive and pleasant.

Diagnosis

AXIS I: Depressive disorder; psychological factors affecting physical condition
AXIS II: None
AXIS III: History of tension/migraine headaches
AXIS IV: Interpersonal stress, stress associated with medical illness
AXIS V: 55

Summary statement and goals

In summary, the patient is a 38-year-old woman experiencing headaches associated with stress. In addition, she is experiencing feelings of depression as well as poor sleep. Stresses include parenting, work, family issues, and issues associated with medical illness. Social support is good, and her marital relationship is described in positive terms.

Goals include: *(1) reduce headaches; (2) improve stress management; (3) improve sleep; (4) decrease depression; and (5) increase self-acceptance and coping skills.*

Strengths and weaknesses

Strengths: *Good insight, motivation, social support, and moderate hypnotic ability.*

Weakness: *Multiple stresses and chronic symptoms. Headaches may be reinforced by avoidance of stressful activities.*

Management plan

1. *Hypnotic relaxation therapy directed toward managing stress and reducing headache frequency and severity. Suggestions for relaxation combined with suggestions for warmth, dissociation to a safe place, and calmness will be provided during sessions.*
2. *Behavioral recommendations for sleep hygiene combined with hypnotic relaxation therapy directed toward improving sleep onset will be given.*
3. *Hypnotic relaxation therapy will be integrated with cognitive therapy to reduce maladaptive self-statements such as, "I am overwhelmed, I can't cope, I should. . . ." Mental imagery for lifting a "dark cloud" of sadness and guilt will be integrated with suggestions for positive cognitive changes.*
4. *Increasing feelings of self-acceptance will be addressed through hypnotic suggestions for letting go of self-criticism and increasing feelings of self-love and compassion.*
5. *The patient will be encouraged to continue daily activities and express her thoughts and needs in a more assertive manner. Social support is a strength, and her husband may be of assistance in dealing with stresses.*
6. *Progress will be determined through self-ratings using a visual analog 0 to 10 scale to rate headache severity, sleep, depression, and self-esteem. Also, frequency of headaches will be monitored.*

CHAPTER 6

The First Hypnotic Relaxation Therapy Session

The first hypnotic relaxation therapy (HRT) session contains a number of critical components that are meant to set the stage for successful treatment. These include: (1) presenting HRT to the patient; (2) dealing with myths and misconceptions; (3) setting the treatment session goals; (4) rating of symptoms; (5) preparatory talk; (6) hypnotic induction; (7) post-hypnotic inquiry; and (8) ending the session. It is important to keep in mind that preparing the patient, answering any questions, and ensuring a collaborative relationship of trust are essential before beginning the actual hypnotic induction. Therefore, the first session may proceed more quickly or more slowly depending on the patient's readiness and the complexity of the presenting problem.

> It is important to keep in mind that preparing the patient, answering any questions, and a collaborative relationship of trust are essential before beginning the actual hypnotic induction.

PRESENTING HRT TO THE PATIENT

It is recommended that the clinician review the patient's previous experience with hypnosis,and specifically discuss the use of hypnotic relaxation for treatment of the patient's presenting issue. Additionally, it is helpful to provide the patient with a brochure regarding HRT (see Appendix).

As the brochure is reviewed, the hypnotherapist should discuss the underlying basis of HRT and clarify any myths or misconceptions the patient may have about hypnosis. For example, the clinician might say:

> "This brochure provides some additional information about HRT. Please take a moment to look it over and see if you have any questions. This includes some information about myths and misconceptions that

people sometimes have about hypnosis. For instance, it discusses that hypnosis does not involve any type of loss of consciousness; rather, you will be aware of what is happening throughout our session. Also, hypnosis does not involve any weakening of the will or loss of control; rather, the focus is on giving you more control to achieve the things you want to achieve."

The process of HRT should be discussed as a collaborative process with the goal of empowering the patient. In this regard, it is important to orient patients to the idea of being actively involved in learning how to use hypnotic relaxation and that their at-home practice between sessions is essential. An example of how this information can be conveyed might be:

The process of HRT should be discussed as a collaborative process with the goal of empowering the patient.

"HRT is a mind–body therapy that involves the use of deep relaxation and mental imagery. During each session, we will go through a hypnotic induction that will involve suggestions to become deeply relaxed. Additionally, at each session, you will be learning more about self-hypnosis and how to make hypnosis work best for you. It is very important that you practice self-hypnosis on a daily basis. At the end of our session today, I will most likely provide you with an audio recording to help you with your practice at home. The goal is to empower you to have more control over your symptoms. At the end of each session, I will ask you to comment on your personal experience during that session so we can learn how to make hypnosis work best for you."

DEALING WITH MYTHS AND MISCONCEPTIONS

While use of the term "HRT" is useful in distinguishing the intervention from other presentations of "hypnosis," some patients may still have misconceptions. Patients that have rigid beliefs or limited personal experience with hypnotic relaxation inductions may have formed conceptions of "hypnotic" interventions from movies, stage shows, or novels in which individuals are made to act in an odd or embarrassing manner. The patient should be reassured that he or she will remain in control, will experience relaxation, and that the experience of trance is a naturally occurring state of consciousness. The therapist can provide everyday examples of a hypnotic or trance state, such as becoming absorbed in reading an interesting novel or watching a movie or daydreaming. The best way to learn what happens during hypnotic relaxation is through experiencing it. Following are some of the usual questions that patients may ask and sample responses.

The best way to learn what happens during hypnotic relaxation is through experiencing it.

1. *Is the hypnotic state the same as sleep?*
   No, the altered state of consciousness associated with hypnotic relaxation is completely different from a sleep state. Brain activity during sleep is different from that which occurs during a hypnotic induction, and for a HRT session, no suggestions for sleep will be given, as that would not be the goal. It is possible that a person can fall asleep during a hypnotic induction; however, that is most likely when suggestions for sleep are actually given. You may experience a lapse in time from being very absorbed in the process, and with even a light hypnotic state, you can at times feel very relaxed. You may also feel a sense of heaviness, a floating sensation, or a kind of detached feeling.

2. *Can everyone be hypnotized?*
   Not everyone can be hypnotized. However, the vast majority of people can achieve some degree of response to hypnotic suggestion. For some people, the benefit from experiencing hypnotherapy is very quick and may occur during the first session. For others, it may take more practice and experience in hypnotic relaxation to enter a deeper hypnotic state and achieve their goals. There are no personality characteristics that predict response to hypnotic suggestion. However, characteristics such as creativity, the ability to become absorbed in experiences, openness, and motivation are all positive predictors of being able to experience response to hypnotic suggestions.

   There are no personality characteristics that predict response to hypnotic suggestion.

3. *Will I be unconscious?*
   You will not be unconscious. You will be able to hear and be aware of things around you as much as you want. However, hypnotherapy is a process that involves "letting go" of conscious effort and allowing your unconscious mind to respond to hypnotic suggestions. We all have a divided mind: a conscious mind and an unconscious mind. The conscious mind engages in more logical thought and rational thinking. The unconscious mind processes information in a more experiential manner and responds to feelings, images, and suggestions more automatically. Therefore, during your hypnotic relaxation sessions, you may find that you are able to "observe" your own responses and feelings. One characteristic of hypnotherapy is involuntariness; that is, responses can occur without a great deal of "trying" or conscious effort. For example, if suggestions are given for your arm to feel light and weightless, it can seem to float up on its own, as you allow it to happen.

4. *Is HRT dangerous?*
   The use of hypnotic relaxation is not dangerous when facilitated by experiences that can be beneficial. You may become aware of thoughts or feelings that cause some stress; however, this may be a part of your therapy to deal with such feelings. Your progress will be monitored and you will be asked to provide feedback throughout the session.

5. *Will I go into a deep trance state?*
   People vary in their hypnotic ability. At times you may feel that you are in a deeper hypnotic state, and at other times, lighter. Research has indicated that even a light hypnotic state can be beneficial. Going into a deeper trance can sometimes occur, but it is often not necessary.

6. *Is it possible I won't be able to wake up from the hypnotic induction?*
   No, it is not possible to become "stuck in a trance state." You will be aware of your therapist's voice and be able to respond to suggestions for alertness at the end of the session, or you can return to conscious alertness at any time you choose. Either way, you will be able to return to conscious alertness at your own pace. It is important that you give yourself permission to return to alertness without feeling rushed. It is also possible that, when practicing hypnotic relaxation at home, you may want to drift into natural sleep and then return to alertness when you awaken.

The fact is that no one can be hypnotized against his or her will.

7. *Can you hypnotize me and make me do something I don't want to do?*
   The fact is that no one can be hypnotized against his or her will. Suggestions will be given for you to accomplish the things that you want to accomplish. Further, research has indicated that if a person is asked to do things that are unacceptable according to one's beliefs, the person will come out of the hypnotic state.

SETTING THE TREATMENT SESSION GOAL

It is usually helpful to review the overall goal of hypnotherapy and then discuss the goal of the session. The goals for the first session can include helping the patient to become more familiar with hypnotherapy, reduce anxiety, gain insight, or reduce symptoms of the presenting problem. It is also important to gain greater knowledge of the patient's personal preferences and experiences so that this information can be used in later sessions for individualization of the hypnotic inductions and suggestions. In the case of Linda, the following exchange took place.

It is important to gain greater knowledge of the patient's personal preferences and experiences so that this information can be used in later sessions for individualization of the hypnotic inductions and suggestions.

> **Therapist:** *Alright, Linda, let's review our goals for hypnotherapy. The overall goals are to reduce your headaches, decrease stress, and improve your sleep and emotional well-being. Does that sound about right to you?*
>
> **Linda:** *Yes, that would be great if we can do all of that!*
>
> **Therapist:** *Well, let's get started! I know we can't accomplish all of those things in one session. However, I think we can make a lot of*

progress today and over the coming week. It seems to me that if you can begin to use hypnotic relaxation to decease feelings of anxiety and stress today and learn to reduce the headaches, that would be good.

Linda: *Sounds good to me. I feel pretty tense right now and have a headache. Will that be a problem with my being able to be hypnotized?*

RATING OF SYMPTOMS

It can also be very helpful to ask the patient to rate his or her symptoms. For example, the clinician can use a 0 to 10 scale, with "0" representing no problem and "10" representing the worst possible experience with a symptom. Patients can also use daily diaries, questionnaires, psychological measures, or rating scales to measure their symptoms. With Linda, rating symptoms was introduced in the following manner:

It can also be very helpful to ask the patient to rate his or her symptoms.

Therapist: *Thank you for letting me know how you are feeling. I don't think that will interfere with you being able to have a good experience with the hypnotic induction. In fact, as you are able to become more comfortable, it may actually help you go into a deeper hypnotic state. Could I ask you to rate those feelings? How would you rate the headache on a 0 to 10 scale, with 0 indicating you have no pain at all and 10 being the worst headache you have ever experienced?*

Linda: *It is pretty bad . . . I would say it is about a 7 right now. I can stand it, but I've had it all day.*

Therapist: *OK, a 7, and how would you rate the level of anxiety you feel right now? Zero is no anxiety and 10 is as anxious as you could be.*

Linda: *I guess I'm a little nervous about the hypnosis. I'm going to say about a 6. It has been worse.*

Therapist: *OK, a 6. I'd like to give you some idea about the hypnotic induction for today.*

Before beginning the hypnotic induction it is advisable to describe the type of induction and suggestions that will likely be provided during the session.

PREPARATORY TALK

Before beginning the hypnotic induction it is advisable to describe the type of induction and suggestions that will likely be provided during the session. This is to give the patient information, ensure that the planned hypnotic induction is acceptable to the patient, and enhance the sense of collaboration and cooperation within the relationship. This was accomplished with Linda as follows:

> **Therapist:** *In a few moments, we will begin your first hypnotic induction. I will ask you to focus your attention by looking at a spot on the wall. I will then give you suggestions to become relaxed and to drift into a hypnotic state where you can respond to suggestions.*
>
> *There is nothing you have to do and nothing you have to try to do. . . . Just allow yourself to respond in whatever way you respond. I will give you suggestions to go to a safe and peaceful place and I will give you suggestions for comfort and calmness. The suggestions for comfort will be to reduce the headache you have right now and to become relaxed enough that the anxiety becomes less and less. Does that sound OK to you?*
>
> **Linda:** *Sounds good.*
>
> **Therapist:** *OK, so would it also be alright with you if I suggest you see yourself in a place where you experience calm feelings, such as being near a lake, or another place where you might like to be and feeling as if you are there? I will also plan to give you suggestions to reduce anxiety, so that your mood will improve. There will also be suggestions for you to practice self-hypnosis. Is that OK with you?*
>
> **Linda:** *Yes, I remember last summer going on a vacation to Fort Parker. There is a beautiful lake there that I remember.*
>
> **Therapist:** *Good. I will also be recording today's session, and at the end of today's session, I will be providing you with the recording of the hypnotic induction. You will benefit most by listening to this recording at least once a day.*

HYPNOTIC INDUCTION

A standard hypnotic induction is usually sufficient in the first session. Specific suggestions toward the goal of the session can also be integrated. For Linda, this included suggestions to target the headache and stress.

Eye focus induction

"Begin by focusing your attention on a spot on the wall. As you concentrate, begin to feel more relaxed. Concentrate intensely so that other things begin to fade into the background. Now take a deep breath of air, hold it . . . hold . . . and now as you breathe out let all of the tension go . . . good. As this occurs, allow your eyelids to close, and notice, more and more, a relaxed and heavy feeling. Now take another deep breath of air, hold it, and as you release the air and breathe out . . . begin going into a very deep state of hypnosis. Each time you breathe out . . . thinking the word 'relax' silently to yourself . . . the mind and the body working together to achieve a deep state of comfort and relaxation."

Setting the overall goal

"And today, finding that it is possible to find comfort . . . real comfort . . . so that the headache becomes less . . . as the relaxation becomes deeper . . . and stress just drifts away."

Relaxation

"And with each breath, let go of all of the tension and drift, so deeply relaxed . . . every muscle and every fiber of your body becoming so deeply relaxed. More and more noticing a feeling of 'letting go' and becoming so deeply relaxed. Your thoughts and feelings can become deeper and deeper relaxed with each suggestion that I give you, finding more and more comfort and calm feelings. Going so deeply relaxed that it would take too much effort to even try to open your eyelids . . . and this is a good feeling that allows you to relax even deeper . . . and as you go deeper relaxed you're drifting into an even deeper level of hypnosis."

Comfort

"As you become and remain more relaxed, finding a feeling of comfort, feeling safe and secure, a peaceful feeling, calm and secure . . . feeling so calm that nothing bothers or interferes with this feeling of comfort . . . From time to time you may notice a floating feeling, drifting and floating as if you were on a cloud . . . more and more relaxed . . . and as you hear my voice count from 1 to 10, with each number you find yourself drifting into an even deeper level of hypnosis . . . at times my voice may seem far away, or you may drift to other times and places where you have felt coolness and relaxation."

Mental imagery for relaxation and deepening trance

"A wave of relaxation spreading from the top of your head to your feet. spreading over you like a cool wind on a warm summer day."

> 1 . . . Deeper and deeper relaxed . . . letting all the tension go from your forehead, face, neck, and shoulders . . . letting go of all of the tension . . . for this time . . . nothing bothers and nothing disturbs this calm relaxed feeling . . . 2 . . . Deeper relaxed . . . your neck can go limp, your jaw can go slack as all the tension drifts away . . . 3 . . . Deeply calm, perhaps noticing special colors associated with calmness . . . or your favorite music . . . and letting that wave of relaxation spread across your arms and shoulders . . . arms become so deeply relaxed that they become limp and heavy . . . all of the tension drifts away . . . 4 . . . Your upper back and your lower back, relaxed and calm and filled with comfort . . . perhaps so comfortable and relaxed that you just don't notice your fingers

and arms . . . 5 . . . Deeper and deeper relaxed, halfway there, twice as relaxed . . . all of the tension drifts away and finding a feeling of peace . . . more at peace within yourself . . . more and more everyday, no matter what is going on around you . . . noticing the relaxation and the comfort . . . 6 . . . Deeper and even more calm . . . back, chest, and stomach relax . . . letting all the tension go now . . . and going deeper and deeper within yourself to find comfort . . . 7 . . . Arms, legs, and feet . . . become so deeply relaxed as that wave of relaxation spreads down your legs and into your feet . . . going into an even deeper level of hypnosis . . . And perhaps you notice how relaxed and heavy your arms and legs have become . . . so pleasant that you just allow the relaxation to become more complete, and with this comes a feeling of control and comfort . . . drifting and floating . . . deeper and deeper relaxed . . . 8 . . . deeper and calmer and at ease . . . 9 . . . almost there . . . deeply relaxed, nothing bothers and nothing concerns . . . 10 . . . all the way there, deeply, comfortably relaxed."

Mental imagery for reducing anxiety and headache

"Now in a moment, I am going to ask you to notice some images in your mind . . . You can hear my voice with one part of your mind while another part of your mind goes to a pleasant, peaceful place where you notice and experience everything that is there . . . images and scenes that allow you to experience even more comfort and so relaxed . . . no headache . . . no stress . . . going to a place where you find the comfort that you need . . . Learning to use hypnosis to remain more comfortable and relaxed, finding that you are near a beautiful lake . . . a lake near Fort. Parker . . . and it is pleasant to notice the tranquil water . . . You might want to take a deep breath of the air . . . this is a very beautiful place . . . and the relaxation becomes more complete . . . relaxed . . . comfort in your face and across your forehead."

Deepening and dissociation

"Now it is possible to enter an even deeper state of hypnosis . . . deeper and deeper relaxed . . . now letting all the tension go . . . And as you do, beginning to enter an even deeper level of hypnosis . . . now as this occurs you may notice a change in sensations . . . this may be a floating sensation . . . a drifting sensation . . . and perhaps you are just less aware of your body . . . just floating in space. Your body floating in a feeling of comfort . . ."

Reinforcment

"And as you are aware of the comfort . . . just nodding your head . . . yes . . . very good . . . you have done very well . . ."

Post-hypnotic suggestions

". . . and each time you experience this hypnotic relaxation . . . you will find a sense of being more comfortable . . . And as this occurs you will find that more and more, you are more relaxed every day . . . less anxiety . . . less stressed, your feelings of well-being will improve . . . you will be pleased as headaches become less and less frequent and less severe."

Alerting

"In a few moments you will be returning to conscious alertness. Returning to conscious alertness in your own time and at your own pace . . . in a way that just feels about right for you today. Feeling very good . . . normal . . . with good and normal sensations in every way as you return to full conscious alertness . . . returning to conscious alertness as I count from the numbers 4 to 1 . . . now, 4 . . . 3 . . . 2 . . . 1 . . ."

POST-HYPNOTIC INQUIRY

Once the patient returns to conscious alertness, a rating of symptoms is taken for a second time. This can be very validating to the patient and can help guide future inductions depending on the patient's feedback. Notes should be taken for future individualization of hypnotic inductions. Also, the patient should be given additional instruction in using the CD recording at home as a "homework assignment." This is illustrated in the following dialogue with Linda.

Therapist: *Do you feel alert? Good. Now, please tell me the number that best reflects how much anxiety you feel right now.*

Linda: *Oh, I guess I would say a 1 or a 2, I feel pretty relaxed . . . not too anxious at all.*

Therapist: *Great. How about the headache? What happened to it?*

Linda: *I feel better . . . it's less. I think, maybe a 3. It's definitely better! Thank you.*

Therapist: *You did great. I am very pleased you were able to achieve this accomplishment today.*

After obtaining the second rating of anxiety, the clinician should ask the participant about her experience with hypnosis to determine any type of preferences for mental imagery. This is illustrated in the following example:

> The therapist should emphasize that practice will help the patient accomplish more and make better progress.

Therapist: *Please tell me about your experience with hypnosis today. Did you experience being by the lake? Did you notice any other* *images or memories that helped you to become relaxed and to find comfort?*

The hypnotherapist should make notes of the patient's responses to these questions. The hypnotherapist should also list any specific imagery or statements about preferences for imagery. Sufficient details should be elicited and recorded so that this information can be used to individualize imagery in future sessions.

ENDING THE SESSION—PROVIDE RECORDING OF HYPNOTIC INDUCTION

Following the induction, the therapist should discuss using a CD recording to practice hypnotic relaxation—and eventually, self-hypnosis. The therapist should emphasize that practice will help the patient accomplish more and make better progress. The patient is typically asked to practice with the CD four or more times per week, with daily practice highly recommended. For example:

> **Therapist:** *As I mentioned earlier, I want you to have a CD recording of the hypnosis session for your home practice and to begin to learn self-hypnosis. You should practice with the CD at least once a day. It doesn't matter if you practice with it in the morning, middle of the day, or before you go to sleep. It is important that you practice with it and learn self-hypnosis and how hypnosis can work best for you.*
>
> *When you listen to the CD you should be either lying down or sitting in a recliner or similar chair as you have been doing today. It is important that you be able to practice for about 30 minutes without interruptions. You can find the time to practice that works best for you. You should only practice when you can close your eyes and be without distractions. You should not listen to the CD when you are driving a car or engaging in any other activity . . . OK?*

It is important to ensure the patient is fully alert and that the homework assignment is understood. Additionally, the clinician should encourage the patient to notice any particular imagery or responses that may be beneficial to integrate into future sessions.

CHAPTER 7

The Second Hypnotic Relaxation Therapy Session

The focus of the second hypnotic relaxation therapy (HRT) session is to begin the process of individualizing hypnotic suggestions and intervention. Individualization does not end in the second session; rather, it is an ongoing process across sessions. However, it is likely that sufficient information can be gathered early on to begin tailoring suggestions within a clearly defined approach. As previously mentioned, HRT is both structured and individualized in order to best achieve the patient's goals. The individualization process will be discussed and illustrated in this chapter.

HRT is both structured and individualized to achieve goals and personal relevancy.

STRUCTURE OF THE SECOND SESSION

The session begins with a review of the patient's progress and experiences with hypnotic relaxation to date. A pre-induction discussion is utilized to monitor progress, review the patient's experience to date, refine the hypnotic induction based upon the patient's experience, and gather information for individualizing hypnotic suggestions. If the patient was provided with a recording of the previous session, the frequency of practice, perceived benefit, imagery preferences, and general observations should be discussed, all of which will serve to further enhance individualization. The patient's overall treatment goals are also discussed, and a goal for the session is identified. This helps to focus the session and communicates the cooperative nature of the hypnotherapeutic relationship. Any problems or concerns are also discussed. If the patient comes into a session experiencing a symptom of concern, (i.e., pain, anxiety, stress), the clinician should obtain a symptom rating pre- and post-hypnotic induction. The hypnotic induction is then provided in a manner that integrates the patient's individualized preferences according to information gathered in the pre-induction discussion. The session may be recorded and provided to the patient for use at home. After the induction, the clinician should conduct a post-hypnotic inquiry to gain additional information for further individualization in the future. The session ends with a review of "homework assignments," which may include monitoring progress and practicing hypnotic relaxation with the CD recording.

The specific components of the second hypnotic relaxation session consist of: (1) a review of the patient's experiences and progress; (2) gathering information for individualization; (3) setting the session goal; (4) symptom rating; (5) individualized hypnotic induction; (6) post-hypnotic inquiry; and (7) ending the session. These individual components are discussed below and are illustrated with excerpts from the second session with Linda.

REVIEW OF THE PATIENT'S EXPERIENCES AND PROGRESS

At the beginning of the session, it is helpful to begin the review of the patient's progress with open-ended questions such as, "Please bring me up to date on your progress. How often have you used the CD recording of hypnotic relaxation? What has been your experience with your practice?" The patient may volunteer relevant information and give some insights into his or her progress and areas to focus upon. For example:

> **Therapist:** *Linda, how have you been doing over the last week? How often have you used the CD recording of the last session?*
>
> **Linda:** *I like the CD and I guess I've listened to it almost every day. Usually before I go to sleep at night.*
>
> **Therapist:** *Tell me about your experience with the CD; is there anything that you especially like or seems less effective for you?*
>
> **Linda:** *I like the suggestions for relaxation. It might be a little long, because I usually fall asleep before I hear the end.*
>
> **Therapist:** *So, it sounds like your sleep is better and you are able to become more relaxed. That sounds like progress.*
>
> **Linda:** *You are right, I am sleeping better. I go to sleep pretty quickly. I do feel more relaxed.*
>
> **Therapist:** *Well, this is good progress. As far as the hypnotic induction today, we can make it a little shorter, but I wonder if during the next week it would help you to practice at times other than bedtime, when you are going to sleep. It might be helpful to listen to the CD occasionally when you are sitting in a recliner and not really sleepy.*
>
> **Linda:** *That makes sense. I could try it in the morning before I leave for work.*

Therapist: *Great. How about your headaches? How have they been this past week? About how many and how would you rate them on the 0 to 10 scale?*

Linda: *It seems like they have been a little better. I have had a couple. Maybe a "7" or "8," so they were still pretty bad.*

GATHER INFORMATION FOR INDIVIDUALIZATION

Before beginning the second hypnotic induction, it is important to engage the patient in a conversation about the process of individualizing suggestions. The patient should be encouraged to share personal preferences and experiences, images, and responses to suggestions. A trusting, collaborative relationship that includes acceptance and unconditional positive regard facilitates the patient's willingness to share this type of personal information. The hypnotherapist should gather as many details as necessary to assure understanding of the patient's individualized preferences. This can include information about the types of suggestions that seem to be most relevant to the patient. Additionally, the clinician should ask the patient to relate his or her personal experience at various points throughout this session, as well as future sessions (e.g., during the pre-hypnotic interview, post-hypnotic inquiry). Individualization can be further enhanced by asking the patient about his or her background and experiences. The clinician should also ask the patient what he or she liked or disliked about the initial hypnotic relaxation induction.

The hypnotherapist should gather as many details as necessary to assure understanding of the patient's individualized preferences.

Information that is directed toward a specific goal can be elicited. For example, suggestions for "safe place imagery" are likely to be useful at some point in the intervention. This involves suggestions for the patient to visualize and dissociate to another place where he or she feels safe, secure, and relaxed. Thus, the process of gathering information can include a discussion of a place where the patient feels safe and calm. The following questions and prompts may be used to help the clinician gain sufficient information to individualize the intervention:

- "Tell me about a time in your life that was very pleasant."
- "If you could go to a very safe and pleasant place, where would it be?"
- "What did you like or dislike about the imagery used in the hypnotic relaxation induction?"
- "What makes, or has made you, feel safe and pleasant?"
- "What feelings or sensations do you notice when you have felt safe and secure?"

The clinician can gather information about the types of suggestions that will be most relevant to the patient by simply asking about the types

It is important to elicit as many details as possible to maximize the degree to which individualization can be achieved.

of sensations or experiences he or she associates with comfort and symptom relief. These are likely experiences from the patient's past (even dating back to childhood) that are personally relevant. For example, if a feeling of warmth or coolness is going to be suggested, the patient may be able to relate these feelings to a time or place where he or she has actually experienced them. Providing suggestions to experience being at a specific beach, where the patient has actually been, may be preferred over general suggestions. For this reason, it is important to elicit as many details as possible to maximize the degree to which individualization can be achieved. Often, the most productive way to gather information for this purpose is to have the patient describe an experience during a prior hypnotic induction. The therapist should encourage the patient to "notice" the experience rather than "trying to think of a time or place." For example, during the process of individualization with Linda, the following areas were explored:

- "In the past, what places or times do you recall when you felt calm and relaxed?"
- "Do you prefer warmth, coolness, a tingly sensation, or numbness in finding comfort as headaches become less intense?"
- "Can you imagine the headaches 'flowing out of your body'?"
- "Can you imagine becoming so relaxed that you are, in a sense, floating outside your body and going to another place? Where might that be?"
- "Would it be alright with you to go back in time, within your mind, to another day and time, when you felt relaxed and comfortable? When would that time be? Tell me about the details of that experience."
- "What types of suggestions help you feel the most calm and relaxed?"
- "Did you find your thoughts drifting to another place during the last hypnotic induction . . . a place that you found familiar in some way, but that was unexpected?"

In the case of Linda, the hypnotherapist summarized her responses to these questions:

> **Therapist:** *Thank you for sharing your experience. I think this gives us some details to use to make today's hypnotic induction more individualized for you. It sounds as if you might begin the induction with your eyes closed and just focusing on your breathing.*
>
> **Linda:** *That sounds good. That's how I do it at home.*
>
> **Therapist:** *Great, then that is how we will begin the induction in a few minutes. Also, based on our discussion today you mentioned*

that you can recall being at Fort Parker State Park. Also, we discussed that you might experience a tingly feeling across your forehead as the headache becomes less intense, and that you could imagine the headache as a loud sound that becomes softer and softer. Is that right? Also, you found that when you practiced with the CD recording your thoughts also drifted to a time when you were on another vacation to the beach in Galveston. You especially recall the texture of the sand on the beach, the sound of the waves coming in on the shore, and you were there feeling relaxed and happy—no stress, no headache. Would it be OK if I give you suggestions to re-experience that time and place?

Linda: *Sounds wonderful.*

SETTING THE SESSION GOAL

The goal of the second session is likely to have two parts: (1) symptom reduction or insight, and (2) greater individualization. It is helpful to communicate these goals to the patient and to discuss how they may be achieved. For example, in the session with Linda, the following excerpt illustrates goal setting:

Therapist: *You have made some progress in becoming familiar with hypnotherapy and becoming more relaxed. It also sounds as if your sleep has already gotten better.*

Linda: *It has. I think this will help me.*

Therapist: *I agree. Let's talk about the goals for today's session. It seems to me that we should focus on reducing the headaches. How does that sound?*

Linda: *I have a headache right now.*

Therapist: *So, would it be OK with you if we used the hypnotic relaxation induction today to see if the headache could become less by the end of the session?*

Linda: *Absolutely, yes!*

RATING OF SYMPTOMS

Once the session goal has been identified, and before the hypnotic induction, a brief rating of the symptom on a 0 to 10, 0 to 100, or visual analog scale can be helpful to track progress and validate the patient's response to hypnotic intervention. In Linda's case, she rated her headache as a "7" at the beginning of the hypnotic induction. As the patient recognizes positive change, the therapist's encouragement and positive reinforcement will contribute to the patient's motivation.

INDIVIDUALIZED HYPNOTIC INDUCTION

As information for individualization was gathered, the hypnotherapist used this information in the hypnotic induction for session two with Linda:

Focusing of attention

"All hypnotic inductions begin with a focus of attention, and for our purposes today . . . you can settle into the chair where you are sitting . . . and when you are ready to begin to enter a comfortable hypnotic state . . . closing your eyes . . . as the eyelids close . . . focusing your attention on your breathing . . . And noticing the feelings that go along with breathing in and breathing out . . . notice the coolness of the air in your nostrils as you breathe in . . . and the feeling of letting go . . . as you breathe out . . . soon becoming more and more relaxed . . . Somehow each breath of air can seem to take you into a deeper and more relaxed state . . . where you can accomplish the things you wish to accomplish today . . ."

As the patient is able to recognize positive change, there can be encouragement and positive reinforcement that contributes to motivation.

Initial suggestions for relaxation

". . . and allowing the relaxation to come to you, easily and naturally. . . . At times you may think the word 'relax' as you breathe out . . . and yet at other times, the relaxation just becomes more complete without your having to do anything at all . . . just noticing relaxation . . . more and more . . . Your forehead relaxes . . . your neck . . . your jaw . . . goes limp and so relaxed . . . your shoulders . . . your back . . . And this profound relaxation . . . now . . . can spread into your arms . . . they become limp and heavy . . . the hands relax . . . back and stomach relax . . . legs become relaxed and limp . . . even your toes and feet become more and more calm . . . more and more . . . relaxed . . . as you drift into a deeper hypnotic state . . ."

Encouraging fading of the generalized reality orientation

". . . And as this occurs . . . other things begin to fade into the background . . . aware of calmness . . . and . . . changes in sensations naturally occur . . . At times you may notice a heaviness in your arms and legs . . . and . . . at other times . . . it may change into a floating or rocking sensation . . . as if you were just floating in space . . . And as this occurs the relaxation becomes a little deeper . . . blood pressure may become a little less . . . heart rate a little slower . . . aware of your own inner experience . . . as other things fade into the background . . . more . . . and more . . ."

Deeping suggestions

". . . And it is possible to go into an even deeper hypnotic state . . . the deeper the relaxation . . . the better the response. . . . letting go . . . and finding that as I count the numbers from 10 to 1 it is possible to become so deeply absorbed in this experience . . . the hypnotic state becomes deeper and deeper . . . 10 . . . Allowing a wave of good relaxation to come to you . . . It spreads across your forehead . . . across your face . . . letting go of all tension . . . drifting deeper . . . 9 . . . A relaxation that now spreads across your shoulders . . . they slump . . . any tension that has remained . . . just begins to drift away . . . and is replaced with comfort . . . calmness . . . 8 . . . The kind of calm, relaxed feeling you experienced before on a pleasant day . . . a day at Fort Parker State Park . . . a place where you feel safe and secure . . . a place where it is possible to feel at ease . . . as you go there with a part of your mind . . . noticing everything that is there on this particular day . . . perhaps you are sitting outside . . . so that you can look out . . . and see the lake . . . the peaceful water . . . the surface of the water is calm . . . and it is that time of day . . . when it is peaceful . . . perhaps evening time . . . and notice all the beautiful colors across the sky . . . as the sun is setting . . . 7 . . . and take a deep breath of air and go even deeper . . . more relaxed more calm . . . 6 . . . and the tensions just flows out of you . . . as if it were all flowing out of the bottoms of your feet . . . the shoulders slump . . . the arms become limp . . . even the fingers of each hand are limp and so deeply relaxed . . . 5 . . . The muscles of the back and stomach relax . . . breathing becomes easier . . . so calming . . . as you look out on the lake . . . drifting into a deeper hypnotic state . . . 4 . . . The legs relax . . . your right leg becomes limp and comfortable . . . the left leg . . . so relaxed . . . no tension . . . no stress . . . drifting deeper . . . 3 . . . going deeper as the relaxation becomes more complete . . . Feet become very deeply relaxed . . . they are limp . . . and all the tension . . . any that has remained drifts away . . . flowing out the bottoms of your feet . . . 2 . . . and notice the calmness . . . almost there . . . 1 . . . so deeply relaxed."

Setting the overall session goal

". . . And within this relaxed state it is possible to achieve greater control . . . this headache can become less and less . . . today . . . it soon becomes less and less . . ."

Mental imagery and dissociation

". . . so that . . . your mind can drift to other times and places where you have found comfort . . . real comfort . . . no tension . . . no stress . . . no headache . . . so that as you can hear my voice . . . A part of your mind can take you to the beach at Galveston . . . a part of your mind . . . remembers the comfort that you experienced . . . there . . . and so you do go there again . . . a good place to be . . . nodding your head when you are there . . . very good . . . And it is a pleasant day . . . and you can see the ocean before you . . . Watch the waves as they come in on the shore . . . and hearing the sound of the waves coming in on the shore . . . and feeling happy and relaxed . . . you are there at Galveston beach . . . and it is good . . . and feeling the warmth of the sun on your face . . . is good . . . And you notice a slight tingly feeling across your forehead . . . across your face . . . Do you notice this? . . . Nodding your head yes as you do . . . very good . . . And as you notice the tingly feeling . . . and hear the sound of the waves on the beach . . . the headache becomes less and less . . . as you notice this . . . nodding your head yes . . . very good . . . it becomes less and less . . . like a sound that has been too loud . . . and it becomes softer and softer . . . like soft gentle music . . . the soft gentle sound of the waves coming in on the shore and going back out . . . Each wave takes you to deeper comfort . . . more control . . . no stress . . . no headache . . . so calm . . ."

Reinforcement of response

". . . and you have done very well today . . . and taking from this experience . . . hypnotic relaxation . . . whatever you need . . . to achieve and continue to achieve the control . . . you have done very well . . ."

Post-hypnotic suggestion

". . . and in the future . . . you will find . . . that each time you experience this hypnotic relaxation . . . it will be possible to go to Galveston beach . . . or wherever you need to go . . . and find comfort . . . And as you do . . . headaches will become less and less frequent . . . less severe . . . and this will be a pleasant experience . . . so that headaches . . . more and more become a distant memory . . . that fades into the background . . . "

Alerting

"Now . . . in a moment . . . returning to conscious alertness . . . normal sensations return to your arms . . . your legs . . . returning to conscious alertness in your own time and pace . . . Soon your eyelids can open . . . when you are ready for them to open . . . and as they do open . . . returning . . . all the way . . . back to conscious alertness . . . in your own time and at your own pace as I count from 1 to 4 . . . 1 . . . 2 . . . 3 . . . 4 . . ."

POST-HYPNOTIC INQUIRY

After obtaining the second rating of the target symptom, the hypnotherapist should ask the patient about his or her experience during the session in order to determine any additional or alternative preferences for mental imagery. For example, following is the post-hypnotic inquiry that followed the hypnotic induction with Linda:

Therapist: *How do you feel? Do you feel alert?*

Linda: *Yes. That was great. I feel relaxed.*

Therapist: *Good. I am interested in what happened to the headache. How would you rate it now on the 0 to 10 scale?*

Linda: *Oh, the headache . . . it went away . . . it's a zero right now . . . I'm pretty relaxed.*

Therapist: *That is what I hoped you would be able to achieve. Very good. I also want to know about your experience with hypnotic relaxation today. Did you experience being at the beach? Did you notice any other images or memories that helped you to become relaxed and reduce the headache?*

The hypnotherapist should make notes of the patient's responses to these questions, and record any specific imagery or statements about preferences for imagery. Sufficient details should be elicited and recorded for use in future sessions. For example, a statement from Linda that was documented in her progress notes:

Linda: *When you suggested going to Galveston Beach I recalled walking along the shore . . . and letting the water come up around my legs . . . it was just so cool and refreshing . . . walking along the beach . . . and I was looking for some sea shells . . .*

Therapist: *Did you find any?*

Linda: *Well, yes! There were lots of them. I was looking for the prettiest one to take home to my daughter.*

Therapist: *Linda, this is very helpful information. Would it be OK to include this in your next session . . . walking on the beach and looking for those sea shells?*

Linda: *Yes, it just seemed like it was part of being there.*

ENDING THE SESSION—HOMEWORK ASSIGNMENT AND SCHEDULING

The second session ends with the post-hypnotic inquiry and a homework assignment for the coming week. The homework assignment may involve continued practice of hypnotic relaxation using the CD recording, continuing to record symptoms and/or noticing personal experiences that may be used for further individualization in future sessions. In Linda's case, the second session was recorded and provided to her for home practice between sessions.

> **Therapist:** *OK, we have your next appointment scheduled. Between now and next week, would you please continue to practice with either the CD from the first session or the one today? Good. When you practice, remember that you just need a time and place where you will not be interrupted; and a place where you can either sit with good support for your head, neck, and shoulders, or lay down. It is important that you aim for daily practice. It can be whatever time of the day that works best for you. For example, continuing to practice in the evening or before you go to sleep is fine for some of the times. Also try other times so that you get the full benefit. Please also notice any experience during your practice that may be helpful to let me know about. Just as you did today, notice any images, feelings, or memories that occur as you practice. I am interested in the details of your experience and what helps you the most.*

CHAPTER 8

The Third Hypnotic Relaxation Therapy Session

The focus of approximately the third session is teaching the patient self-hypnosis. I use the word "approximately" because the content, and intent, of sessions 1, 2, 3, 4, and beyond may be repeated several times and expanded upon depending on the complexity of the patient's problem and his or her progress from one session to the next. Teaching the patient self-hypnosis is one aspect of the end-point goal of "empowering the patient" to self-manage, reduce symptoms, and become involved in his or her own healthcare.

Up until the third session, the patient is likely to have used a CD recording of a previous session to gain benefit from hypnotic relaxation and suggestions between sessions. This is a form of "self-hypnosis;" however, it is really "CD-assisted practice of hypnotic relaxation therapy." This practice with audio recordings may continue; however, it is in the third session that the patient begins to learn and utilize actual self-hypnosis that is not assisted by use of live hypnotic inductions or recordings.

> With increased control, a self-hypnosis practice may be reasonably brief, taking only 5 to 20 minutes, making frequent practice more feasible.

The patient's use of self-hypnosis has a number of advantages and benefits. By learning effective use of self-hypnosis, the patient may reinforce hypnotic suggestions multiple times throughout the day. With practice and increased control, a self-hypnosis session may be reasonably brief, taking only 5 to 20 minutes, making frequent practice more feasible. In addition, as the patient learns self-hypnosis, he or she becomes more empowered and will find that he or she can induce a state of hypnosis when most needed, as opposed to waiting for the opportunity to listen to a recording.

As with any skill, self-hypnosis is best learned through experience. Therefore, in this session, the patient is not only provided with clear instructions and information about self-hypnosis, but is guided through practice with increasingly minimal prompts. This process should be repeated during sessions until the patient is confident that he or she can utilize self-hypnosis between sessions.

As with any skill, self-hypnosis is best learned through experience.

STRUCTURE OF THE THIRD SESSION

As with previous sessions, the third session is goal-directed and individualized to meet the patient's needs and preferences. Therefore, the session begins with a review of the patient's progress, experiences, and preferences. The structure of the third session may be outlined as: (1) review patient's progress and experiences with hypnotic relaxation; (2) gather information for individualization and set the session goal; (3) review steps for self-hypnosis; (4) hypnotic induction following steps of self-hypnosis; (5) patient practice of self-hypnosis with minimal prompts: (6) post-hypnotic inquiry; and (7) ending the session. Linda's third session will be utilized to illustrate this structure.

REVIEW PATIENT'S PROGRESS AND EXPERIENCES WITH HYPNOTIC RELAXATION

As the patient continues her practice of HRT, she is likely to identify additional experiences that are either beneficial or less helpful. An open and nonjudgmental attitude from the hypnotherapist can facilitate the patient's sharing of her experiences. The following excerpt from Linda's third session illustrates this approach.

> **Therapist:** *Linda, please bring me up-to-date on your progress with using hypnotic relaxation therapy. I am interested in whatever you have noticed over the past few weeks, whether it is good, helpful, not helpful—just whatever your experience has been thus far, anything that has stood out to you.*
>
> **Linda:** *I have been practicing with the CD during the day as you suggested last time. That has been good. My headaches have been quite a bit less! I guess I just had a couple last week.*
>
> **Therapist:** *That is good to hear. So, your headaches have been fewer; how about intensity? How would you rate the severity of those headaches on a scale of 0 to 10?*
>
> **Linda:** *Not bad; about a 3 or 4 at most.*
>
> **Therapist:** *What would you say seems to be most helpful when you practice?*
>
> **Linda:** *The relaxation. When I listen to the CD, it just helps me get very relaxed. I like the part where I am at the beach.*

GATHER INFORMATION FOR INDIVIDUALIZATION AND SET THE SESSION GOAL

The pre-induction inquiry includes asking the patient about specific experiences during prior hypnotic relaxation therapy (HRT) sessions. Sufficient detail should be elicited to communicate suggestions that are most personally and emotionally relevant to the patient. In addition, by the third session, the patient may have identified some preferences for how to begin the hypnotic induction. For example, some may prefer to begin with open eyes and focusing on a spot, while others may prefer to begin with their eyes closed and focusing on their breathing. In gaining this type of information, the patient's attention can be drawn to the idea that he may be able to achieve a hypnotic state more rapidly now than when he began therapy. Certainly, the hypnotic state is more familiar, and the patient can be more aware of his own personal experiences during an HRT session.

By the third session, the patient may have identified some preferences for how to begin the hypnotic induction.

Also, it is important to communicate the goal of the session, namely to teach the patient how to use self-hypnosis. The information for preferences and individualization can be used in self-hypnosis practice. This is illustrated in the following exchange with Linda:

The information for preferences and individualization can be used in self-hypnosis practice.

> **Therapist:** *The goal of our session today is to help you learn self-hypnosis. This means learning how to practice self-hypnosis without the CD. I will be giving you some guidance on this and will write out the steps for your practice of self-hypnosis. However, before we get to that, I would like to ask you about some of the details on what you notice when you are in a hypnotic state. How does that sound?*
>
> **Linda:** *So, I am going to learn how to do self-hypnosis on my own?*
>
> **Therapist:** *Yes, that is part of our goal today!*
>
> **Linda:** *This is going to be interesting!*
>
> **Therapist:** *OK, so a few more questions before we get into the self-hypnosis practice. When you are going through a session with your CD, when suggestions are given for being in a safe and calm place where you feel warmth, where do you "go" in your mind and experience?*
>
> **Linda:** *The best place for me is at the beach in Galveston; that is a place where I have such good memories and I do feel calm.*
>
> **Therapist:** *So during today's session it would be consistent to suggest that you experience being at the beach. What kind of things do you notice most while you are there, in a hypnotic state? Can you feel the warmth of the sand? What do you see around you?*

Linda: *It is just very pleasant. I can imagine walking on the sand, and as you say, I do feel warm, the sand is warm. I can hear the sound of the ocean. Just walking or sitting.*

Therapist: *Very good. I also want to ask you about when you practice hypnotherapy at home with your CD. Do you like to begin with your eyes open or closed? What seems to work best for you?*

Linda: *I usually just focus on a spot and then close my eyes pretty quickly when the CD goes to the relaxation suggestions.*

Therapist: *OK; that sounds good.*

REVIEW STEPS FOR SELF-HYPNOSIS

The process of learning self-hypnosis is described, and the guidelines or steps to self-hypnosis should be written out and provided to the patient. It is important to review these steps during the session. The patient should be encouraged to ask questions, and to keep the steps as a reference for home practice. The hypnotic induction for teaching self-hypnosis should be reasonably brief; approximately 5 to 10 minutes is recommended. Linda's self-hypnosis instructions included a brief focus of attention, taking a deep breath of air, and eye closure on the exhale as a method of rapid trance induction. This was followed by suggestions for relaxation, deepening the hypnotic state, and dissociation. Suggestions for imagery of being at her favorite beach were given with suggestions to experience warmth in her hands. The suggestions for "hand-warming" imagery were based upon previous research that has indicated that vasodilation and "hand-warming exercises" may be helpful in reducing migraine headaches (Nestoriuc, Martin, & Andrasik, 2008). The specific imagery was consistent with Linda's preferences and past experience. Suggestions were also given for self-acceptance, calmness, and well-being. The practice of self-hypnosis was presented as a method to enhance coping skills for dealing with stress, headache reduction, empowerment, and feelings of control and well-being. Linda was provided with the following outline for self-hypnosis practice. This outline can be adapted for use with other patients, and the suggestions therein can be adjusted for differing problems.

The hypnotic induction for teaching self-hypnosis should be reasonably brief; approximately 5 to 10 minutes is recommended.

SELF-HYPNOSIS INSTRUCTIONS

"The following are suggestions for learning and using self-hypnosis. With practice, you can become skilled in using the following instructions to further help you in achieving hypnotic relaxation and responding to suggestions in a way that is best for you. Learning to practice self-hypnosis has the advantage that you can induce a calm and relaxed state and reinforce suggestions whenever it is best for you. Your practice of self-hypnosis can be as long or as short a period of time as works best for you at any particular time and place. It is flexible in how it can be practiced. Also, you may continue to practice with your CD recording. For example, you may practice self-hypnosis for as little as 5 minutes at a time, while taking longer when you use the CD. You can continue to use the CD at least once or more per day if that works best for you. Learning self-hypnosis is in addition to what you already know; it is not to replace your CD or sessions. You may use the CD or practice self-hypnosis in the mornings, middle of the day, or evenings. The steps to practicing self-hypnosis are as follows:

1. Roll eyes upward and focus on a spot.
2. Take a deep breath and as you exhale allow your eyelids to close.
3. Now, focus on your breathing, and each time you breathe out, think the word "relax" and allow your body to become more relaxed. The mind and the body working together for a common purpose . . . to create feelings of relaxation and comfort.
4. Now, notice a wave of relaxation that spreads from the top of your head down to your feet. Across your forehead, neck, shoulders, arms, back, chest and stomach, legs and feet. Every muscle and every fiber of your body more and more completely relaxed . . .
5. And now, with one part of your mind, go to another place . . . a place where you are safe and feel secure, calm, and at ease. Going to that place now, where you find warmth and comfort. Soon you will be at the beach in Galveston . . . experiencing everything that is there . . .
6. Now, as you are there . . . deepen this hypnotic relaxation . . . going even deeper relaxed. Not only deeply relaxed physically but also emotionally relaxed, calm, more at peace and more at ease. And mentally calm and relaxed, relaxed within your thoughts and feelings, and physically deeply relaxed and comfortable . . .
7. . . . and as you are there, in that pleasant place, so relaxed, you notice warmth on your hands. Hold some of the warm sand.
8. And remaining more relaxed and at ease, feeling more in control of your feelings and allowing a feeling of well-being to be experienced . . . a feeling of self-acceptance, liking yourself, and feeling more confident in yourself.
9. Now, go even a little deeper relaxed . . . deepen the hypnotic relaxation even more now. Head, neck, arms, back, chest, stomach, legs and feet, completely relaxed and comfortable.

The process of hypnotic suggestion in self-hypnosis practice is more like "planting a seed" than like "driving a nail."

Releasing every worry and every tension now. Headache is less, body is relaxed, mind is calm, and you have a feeling of self-acceptance.

10. Now, gently and easily return to conscious alertness, in your own time and at your own pace, in a way that pleases you."

HYPNOTIC INDUCTION FOLLOWING THE SELF-HYPNOSIS STEPS

After the patient has been oriented to the process of self-hypnosis, the instructions are discussed and questions are addressed by the therapist. Based upon feedback from the patient, specific suggestions may be further modified to achieve greatest relevance and emotional significance for the patient.

In addition, it should be explained that the patient's response to self-hypnosis practice should feel effortless. Potential myths and misconceptions should again be explored. Even though the patient has, at this point, considerable experience with HRT from previous sessions, there may still be some remaining misconceptions. For example, some patients may have the idea that self-hypnosis is a way of "driving suggestions into the mind" or that suggestions have to be continually repeated. It should be explained that the process of hypnotic suggestion in self-hypnosis practice is more like "planting a seed" than like "driving a nail." Suggestions are given for relaxation, dissociating, "letting go," and for allowing the suggestion to occur without conscious effort.

For example, in the exchange with Linda, the following pre-induction talk was provided to help her prepare for and understand the practice of self-hypnosis.

Therapist: *OK Linda, as we discussed, the best way to learn how to use self-hypnosis is by going through a hypnotic induction following the steps for self-hypnosis. I will guide you through the hypnotic induction using each step. We will begin with your focusing your attention, taking a deep breath of air, and your allowing your eyelids to close as you breathe out. From there we will go on to the other steps that will be to achieve a deeply relaxed state, then suggestions for you to experience being at the beach and feeling warm sand on your hands and noticing the beauty of being at the beach. Following that will be suggestions for self-acceptance, well-being, and control. Then before alerting, I will go to the next step of just going a little deeper relaxed; and then you can return to conscious alertness in your own time and pace. Does that all sound OK?*

Linda: *Yes, I understand.*

Therapist: *Good, and keep in mind that self-hypnosis is a "process of letting go." Just allowing yourself to respond in whatever way you* do *respond without "trying." It should just feel effortless to you and very pleasant and positive.*

After this discussion, a hypnotic induction was conducted. Each step was clearly stated, and specific suggestions associated with each step were incorporated. The pace of the induction was made consistent with Linda's breathing patterns and the entire induction lasted approximately 6 minutes.

PATIENT PRACTICE OF SELF-HYPNOSIS WITH MINIMAL PROMPTS

It is important to give the patient an opportunity to practice self-hypnosis with minimal prompts during the session. This builds confidence and knowledge about how to use self-hypnosis, and it allows the patient to work out any potential problems ahead of time. As the patient returns to conscious alertness, it is helpful in gauging the patient's progress to ask an open-ended question such as "What are you most aware of . . .?" or "How do you feel . . . now?" After the patient responds, remind him that he will be asked to complete a second self-hypnosis induction, this time with minimal prompts. This reminder is designed to build anticipation, further engage the patient in the process, and to bring to mind any questions. This discussion should be relatively brief so that the patient continues to experience the process of self-hypnosis rather than engaging in an intellectual discussion or critical thinking. The following is an illustration of this in the third session with Linda.

Therapist: *As you return to conscious alertness, what are you most aware of?*

Linda: *My hands are warm . . . I feel very relaxed . . . I can see the ocean.*

Therapist: *Very good! Now that process took about 6 minutes.*

Linda: *Is that all? It seemed like a whole session. . . . I just feel so relaxed.*

Therapist: *And no headache?*

Linda: *None . . . I feel great.*

Therapist: *Alright, now I will ask you to complete another hypnotic induction for self-hypnosis. This time I will just give you a few minimal prompts, such as just saying Step 1, Step 2, . . . etc. Does that sound OK?*

Linda: *So, at Step 1, I focus on a spot . . . and Step 2, I take a deep breath, and then on Step 3 I let my eyes close as I think the word relax . . .?*

Therapist: *Exactly right. I can give you a few more prompts as you get further into the process . . . such as . . . Step 5 . . . going to the beach in Galveston...or if you are unsure, it is always OK to open your eyes and look at the paper with the steps outlined. Ready?*

Linda: *OK, you want me to go ahead and focus now?*

> **Therapist:** *Yes, settle back into the cushions of the chair . . . Step 1 . . . Focus your attention . . . Step 2 . . . Good . . . now going on to Step 3 . . .*

The clinician should closely observe the patient during this second practice session of self-hypnosis in order to help him go at a reasonable speed (5 to 10 minutes for the second practice session) and to provide prompts at a pace that is consistent with his experience. Once the patient begins to return to conscious alertness for the second time, a complete post-hypnotic inquiry is recommended.

POST-HYPNOTIC INQUIRY

It is usually helpful to begin the post-hypnotic discussion by again asking the patient to describe her feelings and experiences during the second self-hypnosis practice. The clinician should draw the patient's attention to anything that was perceived as especially helpful, answer any questions, and discuss how to begin using self-hypnosis. It is helpful to provide the patient with specific examples of how to begin using self-hypnosis. This gives the patient some clear ideas of how and when to use this newly learned skill. The discussion with Linda included the following:

> **Therapist:** *How do you feel now?*
>
> **Linda:** *Good, very relaxed.*
>
> **Therapist:** *That process took about 5 minutes. Was there anything that stood out to you . . . any questions?*
>
> **Linda:** *I don't have any questions . . . wow, it is like I just got back from being in Galveston. . . . I just notice that I feel good . . . I liked the ideas for feeling calm and more self-accepting.*
>
> **Therapist:** *Good. Let's talk about when you can practice the self-hypnosis. Since you now know you can use self-hypnosis in as little as 5 minutes, can you think of times and places where you might take 5 minutes and go through the self-hypnosis steps?*
>
> **Linda:** *I guess I could do it almost anywhere in the day.*
>
> **Therapist:** *Yes, that is the idea. That you could just stop and take a few minutes to put yourself into a state of hypnotic relaxation and go through the steps. It could be in the morning before you begin your day, in the afternoon . . . just when you can have a few minutes where you will be uninterrupted and can engage in self-hypnosis. You could be sitting in the waiting area for your appointment and if you had a few minutes you could use self-hypnosis—experience hypnotic relaxation—and all of the suggestions in your self-hypnosis*

steps, even if you were just waiting for a few minutes for an appointment.

Linda: *That makes sense; so if I have a situation where it is going to be stressful, I could do the self-hypnosis even if I don't have the CD?*

Therapist: *That's the idea—that now you have more control. You can use self-hypnosis as you need it, in times and places that work best for you. You might do the self-hypnosis once, twice, or 10 or more times a day, depending on what works for you. You can also continue using your CD between sessions as you have been doing; but now you have another tool—self-hypnosis—to help you feel more relaxed, control the headaches . . . and I do think the suggestions for well-being and self-acceptance will be helpful.*

HOMEWORK ASSIGNMENT AND SCHEDULING

It is important to reinforce the patient's progress and provide continued support. Ending the third session includes confirming the time and date for the next appointment and reinforcing the "homework assignment"; that is, to practice self-hypnosis. This can be done by simply telling the patient that he will be asked about his experiences with self-hypnosis over the upcoming week and his success in finding time and places to practice. This communicates the importance of empowerment and the patient's involvement in his own care.

It is important to reinforce the patient's progress and provide continued support.

It can also be helpful to review some ideas for the fourth session so that the patient can reflect on goals prior to the next session. This was conveyed to Linda as follows:

Therapist: *Linda, you have done very well today. I think you understand how to do self-hypnosis, you have your outline of the steps to refer to as needed, and I will be interested in your experience when we have our next session. Remember, the purpose of self-hypnosis is to give you more control and it is a way to continue to make progress between sessions. Frequent practice, as needed.*

Linda: *I can do that! I like being able to do it on my own.*

Therapist: *Great! Also, at our next session, I will want to review your overall progress and how we are doing in helping you meet all of your goals. I know your headaches are becoming less; you are sleeping better, and managing stress better. Also, at the next session, I will want to see how you are doing in regard to expressing your feelings, reducing self-criticism, lifting the "dark cloud" of stress and* *whatever that may involve. Will you think about this between now and the next session as you continue to make good progress?*

Linda: *I feel like I am doing better, but I do think it would be good for me to talk about the self-criticism . . . I know I still do that.*

Therapist: *That is good, because being aware of your thoughts and feelings is necessary in order to change them. Just that awareness is helpful. We can integrate your practice of hypnotic relaxation therapy with some ideas to meet these other goals and changing some of your internal thoughts that lead to stress. Have a good week, and I will look forward to seeing you next time.*

This discussion is designed to reinforce the patient's intent to practice self-hypnosis and to acknowledge areas where goals are being accomplished. At the same time, it prepares the patient for the next session and provides a sense of "what we will work on next," which can be helpful in continuing to keep a strong collaborative relationship with the patient.

CHAPTER 9

Session Four and Beyond

INTEGRATION

While hypnotic relaxation therapy (HRT) may be used as the primary modality of treatment, it is often integrated with other evidence-based psychotherapy methods such as cognitive-behavioral therapy. Because of this, the focus of session four and later sessions is *integration*. HRT is goal-directed and may be integrated with any methods that enhance the efficiency in which therapeutic goals are achieved. In many cases, the integration of HRT with other methods results in greater or faster gains. The number of sessions needed in treatment of an individual patient will vary depending on the complexity of the problem and individual patient characteristics. Sessions may range from as few as 4 to as many as 12 or more to achieve treatment goals. This chapter will provide guidance on how to structure and conduct the fourth session and address further sessions as well.

Hypnotic relaxation therapy is goal-directed and may be integrated with any methods that enhance the efficiency in which therapeutic goals are achieved.

The manner in which HRT is integrated with other therapies depends upon the overall treatment goals. HRT can be utilized for (1) symptom reduction, (2) developing coping skills, (3) increasing insight, or (4) relapse prevention. HRT may be the primary therapy for some problems and goals. However, HRT is not, in and of itself, a system of psychotherapy. Rather, it is a method of treatment that involves utilizing hypnotic methods in a step-by-step approach that is structured, but also individualized, to best meet the patient's needs and progress. Examples of HRT integration are provided below.

SYMPTOM REDUCTION

Patients enter therapy because they are suffering in some way. The suffering may be due to physical injury or illness or it may be that the patient is dealing with emotional pain. The reduction of discomfort and alteration of symptoms are often goals in the early phase of treatment. A hypnotic relaxation induction can provide some symptom alteration through suggestions for deepening relaxation. In HRT, the suggestions for relaxation are both physical and emotional. Suggestions for physical relaxation can provide some comfort, but they also provide a pathway to helping the patient achieve a greatly enhanced subjective sense of relaxation and comfort. Hypnosis involves an altered state of consciousness. The patient's awareness of external factors fades into the background and the inner experience becomes more prominent. Suggestions are given for the patient to imagine, to dissociate, and to "go to a pleasant place, within the mind" where comfort is experienced. Suggestions may be given for the patient to experience being in a "safe place," and "feeling the comfort that can be experienced while in this safe place."

In HRT, the suggestions for relaxation are both physical and emotional.

In addition, reduction of symptoms may also involve suggestions for symptom alteration. This use of HRT goes beyond suggested relaxation. Symptom alteration involves working directly with the symptom and providing suggestions for the symptom to be experienced differently. For example, suggestions may be given for the symptom to lessen or to change in how it is perceived. Suggestions may be given for a sensation of pain to begin to change in some way, perhaps to become more of a feeling of "pressure" or of being "tingly" or "warm." This may be suggested with guidance for the patient to "notice where the pain is resting now . . . and certainly it is possible for the pain to change in character or in the way it is experienced . . . as you go into a deeper hypnotic state, this pain can become less and less . . . and as it does . . . it can change into a warmth or a feeling of pressure . . . becoming less and less as you become more comfortable."

Symptom reduction may be an initial goal in some instances where the patient presents with considerable anxiety, tension, pain, or discomfort during the session. When symptom reduction is achieved during the HRT session, it provides comfort and a means for the patient to develop greater confidence in his or her ability to respond to and use hypnotherapy. While symptom reduction may or may not involve insight, it allows the patient to begin to focus on other goals for therapy, and creates the opportunity for enhanced rapport between the therapist and patient. This is especially useful in early sessions of integrating HRT with cognitive–behavioral interventions for problems such as anxiety disorders, subjective experiences related to pain or tension, or reduction of symptoms. This allows for other issues to be addressed.

The use of HRT to develop coping skills involves the patient's use of self-hypnosis in addition to therapist-directed sessions.

DEVELOPING COPING SKILLS

HRT can also be used to help the patient further develop coping skills. The therapeutic process of developing coping skills is likely to involve some cognitive–behavioral techniques, such as identifying self-defeating cognitions or utilizing applied relaxation. The use of HRT to develop coping skills largely involves the patient's use of self-hypnosis in addition to therapist-directed sessions. As the patient learns how to induce a trance state, use mental imagery, and respond to hypnotic suggestions, self-hypnosis can be integrated with other aspects of medical treatment or psychotherapy. This may be achieved in several ways.

First, the practice of self-hypnosis involves using hypnotic relaxation as a coping skill. The patient learns how to use self-hypnosis to reduce stress, decrease pain, or to manage symptoms of a more chronic nature. This is especially effective in improving sleep and decreasing insomnia and is discussed in later chapters.

Second, self-hypnosis can be used to enhance coping skills through reinforcing positive self-talk. For example, a patient that is being treated for chronic pain using cognitive therapy may also benefit from learning and using self-hypnosis, as one focus of cognitive therapy for pain management involves identifying maladaptive thoughts (such as catastrophizing) and replacing them with more positive self-statements. In this way, HRT may be integrated with cognitive therapy (Alladin, 2008).

HRT may be used to reduce tension and to provide a mental state in which visualization and mental rehearsal of real-life situations may be most effective.

Third, HRT may be used to mentally rehearse a particular behavior. For example, if a patient is involved in psychotherapy to develop more assertive behavior, he or she may complete readings, engage in discussion during therapy sessions, role play, and identify underlying cognitions. HRT can be integrated with this therapy by having the patient complete a hypnotic induction in which he or she is guided through a mental rehearsal of the desired behavior. Specific situations may be the focus of HRT with an eventual outcome being that the patient becomes able to engage in real-life situations. As such, HRT may be used to reduce tension and to provide a mental state in which visualization and mental rehearsal of real-life situations may be most effective.

DEVELOPING FURTHER INSIGHT

Developing insight into the underlying dynamics or causes of emotional problems is often a goal of psychotherapy interventions. At times, psychotherapy may reach an impasse when conscious insight is limited or absent. Because the process of a hypnotic relaxation induction involves lowering conscious defenses and permitting unconscious thoughts and feelings to rise into conscious awareness, HRT can be utilized to explore underlying issues when conscious insight is limited. This is illustrated in in Chapter 18 and in the following example.

A 21-year-old female college student was referred for HRT to assist in treatment of her symptoms of severe anxiety. She was in her senior year as a pre-med major with plans to apply to medical school. She stated that her grades were excellent and that she enjoyed her classes and had very good support from family and friends. She was engaged to be married after graduation, and

Developing insight into the underlying dynamics or causes of emotional problems is often a goal of psychotherapy interventions.

she offered that, "Things seemed to be falling into place." She denied any particular stresses other than those associated with maintaining good study habits and balancing a social life. However, over a period of 10 months, she began to experience increasing episodes of health concerns and anxiety. She reported symptoms of unexplained tachycardia, shortness of breath, sweaty palms, and dizziness. At first, she was concerned that she was suffering from cardiac disease. However, after being seen in an emergency room and following up with her physician, she was reassured that her physical health was fine. She was diagnosed with anxiety or panic attacks and referred for psychotherapy.

The patient then entered counseling that focused on learning relaxation techniques and other ways of coping with anxiety. However, she stated that, after 12 sessions, she continued to have difficulty with severe anxiety. She attended her sessions and practiced her newly learned skills faithfully. However, she was frustrated with her lack of progress and continued to experience anxiety attacks that seemed to "come out of nowhere." It was then recommended that she consider hypnotherapy to reduce anxiety and determine if there was an underlying cause of her symptoms.

In the initial consultation, the patient discussed that she felt there was some "deeper issue" related to her anxiety. She discussed that her parents emigrated from Mexico, that she would be the first in her family to graduate from college, and that her family was very proud of her. She described her parents as hard-working people who taught her the values of responsibility, working to achieve your dreams, education, and caring for others. During this discussion, it became apparent that much of her self-worth was related to her accomplishments and to her family's admiration of her academic achievements. She was able to discuss her self-esteem in an intellectual manner and agreed that the drive to success had both positive and negative aspects for her.

The process of HRT was then explained and discussed. A hypnotic induction with suggestions for relaxation and comfort was completed. It was then suggested that the underlying cause of the patient's anxiety could become more apparent, that her "unconscious mind has an understanding of the anxiety that may be different from the conscious mind's understanding." It was then suggested that she would see a picture, that a picture would come to her mind that was related to the anxiety: "And now as you are in a safe and calm place . . . this picture comes to you . . . a picture that is related to the anxiety . . . as if you were looking at a blank screen . . . and yet as you look you begin to see what you need to see . . . what needs to be seen to understand the anxiety . . . just keep looking and tell me what you begin to see." As she focused, tears began to stream down from her eyes and she began to softly sob. She was asked, "What do you see there?" To which she replied, "I see myself in a classroom with children." She was asked, "What are you doing there?" Her reply was "I am teaching, teaching the children . . . that's what I want to do. . . . I don't want to be a doctor . . . I don't want to go to medical school . . . Oh God, my parents . . . they mean so much to me . . . I can't let them down!" It was apparent that there was a disconnection between the patient's real desires and the expectations that had been put upon her for years. As she was able to finally acknowledge these facts, her anxiety symptoms lessened and eventually stopped. In psychotherapy, these issues then became a focus. She was able to tell her parents about her desire to teach in an elementary school and was surprised by their acceptance.

RELAPSE PREVENTION

HRT can also be used to help patients maintain treatment gains. A patient may enter therapy with specific goals to change symptoms or alter behaviors (e.g., smoking cessation, addictive behaviors, anxiety management, or psychophysiological symptom reduction). Typically, once goals are achieved, therapy begins to taper. However, maintaining gains and minimizing relapse risk may be an ongoing issue.

Typically, once goals are achieved, therapy begins to taper. However, maintaining gains and minimizing relapse risk may be an ongoing issue.

Hypnotic relaxation is empowering. It also provides a basis for the patient to engage in quiet self-reflection and to reinforce and continue the practice of effective therapeutic suggestions. Encouraging the patient's continued use of hypnotic relaxation through self-hypnosis, CD recordings, and/or booster sessions can be of benefit in reducing relapse. For example, it has been shown that HRT, when properly applied, can reduce hot flashes among post-menopausal women and breast cancer survivors. However, experience has shown that continued practice of HRT is important to maintain the reduction in hot flashes and related symptoms after formal therapy sessions are concluded. This will be further illustrated in Chapter 15, where HRT is presented in the treatment of post-menopausal hot flashes.

CONSCIOUS AND UNCONSCIOUS INFORMATION PROCESSING

The integration of HRT with other treatment methods is also based upon the conceptualization that the unconscious (experiential) mind operates and processes information in a manner that is different from the conscious (rational) mind. Cognitive therapy and most talk-oriented psychotherapy interventions are largely directed toward conscious information processing. Thus, the patient may develop excellent insight at an intellectual or conscious level, yet the basic problem, or emotion, remains unchanged. This may be due to the fact that understanding at an unconscious level remains unchanged until an intervention directed toward the unconscious is effectively applied. HRT assumes that all information is processed at both conscious and unconscious levels of awareness in a manner consistent with cognitive experiential-self theory (Epstein, 1990). For example, a patient with a social anxiety disorder may come to understand that his anxiety is caused by irrational beliefs that acceptance by others is paramount and that rejection by friends or a respected individual would be terrible. However, this understanding may not be translated into an actual change in emotion. The patient may achieve understanding at a conscious level, yet the unconscious mind may still hold on to the mistaken, irrational beliefs, and change at the experiential level needs to be accomplished. Therefore, HRT may be integrated with cognitive therapy to direct suggestions to the unconscious mind in order to develop the same insight that exists at the conscious level of awareness.

STRUCTURE OF SESSION FOUR AND BEYOND

The content of session four and subsequent sessions will vary somewhat depending on the goals of the intervention and the level of integration with other therapies. However, the general structure involves the following: (1) reviewing the patient's experience and progress; (2) setting the session goal in the context of the overall goal; (3) rating symptom(s) of focus; (4) identifying integration methods: (5) communicating session goals and approach to the patient; (6) hypnotic relaxation induction; (7) post-hypnotic inquiry; (8) homework assignment and scheduling toward endpoint goals.

This will be illustrated with a selected session with Linda in which the goals of increasing self-acceptance and decreasing self-criticism were identified. The integration of HRT with cognitive insight provided positive benefit.

REVIEWING THE PATIENT'S EXPERIENCE AND PROGRESS

As with prior sessions, it is important to review the patient's progress to date, discuss his or her experience with HRT, and review any prior homework assignment.

> **Therapist:** *To begin our session today I would like to review your practice with self-hypnosis. How has it been going for you?*
>
> **Linda:** *Really, pretty well. I have been using the CD about every night and then doing the self-hypnosis during the day.*
>
> **Therapist:** *Very good! Do you find you are able to do the self-hypnosis OK without the CD? How do you do it exactly?*
>
> **Linda:** *I have read over the self-hypnosis sheet you gave me several times. It all seemed kind of natural and fit with the other sessions. I can usually tell when I am starting to tense up and so I just go to a place where I can be mostly alone for a few minutes. I try to find a place where I can sit and close my eyes. I usually start with focusing on my breathing and then the relaxation and suggestions. Most of the time I can do it in about five minutes, but if I have time it might be 20 or so.*
>
> **Therapist:** *Great, so how have the headaches been?*
>
> **Linda:** *Much better. For the most part, I really have not had any headaches at all over the past week. I am happy with that!*

Therapist: *Wonderful. I am pleased to hear of your success and progress. I think last time we discussed that today we would also touch base on the issues of self-criticism, expressing feelings, and overall stress.*

Linda: *I still have some work to do on those issues. I know I hold my feelings inward, but it seems so hard to change that and to stop putting myself down.*

Therapist: *What kind of thoughts come to your mind when you realize that you are not really expressing your true feelings?*

Linda: *That's easy; I can give you an example of how it goes. Last week I had an argument with my husband. He came home from work and asked me what I had been doing that day. I know he was just asking about my day, but it felt like he was accusing me of just staying home and doing nothing. I could feel the anger building up in me . . . and then the guilt . . . but I didn't say anything. I just held it inside and then later that evening it kind of blew up when I asked him to take the trash out and he said OK, but then just kept watching television. I got mad and grabbed the trash can and just said, "I guess I have to do everything around here, you don't do anything!" We got over it but it just seemed like it was unnecessary.*

Therapist: *Let me go back to the thoughts you were having. Earlier, we discussed the relationship between thoughts and feelings. I know you were aware of the feelings, but what thoughts were going through your mind at first, when he asked you about what you had been doing that day?*

Linda: *I know what I was thinking. It went something like, "I should be doing more; I'm just a failure; he thinks I'm lazy; I've had it with everything; what's wrong with me?" I know I have those thoughts, I know they just upset me, but they are hard to change even though I know they are not right.*

Therapist: *Well that is good insight. Let's work on that more today.*

SETTING THE SESSION GOAL IN CONTEXT WITH THE OVERALL GOAL

In addition to reviewing the patient's progress, therapists are encouraged to frequently review the initial case conceptualization for planning hypnotherapy (Chapter 4). The case conceptualization identifies the goals for therapy, contributing factors, strengths and weaknesses, and the overall treatment plan. It provides a kind of "road map" for HRT and helps to avoid "therapist drift." Therapist drift refers to the tendency, after rapport is established, for therapists to drift away from an established treatment plan and toward a conversational style of supportive counseling in which immediate concerns become the ongoing focus. In addition to the case conceptualization, following the aforementioned steps for each session can help keep focus on the overall and session goals. In Linda's case, issues related to self-esteem and self-criticism were identified early on, as was the approach of integrating cognitive insight with hypnotic relaxation experience. Because of her positive progress in reducing headaches, improving sleep, and gaining conscious insight, the focus of the session could shift toward integrating cognitive therapy for increasing self-acceptance, compassion, and expression of her thoughts and needs.

RATING SYMPTOM OF FOCUS

Symptom rating provides an indication of the patient's level of distress or concern and allows the clinician to track change over time. In Linda's case, once self-acceptance had been identified as a primary focus of the session, the therapist asked her to rate this "symptom" or issue.

> **Therapist:** *Would you take a moment and reflect on how accepting you feel you are of yourself at this moment? Let's let 100 represent 100% self-acceptance and 0 represent 0% self-acceptance. How self-accepting do you feel that you are?*
>
> **Linda:** *I would say I am at about 30%. Somewhat, but really it doesn't take much to push me into the self-critical mode.*

IDENTIFY INTEGRATION METHODS

The multiple uses of HRT, in regard to broad goals, should be reviewed. In this case, the goal of further developing coping skills was identified. This was because Linda appeared to have generally good conscious insight, she was using self-hypnosis as directed, and she had achieved primary symptom reduction (headaches). She was able to identify self-defeating cognitions and more positive self-talk; however, she needed to integrate new thoughts and beliefs at the unconscious/experiential level.

COMMUNICATE SESSION GOALS AND APPROACH TO THE PATIENT:

It is most important that the therapist communicate his or her understanding of the issues, session goal, and approach. This assures that the relationship remains collaborative and that the session goals and plan are acceptable to the patient. It also encourages the patient to share his or her perceptions. For example:

> **Therapist:** *OK, so I would like to just share with you the plan for the hypnotic relaxation induction today. The goal is to increase feelings of self-acceptance. While you now know that the self-critical thoughts are false and self-defeating, you have not really changed your internal beliefs at a feeling level. Does that sound about right to you?*
>
> **Linda:** *Yes, I know I should not be so critical of myself, but I just lapse back into doing it.*

> **Therapist:** *During the hypnotherapy session today, I would like to give you some suggestions to create an emotional experience that allows you to change those beliefs and to integrate the sense of greater self-acceptance at both conscious and unconscious levels of processing. To do that, I will begin with asking you to focus your attention and then drift into a deeply relaxed state. As you deepen that relaxation, go to a safe and secure place such as being at a wonderful beach on a warm pleasant day. Now, while you are there, the issue of self-acceptance needs to be addressed, and so I will ask you to see a child . . . of course the child is you. I will ask you to really see and experience a little girl . . . you as your adult self . . . seeing this precious little girl . . . and communicating with her, in a way that she can understand, that she is valuable, loved, accepted, important, and that nothing can change that fact. She needs to know it; just as you know it . . . and as she has this understanding . . . deep emotional understanding . . . your feelings will change . . . you will have a solid and strong sense of self-acceptance . . . less self-critical and more self-loving. Does that all sound OK with you?*

It is important that, during the induction, the therapist is consistent with what has been communicated with the patient about the session and induction process.

> **Linda:** *Yes, I understand. I need to see myself as a child and relate to her and then I can relate to myself as an adult.*

> **Therapist:** *That's right.*

HYPNOTIC RELAXATION INDUCTION

It is important that, during the induction, the therapist is consistent with what has been communicated with the patient about the session and induction process. The conversation is a kind of contract between therapist and patient that is especially important to honor as the patient engages in "letting go" in order to achieve a trance state. The following is an excerpt of the hypnotic relaxation induction and session with Linda.

> **Therapist:** *Linda, just settle back in the recliner and find that point to focus your attention . . . very good . . . focus intently and then as things begin to fade into the background . . . take a deep breath of air . . . and as you exhale . . . allow your eyelids to close . . .*

This was followed by additional suggestions for absorption, relaxation, and dissociation.

> **Therapist:** *Now, Linda, you have come to that very beautiful beach . . . and notice what a pleasant day it is. Notice the sound of*

the waves . . . notice all of the beauty around you . . . and how far you can see across the ocean . . . now when you are there . . . when you are at the beach . . . just nod your head "yes," so I will know you are there.

Linda: (Indicates "yes" with slight head movement.) *And, Linda while you are there, soon you will see a child . . . a little girl . . . and I want you to take the time to really look at her . . . look at her face . . . look into her eyes . . . When you see her, again nod your head, "yes."*

Linda: (Again, indicates experiencing the suggestions through a slight head nod of "yes.")

Therapist: *Good. Now you know this little girl is you . . . and you know that she doesn't believe in herself . . . she has been criticized . . . she has come to believe that she is less than . . . that she is bad in some way . . . that she really does not love herself . . . does not accept herself . . . but that can change. She needs love, she needs your help and your understanding. Do you agree?*

Linda: *Yes.*

Therapist: *Now, bring her close to you . . . do you see her crying? . . . now hold her . . . and you can say to her the things she needs to hear . . . soon saying to her . . . that you love her . . . that you will always love her . . . that she is OK just as she is . . . that you believe in her . . . and that you will never put her down . . . criticize her unfairly . . . and that you will always treat her with respect and kindness . . . Hear yourself talking with her . . . in a way that she will feel your caring and your love for her . . . and just take your time . . . and nod your head "yes" when she understands . . .* (Pause.)

Linda: (Nodding her head "yes" very definitively and starting to cry.)

Therapist: *Now, this experience today will be life-changing . . . From this time forward you will feel a greater sense of self-love, self-acceptance, and compassion for yourself . . . you will keep the promise made to this little girl . . . this little girl that is you . . . and deep within yourself now knowing and feeling a sense of love . . . compassion . . . no more of the old, worn-out criticisms . . . love and compassion . . . become stronger and stronger each time you think of this experience today . . . and this little girl that you have seen today.*

POST-HYPNOTIC INQUIRY

To assure a feeling of safety, it is advised to provide suggestions that the patient return to a calm and peaceful place. The hypnotic induction session is concluded with suggestions for post-hypnotic responses and then returning to conscious alertness. The post-hypnotic inquiry allows for further exploration of the patient's experience and insight and reinforcing changes that are most in the patient's awareness at that time. It is also helpful to ask the patient to again rate the target symptom or feeling in order to gauge progress.

To assure a feeling of safety, it is advised to provide suggestions that the patient return to a calm and peaceful place.

Therapist: *As I begin to count from the numbers 4 to 1, returning to conscious alertness . . . 4 . . . becoming more aware of this time, this room and place . . . 3 . . . Soon your eyelids can begin to open . . . feeling calm and with a sense of self-love and acceptance . . . 2 . . . Eyelids opening . . . and 1 . . . Returning to conscious alertness. How do you feel? What are you most aware of now?*

Linda: *I feel relaxed . . . I feel positive . . . I'm calm.*

Therapist: *Good. Now let's go back to the rating of self-acceptance. How self-accepting do you feel now on the 0 to 100 scale?*

Linda: (Wiping away tears.) *I feel better. I don't have any self-criticism right now . . . it's at like 90%. I feel calm inside, like I'm at peace with myself. I'm OK . . . just as I am . . . I'm going to love myself.*

Therapist: *And the little girl?*

Linda: *She was smiling . . . she will remind me of who I am . . . it was good.*

HOMEWORK ASSIGNMENT AND SCHEDULING TOWARD ENDPOINT GOALS

It is helpful to discuss the patient's progress and the therapist's estimations of future sessions to move toward endpoint goals. It is also important to discuss any homework assignments, including practice of self-hypnosis, reading, or other individualized activities. Linda was seen for a total of six sessions and made excellent progress that was confirmed at a 6-month follow-up appointment.

CHAPTER 10

Assessment of Hypnotizability

Hypnotizability is defined as the ability to become hypnotized and to produce the subjective and behavioral phenomena associated with hypnotic depth. In this chapter the terms "hypnotizability" and "hypnotic ability" will be used interchangeably to emphasize that the ability to respond to hypnotic suggestions represents an ability or talent that individuals may possess to varying degrees. Research has well established that there are individual differences in the ability to respond to hypnotic suggestions. However, easily administered and clinically relevant measures of hypnotizability have been limited, and hypnotizability is not often assessed in clinical settings. This chapter presents the first publication of a new assessment instrument, the Elkins Hypnotizability Scale (EHS).

> Research has well-established that there are individual differences in the ability to respond to hypnotic suggestions.

Normative data from participants recruited in an outpatient clinical setting is also presented. In addition, validity and reliability data are reported. A 9-item clinical version of the scale, the EHS—Clinical, is presented along with a longer research version (12 items). The clinical version of the scale takes approximately 15 to 20 minutes, and the research version requires approximately 25 to 30 minutes to administer and score. The EHS, scoring forms, and interpretation are included in this chapter. The use of information on hypnotic ability in providing hypnotherapeutic interventions is also discussed.

WHY ASSESS A PATIENT'S HYPNOTIC ABILITY?

Research has shown that most people are hypnotizable (Fromm and Nash, 1992); however, individuals vary in their ability to respond to hypnotic suggestions and hypnotherapy (Bates, 1993). About 66% of adults are hypnotizable and 10% are highly hypnotizable (Hilgard, 1965). Persons who are highly hypnotizable may demonstrate greater or quicker response to suggestion

(Hilgard & Hilgard, 1975; Patterson & Pacek, 1997) in comparison to persons who are less hypnotizable. Notably, hypnotizability is a relatively stable trait that can be accurately measured over time (Piccione, Hilgard, Zimbardo, 1989).

Hypnotic ability can be estimated through informal (clinical intuition) means or through use of a standardized scale. Though not essential in all cases, using a standardized scale does provide an advantage over informal assessment. It is important that clinicians who use hypnotherapy understand hypnotizability and have the knowledge and skills needed to assess the hypnotic ability of their patients.

TREATMENT PLANNING

Knowledge of patients' hypnotic ability can be helpful in treatment planning. As mentioned, more highly hypnotizable individuals may benefit from hypnotherapy more quickly, and their response may be more profound. Hypnotherapy has a wide range of applications, and individuals who are most highly hypnotizable may be able to use hypnotic relaxation to a greater degree than those with less hypnotic ability. For example, hypnotherapy has been used as the sole anesthesia in surgery and in successfully coping with extended medical procedures (Lang et al, 2000; Patterson & Ptacek, 1997). The person with higher hypnotic ability is more likely to be successful in the use of hypnosis to achieve difficult tasks such as these. By assessing the patient's hypnotizability, the clinician can gain insight into how a particular patient can best use hypnosis and whether hypnotherapy should be used as a primary or secondary intervention. The clinician's primary consideration should be that the patient benefit and achieve his or her goals.

It is important for clinicians who use hypnotherapy to have the knowledge and skill needed to assess the hypnotic ability of their patients.

DETERMINATION OF RESISTANCE VERSUS HYPNOTIC ABILITY

As will be discussed further in Chapter 11, the assessment of hypnotizability can be useful in determining the degree to which a patient may be resistant to hypnotic interventions. This is very important in clinical applications of hypnotic relaxation therapy (HRT) and in helping patients achieve their therapeutic goals.

DIAGNOSIS

Assessment of hypnotizability can assist in diagnosing some disorders. Hypnotizabilty has been shown to be associated with several diagnoses, including dissociative identity disorder (DID), post-traumatic stress disorder (PTSD), certain phobias, and some eating disorders.

Assessment of hypnotizability can be useful in differential diagnosis of DID, as patients with this disorder

Assessment of hypnotizability can assist in diagnosing some disorders.

typically score within the top 10% using a standardized hypnotizability scale (Bliss, 1983, 1986; Frischholz, Braun, Sachs, & Schwartz, 1991).

PTSD has also been associated with higher hypnotizability. It is unclear whether hypnotizability is a risk factor for developing PTSD. However, two studies (Spiegel, Hunt, & Dondershine, 1988; Stutman & Bliss, 1985) found that veterans diagnosed with PTSD scored higher on measures of hypnotizability compared to those without PTSD symptoms or other psychiatric disorders.

Several studies have also found higher hypnotizability among patients with phobias. Crawford and Barabasz (1993) suggested that the relationship between hypnotizability and phobias may be due to a more highly hypnotizable person's ability to become intensely absorbed in memories of an initially fearful experience. Following the intense encounter with the fearful memory, the person engages in avoidance, contributing to the development and maintenance of the fear.

Assessment of hypnotizability may also be helpful in understanding and diagnosing patients with eating disorders. An important study by Pettinati, Horne, and Staats (1985) showed that female patients with a diagnosis of bulimia were highly hypnotizable, while patients with a diagnosis of anorexia fell into the mid-range of hypnotizability. These findings are consistent with a study reported by Barabasz (1991), who also found that patients diagnosed with bulimia were more highly hypnotizable compared to those without bulimia. While the relationship between hypnotizability and eating disorders is not fully understood, researchers have hypothesized that patients with bulimia may engage in binging and purging while in a dissociated, hypnotic-like state (Barnier & Council, 2010).

The assessment of hypnotizability can serve as a means to familiarize the patient with the experience of hypnotic relaxation.

INTRODUCTION OF HYPNOTIC EXPERIENCE TO THE PATIENT

The assessment of hypnotizability can serve as a means to familiarize the patient with the experience of hypnotic relaxation while providing insight into his or her ability to respond to suggestion. In order to measure hypnotizability, it is necessary to complete a hypnotic induction and then determine the individual's response to specific hypnotic suggestions. When done skillfully and with clinically relevant measures, this can be achieved in a relatively brief amount of time.

Research into applications of hypnotherapy is enriched by evaluating hypnotizability.

RESEARCH

Assessment of hypnotizability is also important for clinical research. Research into applications of hypnotherapy is enriched by evaluating hypnotizability, as it provides a means to better understand hypnosis and to examine the role of hypnotic ability in the treatment of a particular disorder. In this regard, assessment of hypnotizability is somewhat underutilized, due in part to some of the strengths and weaknesses of current measures as discussed below.

OVERVIEW OF HYPNOTIZABILTY SCALES

The development of the EHS was motivated by the need for a brief, clinically relevant, reliable, and valid measure to evaluate a full range (very low to very high) of hypnotic ability. Before describing the EHS, some of the more prominent existing scales will be discussed. This is because it is important for practitioners of HRT to have an understanding of the current scales and their relative strengths and weaknesses.

More than 50 years have passed since Weitzenhoffer and Hilgard introduced the first viable measure of hypnotizability into clinical research. In 1959, the Stanford Hypnotic Susceptibility Scale, Forms A and B (SHSS: A, B; Weitzenhoffer & Hilgard, 1959) was developed with a college student population and introduced as a measure of hypnotizability in research subjects. This scale was a major advancement in the measure of hypnotizability, but it was found to have limited usefulness due to a predominance of motoric items (i.e., items that rely on movement as opposed to mental processes) and its lack of sensitivity to differences among high hypnotizables (Hilgard, 1965; Perry, Nadon, & Button, 1992; Council, 2002).

Because of these problems, the Stanford researchers developed the Stanford Hypnotic Susceptibility Scale, Form C (SHSS: C; Weitzenhoffer & Hilgard, 1962) to provide a better measurement of the cognitive processes associated with hypnosis and to better differentiate those subjects at the high end of hypnotizability. This scale, which was also developed and normed with a college population, provides a range of scores from 0 to 12. It is the most highly regarded scale and the most accepted research measure for determining hypnotizability in current use (Barabasz & Barabasz, 1992). However, the SHSS: C also has some major drawbacks that severely limit its use in research and clinical practice. For example, the instrument takes up to an hour to administer and score. This is impractical and overly burdensome for most clinical applications, especially when patients are in pain or emotional distress. Also, the scale includes suggestions for "age regression." This is controversial not only because such items may be uncomfortable for patients who were victims of childhood trauma, but also because the validity of temporal "age regression" has been brought into question (Nash, 1987). Further, the scale includes additional items, such as the suggestion for anosmia (i.e., suggesting that the person will be unable to smell ammonia). This might be inappropriate for some persons sensitive to ammonia. It also includes suggestions that might be uncomfortable for some patients, such as the suggestion to hallucinate a mosquito (Elkins, Marcus & Rascoe, 2003).

In an effort to develop a shorter scale to measure hypnotizability in clinical research, the Stanford Hypnotic Clinical Scale was developed.

Because of these difficulties, efforts have been made to reword some items and make substitutions for others (Perry, Nader, & Button, 1992). Despite these changes, the SHSS: C is still rarely used in clinical practice because of the concerns described above.

In an effort to develop a shorter scale to measure hypnotizability in clinical research, the Stanford Hypnotic Clinical Scale was developed (Morgan & Hilgard, 1978–1979a). This scale, like the aforementioned measures, was developed using a college-age population. The instrument is based upon the SHSS: C, takes approximately 20 to 25 minutes to administer, and includes suggestions for hands moving together, a dream, a post-hypnotic response (throat clearing), age regression, and amnesia. A score from 0 to 5 may be obtained. While this scale is more time-efficient, it does not measure the full range of hypnotizability and cannot distinguish very highly hypnotizable persons. It also retains the "age regression" item, which, as mentioned, may be inappropriate for some patients.

A number of group-administered scales to measure hypnotizability have been developed. These include the Harvard Group Scale of Hypnotic Susceptibility, Form A (HGSHS: A; Shor & Orne, 1962) and the Waterloo–Stanford Group Scale of Hypnotic Susceptibility (Bowers, 1993; Bowers, 1998). These scales are generally used only as a screening tool followed by the SHSS: C. While these group scales are useful as screening instruments in experimental situations, they lack the discrimination found in individually administered scales. Further, the combined use of group and individual measures places too much burden on research subjects or patients.

Many researchers have recognized the continuing need to develop a scale that is time-efficient and appropriate to measure hypnotizability in clinical populations. In this regard, the Hypnotic Induction Profile (HIP; Spiegel & Spiegel, 1978) was standardized on a clinical population (smokers and psychiatric patients) and takes approximately 5 to 10 minutes to administer. However, this scale includes an "eye roll" test that does not correlate very well or consistently with standard measures of hypnotizability, such as the SHSS: C. Further, because the HIP relies on suggestions for "arm levitation," it is essentially a one-item scale and simply contains too few items to provide a representative assessment of hypnotic responsiveness (Kihlstrom, 1985). This severely limits the effectiveness of this scale to discriminate between low, mid-range, high, and very high hypnotizables. Further, the correlation between results from the HIP and those from standardized scale scores such as the SHSS has ranged from .19 (Orne et al., 1979) to .63 (Frischholz et al., 1980). Thus, the relationship between the HIP and the SHSS: C, as well as the instrument's validity, remain very controversial (Hilgard & Hilgard, 1979; Hilgard, 1981a; Hilgard, 1981b; Frischholz, Spiegel, Tryon, & Fisher, 1981; Spiegel, Tryon, Frischholz, & Spiegel, 1982).

Many researchers have recognized the continuing need to develop a scale that is time-efficient and appropriate to measure hypnotizability in clinical populations.

In addition to the HIP, Hilgard, Crawford, and Wert (1979) reported on a brief scale referred to as the Stanford Hypnotic Arm Levitation and Induction Test. This is a 6-minute hypnotic induction and measurement scale. While its brevity is advantageous, it has the same weakness as the HIP because of its dependence on one item.

A number of other scales have been developed and standardized with college students, including the Barber Suggestibility Scale (Barber and Glass, 1962). This scale is not widely used by clinical researchers because of the time required for administration and controversy among clinical researchers about the validity of the scale. The Barber Suggestibility Scale has been largely replaced by the Carleton University Responsivity to Suggestion Scale (Spanos, Radtke, Hodgins, Bertrand, Stam, & Dubreuil, 1983). However, it has been suggested that the scores on this instrument represent more cooperativeness rather than an ability to experience subjective alterations that many clinical researchers associate with hypnosis (Bowers & Davidson, 1991; Bates & Brigham, 1990). Because of this concern, it has been suggested that the Carleton University Responsivity to Suggestion Scale may be more of a measure of social compliance (Kihlstrom, 1985) or expectancy than hypnotizability. Further, the scale requires almost an hour to administer, creating too much of a burden to be widely used in clinical practice. These concerns not only lead researchers and clinicians to avoid measurement of hypnotizability (Cohen, 1989); they leave unanswered the need for a scale to effectively and quickly measure hypnotizability within clinical populations.

DEVELOPMENT OF THE EHS

The EHS was developed over several years of study and is based upon extensive experience with using hypnosis in both clinical care and research. The EHS was developed according to several considerations:

Hypnotic depth is associated with the ability to respond to increasingly difficult suggestions.

1. The experience should be perceived as pleasant (in terms of item content).
2. The scales should be time-efficient (i.e., take 25 minutes or less to administer).
3. The instrument should include enough items, and those items should be sufficiently difficult and discriminate between low, moderate, high, and very highly hypnotizable patients.
4. The instrument should have acceptable reliability and validity to be a useful clinical and research tool.

For assessment purposes, hypnotizability refers to the depth of hypnosis achieved under the standard conditions of a hypnotic induction and suggestion.

It has long been recognized that a hypnotic induction increases the subject's responsiveness to suggestion (Weitzenhoffer & Sjoberg, 1961), and for assessment purposes, hypnotizability refers to the depth of hypnosis achieved under the standard conditions of a hypnotic induction and suggestion. Therefore, the EHS begins with standard instructions and a well-defined hypnotic induction with suggestions for a deeper level of hypnosis.

Hypnotic depth is associated with the ability to respond to increasingly difficult suggestions, and it is generally supposed that the successful response to a suggestion increases the likelihood of successful response to later suggestions (Hull, 1933; Hilgard, 1965). Therefore, items within the EHS are arranged from least difficult (items that the majority of persons can experience) to most difficult (items that only a few persons can experience). For example, it has been demonstrated that 92% of the population can respond to motor behavior items such as suggestions for "hand lowering" (suggestions that an outstretched hand can feel heavy and lower). However, more difficult suggestions, such as those for a positive hallucination (i.e., suggestions to see a light or object that is not really there) are experienced by less than 9% of the population (Weitzenhoffer & Hilgard, 1962).

Items that appear to sample a range of hypnotizability from low, mid-range, high, and very high hypnotic ability were chosen for the EHS. Because hypnotic responding is highly subjective, responses are scored using both behavioral observation as well as the patient's or research participant's description of his or her subjective experience. Using the Principal Investigator's (PI) clinical experience and normative data from the Stanford Hypnotic Susceptibility Scales (Forms A, B, and C and the SHALIT), the PI and a panel of experts developed the scale using the following items.

CONSTRUCTS AND ITEMS OF THE EHS

The EHS is composed of twelve items clustered within six theoretical constructs from the domain of hypnotizability: (1) arm heaviness, (2) arm lightness, (3) mental imagery/dissociation, (4) rose-scent olfactory hallucination, (5) positive hallucination, and (6) post-hypnotic amnesia. These common hypnotic factors were chosen as the most parsimonious to determine individual differences. All but post-hypnotic amnesia have at least two indicators, which were designed to indicate the strength of the response. The amnesia factor, a hypnotic ability that is less common, has only one indicator. The EHS constructs and associated indicators are shown in Figure 10.1, and their descriptions follow.

Arm heaviness/arm immobility

This comprises two items—suggestions for heaviness in one arm and a challenge for the subject to "try" to lift the arm. These items, which may be similar to items for arm rigidity or hand lowering, were selected as being relatively "easy" items because the majority of persons can experience them. Clinical experience also suggests that these items are appropriate for clinical populations and provide clinically relevant information. These items are scored

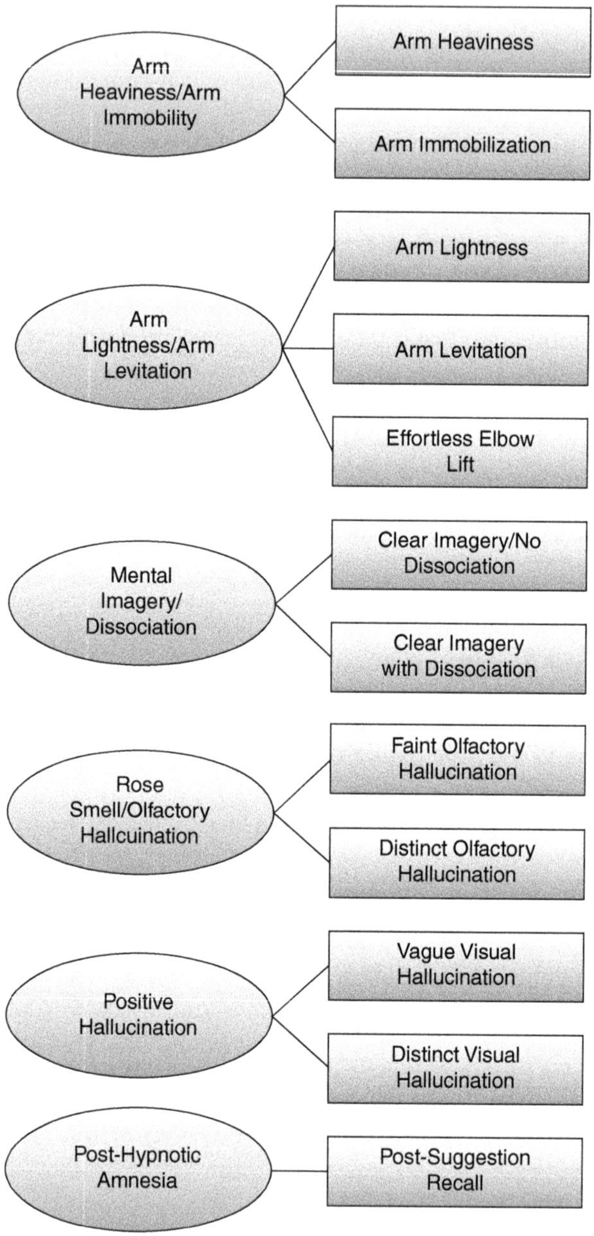

Figure 10.1
Constructs of the Elkins Hypnotizability Scale.

based on both behavioral observation (i.e., does the patient lift his or her arm?) as well as the patient's report that his or her arm felt heavy.

Arm lightness/arm levitation

Research (Spiegel & Spiegel, 1978; Hilgard, Crawford, & Wert, 1979) suggests that arm levitation can be useful in determining hypnotizability. This is because suggestions for arm levitation, when appropriately presented, are sensitive to ideomotor responses (responses that seem automatic and occur outside of the subject's awareness) and involve a subjective sense of dissociation. In the EHS, this construct includes suggestions that: (1) the participant's arm feels light; (2) the arm feels weightless; and (3) the arm lifts by itself without any conscious or willful effort by the subject.

Mental imagery/dissociation

Items in the construct of mental imagery/dissociation involve suggestions for dissociating from the present time and place and experiencing imagery associated with walking through a garden. These items likely share some similarities with the suggested "dreams" and "age-regression" items on the SHSS: C. The choice to suggest a walk through a garden was made to overcome some negative aspects of "age regression" items while capturing the responsiveness to suggestions for mental imagery and dissociation. By scoring items for mental imagery and dissociation separately, the EHS can distinguish persons who are able to experience a complete dissociation and those who are only able to experience mental imagery. Our clinical experience suggests that this item identifies individuals who are in the moderate range of hypnotizability.

By scoring items for mental imagery and dissociation separately, the EHS can distinguish persons who are able to experience a complete dissociation and those who are only able to experience mental imagery.

Rose-smell/olfactory hallucination

The items in this construct involve suggestions for imagery and smelling a rose while walking through a garden. These items likely share some similarities with those that suggest that subjects "taste of something sour or sweet" on the SHSS: C. These items were chosen to easily assess response to suggestions for sensory change. Scoring allows for differentiation between individuals who are able to experience a faint perception of smell and those who can distinctly smell a hallucinated rose.

Positive hallucination

The items in this construct likely correspond to the positive hallucinations factor in the SHSS: C (Hilgard, 1965). These items are the most difficult within the

EHS. The clinician suggests that the subject or patient "see" a box that does not exist in reality. The items that comprise the Positive Hallucination construct were selected to distinguish the 9% to 10% of individuals who are able to respond to suggestions for a positive hallucination (Hilgard, 1965). Thus, the items, which are easy to administer, are useful in identifying individuals in the very high range of hypnotizability.

In order to ensure acceptable content validity, the items were submitted for review to a panel of experts in clinical and experimental hypnosis.

Post-hypnotic amnesia

This construct involves suggestions for an inability to recall the items in the administration of the EHS until a "cue" is given. This item evaluates a person's ability to experience a suggested inhibition of recall and sensory impressions. Approximately 27% of individuals can experience a hypnotically suggested amnesia (Hilgard, 1965).

PSYCHOMETRIC PROPERTIES OF THE EHS

The wording for each item was based upon clinical experience and from patient feedback following clinical administration of the EHS. In order to ensure acceptable content validity, the items were submitted for review to a panel of experts in clinical and experimental hypnosis. As evidence of face validity, there was a consensus that the scale includes items that are appropriate to measure hypnotizability. Additionally, the EHS contains an adequate number of items to gather enough information and includes items of varying and sufficient difficulty so that it can discriminate among minimally, moderately, and highly hypnotizable patients and have adequate content validity (Elkins, Marcus, & Rasco, 2003).

A sample of 252 adults (129 men and 123 women) was recruited from outpatient clinical settings. Subjects were recruited through mailing and posting flyers in hospitals and medical clinics. The EHS and the SHSS:C were administered in balanced order during individual sessions. Masters- and doctoral-level practitioners who were trained according to guidelines set forth by the American Society for Clinical Hypnosis administered and scored the scales. There were no order effects for any item or scores; therefore, the data reported were based on the total sample.

The mean age of participants was 41.53 years, with the majority being Caucasian (85.3%) and predominantly married (71.8%; Table 10.1). Females in the sample ranged in age from 19 to 65 years ($M = 40.03$, $SD = 11.74$). Male participants' ages ranged from 19 to 67 ($M = 42.96$, $SD = 11.66$).

Score distributions for the EHS are shown in Figure 10.2. The average EHS score for females was 5.95 ($SD = 3.27$), while the average for males was 5.71 ($SD = 3.198$). There was no significant difference in mean scores for males and females ($F[1,249] = 0.563$, $p = .563$). The average time for administration of the full EHS was 25.8 minutes ($SD = 5.1$ minutes).

Table 10.1
Participant Demographic Characteristics (n = 252)

Characteristics	
Age in years, mean (range)	41.53 (19–67)
Race, No. (%)	
American Indian or Alaskan Native	1 (0.4)
Asian	4 (1.6)
African American	13 (5.2)
Caucasian	215 (85.3)
Hispanic	19 (7.5)
Marital status, No. (%)	
Married	183 (71.8)
Divorced	35 (13.9)
Single	33 (13.1)
Widowed	1 (0.4)
Education in years, mean (range)	15.44 (9–25)

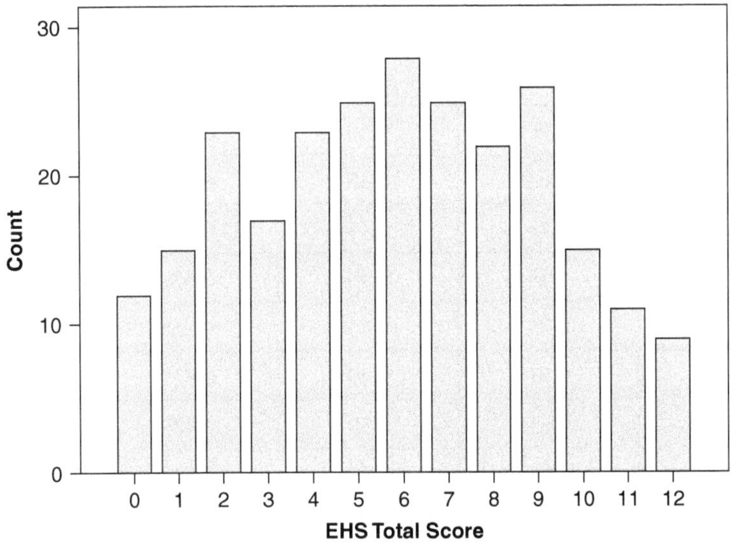

Figure 10.2
Distribution of EHS Scores

Reliability analysis indicated that the EHS is highly reliable (Cronbach's α = .849). The means, standard deviations, and percent passing each item are shown in Table 10.2. The items are listed by number and order of administration:

EHS 1 (subjective arm heaviness)
EHS 2 (arm immobility)

EHS 3 (subjective arm lightness)
EHS 4 (arm levitation)
EHS 5 (elbow lift)
EHS 6 (clear imagery)
EHS 7 (dissociation experience)
EHS 8 (faint rose smell)
EHS 9 (distinct rose smell)
EHS 10 (vague visual hallucination)
EHS 11 (distinct visual hallucination)
EHS 12 (post-hypnotic amnesia)

In order to examine convergent validity, correlational analyses were completed for the EHS and SHSS: C, revealing a strong relationship ($r = .821$, $p < .001$). Additionally, correlational analyses were completed for the first nine items of the EHS (referred to as the EHS—Clinical Form, EHS:C) and SHSS:C,

Table 10.2
Means, SDs, and Estimates of Reliability

	Mean	*SD*	*Cronbach's alpha**	*% Pass*
EHS 1	0.90	0.30	0.843	84.20%
EHS 2	0.64	0.48	0.832	63.50%
EHS 3	0.73	0.45	0.836	69.40%
EHS 4	0.43	0.49	0.829	39.20%
EHS 5	0.24	0.43	0.835	22.60%
EHS 6	0.81	0.39	0.839	77.40%
EHS 7	0.53	0.50	0.829	50.60%
EHS 8	0.54	0.49	0.838	51.30%
EHS 9	0.18	0.38	0.847	30.90%
EHS 10	0.38	0.48	0.839	17.50%
EHS 11	0.12	0.35	0.845	10.90%
EHS 12	0.35	0.47	0.834	32.80%
9 Item EHS:C	5.02	2.54	0.822	
EHS	5.82	3.23	0.849	
SHSS-C	6.52	3.38	0.856	

* Cronbach's alpha values for items indicate value if item was deleted; values for scales are indicators of total scale reliability.

also showing a strong and significant relationship ($r = .789$, $p < .001$). The correlation between the EHS and EHS:C was also strong ($r = .962$, $p < .001$), indicating that the shorter EHS:C provides a good estimate of total EHS scores. Thus, both the EHS and EHS:C appear to be valid and reliable estimates of hypnotic responsiveness. The results of the correlational analysis are shown in Table 10.3.

Table 10.3
Correlational Analyses for Convergent Validity

	9-Item EHS:C	*EHS*	*Stanford*
9-Item EHS:C	1.00		
EHS	.962*	1.00	
Stanford	.789*	.821*	1.00

*Correlation is significant, at $p < .001$.

Participants were also asked to rate how pleasant the experience was of completing the EHS. Upon completion, participants were asked to rate pleasantness on a 0 to 10 scale (0 = completely unpleasant; 10 = completely pleasant). The results indicated that one-half of the participants rated the EHS as 10 (completely pleasant). The average rating of pleasantness was 8.97, which strongly indicates that the EHS is likely to be experienced as very pleasant by the majority.

To summarize, both the EHS and EHS:C appear to be valid and reliable measures of hypnotizability. The EHS is experienced as pleasant and is well-received. With this information, the administration protocol for the EHS is presented here, followed by a specimen scoring form and guidelines for item scoring.

The EHS and EHS: C both appear to be valid and reliable measures of hypnotizability. The EHS is experienced as pleasant and is well received.

PROTOCOL FOR ADMINISTERING THE EHS

Ensure that the subject is seated in a comfortable chair with support for the head, neck, and shoulders. A foot stool may be provided to allow the subject to elevate his or her legs; however, if seated in a recliner, the back of the chair should *not* be reclined. See the "General Instructions for Administration and Scoring of the EHS" for further information.

INTRODUCTORY REMARKS

"This is a scale to measure your ability to experience hypnosis and respond to hypnotic suggestions. It is a standardized scale and therefore I will be reading from these papers. You may occasionally hear me writing or hear the sound of things outside this room. You can pay as much or as little attention to such sounds as you wish.

"The best way to determine a person's ability to experience hypnosis is to complete a hypnotic induction. This will involve focusing your attention on a spot on the ceiling and suggestions for calmness. After your eyes close I will give you some hypnotic suggestions. It is important to *just respond to what you are feeling and experiencing*. There is nothing that you have to try to do; just allow yourself to respond to whatever you experience. Not everyone experiences the same things and not everyone is equally hypnotizable. At times during hypnosis I will ask you to verbally describe what you are feeling or experiencing. You will be able to do so without interrupting your experience of hypnosis. As you listen to my words, just let whatever happens happen so that we can see how you experience hypnosis and how we can learn to make hypnosis work best for you."

(NOTE: Place a small table with a white top in front of the participant before beginning the induction. Ask the participant to extend his or her arms and bring them down to a relaxed position on the arms of the chair.)

INDUCTION

"Now, please roll your eyes upward and focus on a spot on the ceiling. That's right. Now, *focus on that spot so intently* . . . that everything else begins to fade into the background . . . more and more . . . Good . . . Now take a breath and hold it for a moment . . . hold . . . and as you exhale allow your eyelids to close normally and naturally . . . Good . . . Now, allow your body to relax . . . notice a wave of relaxation spreading from the top of your head . . . down to your feet . . . letting all the tension go . . . Head, neck, shoulders . . . relax . . . arms and legs . . . relax . . . as you enter a hypnotic state, finding a calm . . . relaxed feeling . . . more calm and more at ease . . . comfortable and calm . . . Now, as I count from the number 10 down to 1, with each number that I count . . . going into *an even deeper state of hypnosis*."

(NOTE: During the deepening suggestions, numbers are counted on the subject's exhalation.)

"10 . . . A wave of relaxation spreading across your forehead . . . neck . . . and shoulders . . . 9 . . . More relaxed . . . your jaw goes slack . . . shoulders slump . . . and arms become very relaxed . . . 8 . . . That wave of relaxation now spreads across your back . . . your upper back . . . and lower back . . . deeply relaxed . . . 7 . . . A deeper level of hypnosis now as your legs become very relaxed, letting all the tension go . . . feeling more calm . . . feeling more peaceful . . . 6 . . . Entering such a deep level of hypnosis now . . . that you may notice a drifting or floating sensation . . . just drifting . . . and floating . . . deeper and deeper into this hypnotic state . . . 5 . . . Deeply calm and deeply hypnotized . . . 4 . . . Now allowing that calmness to become *even more complete* . . . and entering *the deepest level of hypnosis* . . . 3 . . . so deeply hypnotized that you are able to respond to each suggestion . . . and experience each thing that I suggest . . . 2 . . . Calm and peaceful . . . so deeply relaxed . . . any tension that has remained is released . . . *Now* . . . 1 . . . *all the way there* . . . deeply hypnotized . . . calm and peaceful.

"And it is possible to feel a special sense of calmness . . . and you will be able to experience and respond to each suggestion during hypnosis today . . . Just listen to my voice and let whatever happens happen so we can see how you experience hypnosis"

Arm heaviness/immobilization

"Now, as you remain deeply calm . . . you will *soon* become aware of a change in sensation in your *right* arm and hand . . . Soon you will notice that your right arm will become *very, very heavy* . . . just as *heavy as lead* . . . That heavy feeling begins to occur now . . . that arm becomes *heavier and heavier* . . . and as this occurs it can feel as if the arm is becoming *less a part of you . . . as you allow it to become as heavy as lead*."

(Pause for 5 seconds.)

"And now that arm will become *even heavier* . . . so very heavy that you will find that you *cannot lift this right arm* . . . No matter how hard you *try* to raise it . . . it will be too heavy to lift . . . and finding that *you just don't want to lift it* . . . In fact . . . the harder you *try*, the *heavier* the arm and hand will become . . . and now the arm, the wrist, the hand, *and even the fingers* have become *stuck to the chair . . . they just won't move* . . . they are so very heavy."

(Pause for 5 seconds.)

"*Now* . . . as this hand and arm remain as *heavy as lead* and too heavy to lift, I want you, *in a moment*, to try to lift them, but *they* will not move . . . The arm, the wrist, the hand *and even the fingers are stuck to the chair and too heavy to move*. Go ahead and *try* to lift them, genuinely try, but they are just stuck to the chair and they are too heavy."

(Pause for 5 seconds.)

"Very good. Now allow your arm to relax, this heavy feeling passes and the right hand and arm rest . . . normal sensation returns . . . and as *this* occurs going into an *even deeper level of hypnosis*."

Record Observations:
1. Did the arm lift?
2. Was there obvious effort to lift the hand and arm?
3. Other observations (note finger movements etc.):

ARM LEVITATION

"Now as you go into an *even deeper level of hypnosis* . . . you will *soon* become aware of a change in sensation in your *left* arm and hand . . . Soon you will notice that your *left* arm and hand will become very, very light . . . and weightless . . . *just as light as a feather* . . . That light feeling begins to occur . . . *now* . . . *it* becomes lighter and lighter . . . and as this occurs it can feel as if the arm is becoming *less a part of you* . . . as you allow it to become so . . . *light and weightless*."

(Pause for 5 seconds.)

"And now . . . there is a *ribbon* around the left wrist . . . and at the other end of that ribbon are several *balloons* . . . red, yellow, green, blue . . . all different colors . . . there are quite a few of them . . . *four or five balloons* . . . And these balloons are lighter than air and *they begin to float upward* . . . and as they do . . . the left hand begins to *float upward* . . . Just notice the balloons are tugging . . . pulling . . . lifting the wrist *up* . . . *up* . . . *up* . . . *it just drifts and floats up* . . . feeling lighter and lighter . . . floating up *higher and higher* . . . just allowing the *arm* to float up . . . *all by itself* . . . just as high as *it* wants to go . . . floating up *now* . . . higher and higher."

(Pause for 5 seconds for the response to occur; wait until levitation stops.)

"Very good. Now this feeling passes and your hand and arm begin to drift downward to their comfortable resting position . . . *(Wait for the arm to begin to lower. Additional suggestions for normal sensations and arm lowering may be given)* . . . The balloons are gone . . . normal sensation returns to your arm and hand, and as this occurs *you go into an even deeper level of hypnosis.*"

(If the arm remains lifted, instruct the participant to lower the arm to the chair. Note the responses to each question.)

Record Observations:
1. Did the hand or arm lift?
2. Was there obvious effort to raise the arm and hand?
3. Did the elbow raise from the arm of the chair?
4. Other observations:

IMAGERY INVOLVEMENT/DISSOCIATION

"And now something *very interesting* is going to happen . . . It is possible to *hear my voice with one part of your mind* . . . and with another part of your mind . . . to find that *you are in a different place* . . . Soon you will find that you are *no longer in this room* and *instead* you will *be in a beautiful flower garden* . . . and when this occurs, you will be able to see everything there . . . you will experience every sight . . . sound, smell . . . and feeling in this garden . . . When this occurs you will find that . . . you are no longer in [state present place] and instead you will be in a flower garden experiencing everything *there* . . .

"Now, as you hear my voice, at the same time seeing before you a gate that leads into the flower garden . . . seeing the gate now . . . and as I *count from 1 to 4* you will find that you are walking through that gate and into the flower garden . . . More than just imagining it . . . soon *you will be in a flower garden* . . . walking through the garden.

"1 . . . going through the gate now . . . 2 . . . as you go into the garden you can see the flowers that are there . . . 3 . . . Able to continue to hear my voice as you are there . . . experiencing every sight, sound, smell and feeling in this *flower garden* . . . 4 . . . *Now* you are there . . . you are *in a flower garden* . . ."

(Pause for 5 seconds and then proceed.)

"*Good.* It is a warm day . . . and yet you can feel a gentle, cool breeze in the air . . . it is very pleasant . . . feeling safe, secure, and relaxed . . . Before you is a path . . . and you notice that there are flowers all along the path . . . the grass is very green and there are many beautiful flowers . . . Now notice the colors of the flowers . . . whether you see red, yellow, or any other colors . . .

"*There* . . . *there* is a very beautiful red *rose* . . . you can see this rose . . . now, stopping there for a moment . . . Go close enough to *smell the wonderful sweet aroma* of this beautiful rose . . . the aroma of the rose becomes stronger now . . . it is a pleasant smell . . . Now take a breath and . . . *just smell the rose* . . . and notice how *strong* the smell is,"

(*Pause for 5 seconds.*)

"Now . . . as you are *there* . . . you can describe what you are experiencing without interrupting your experience of hypnosis. Please describe what you are experiencing."

(If the subject does not respond to the first question, prompt with, "You can answer verbally, . . . ," and so on. Record responses to each question.)

Record Responses:	
Where are you?	
What do you see around you?	
Do you see the rose?	
Do you smell the rose?	
Other comments:	

"*Very good* . . . Now, soon returning back to this room at state present place and the present time . . . as you remain *deeply hypnotized* . . . Now walking back through that gate and returning to the present time and back to state present place . . . you are now here, deeply hypnotized and comfortably experiencing hypnosis."

POSITIVE HALLUCINATION

"And now . . . going into an *even deeper state of hypnosis* . . . In fact, *going very deeply hypnotized and very deeply calm* . . . Good . . .

"Now, in a few moments I will ask you to open your eyes as you continue to remain in a deep state of hypnosis . . . When you open your eyes *you will see a small blue block on the table in front of you* . . . a little square block . . . *the kind of block that a child might play with* . . . the block is *bright blue* . . .

"In order for you to be able to *see the block* on the table it may be helpful to first *see it in your mind* before you open your eyes . . . a little *blue* block . . . sitting on the table . . . the kind of block a child might play with . . . just really see it in your mind . . . and, in a moment, when you open your eyes *you will see the block on the table*."

(Pause for 5 seconds.)

"Alright . . . now, as I count from 1 to 3 I will ask you to open your eyes . . . You will remain deeply hypnotized and you will see *a small blue block on the table in front of you* . . . some people see the block right away, while others see more of a *blue color* . . . *a shape or shadow at first.*

"1 . . . Beginning to open your eyes . . . 2 . . . eyelids opening . . . 3 . . . eyes open *now* . . .

"Now, look at the table in front of you . . . just continue looking . . . and notice what you see on the table . . . just really looking . . . and noticing . . . whatever you see there . . .

Record Responses:	
What do you see on the table? (*Inquire as needed: Do you see the block?*)	
If no description of a block, inquire as needed to determine if there is any perception of a color, shape, or shadow, etc.: *Do you see anything on the table? Do you see any color, shape, or shadow of a block?* (Note detail of any evidence of a positive hallucination such as a color, shape, or shadow, etc.)	

(Note: If no perception of a block is reported, then add, *"Not everyone sees something on the table."* and proceed as below.)

"Very good . . . now allow your eyelids to close and go *into an even deeper state of hypnosis* . . . relaxing deeply and feeling calm and relaxed."

POST-HYPNOTIC AMNESIA

"Now, while remaining in a deep state of hypnosis . . . you can hear my voice and all of the suggestions that I give to you . . . In a few moments I will suggest that you return to conscious alertness . . . however, when you return to alertness you will find that *you are not able to recall any of the things that happened* during the hypnosis session today.

"You have been *so deeply absorbed* in experiencing hypnosis that you will have a great deal of difficulty recalling any of the suggestions I gave you and the things you experienced . . . In fact, the harder you *try* the more difficult it will be to recall these things . . . it will be much easier to just forget . . . You will not be able to recall anything about the hypnosis session today . . . it will seem as if there is a wall between you and the memory . . . just allow this to occur . . . so that the wall is there *now* . . . and you will find that you just *don't want to remember at all. You will not be able to recall anything that happened during hypnosis* today until you hear me say these words . . . '*Now you can recall everything.*'

"*Then the wall will lift* and then you will be able to recall all of your experiences . . . Now, as I count from 1 to 10 you will return to alertness."

ALERTING

"Alright, returning to conscious alertness now. [*Note: Increase volume of voice as counting.*]

"1, 2, 3	. . . Beginning to return to conscious alertness. . .
4, 5	. . . more alert and eyes beginning to open. . .
6, 7	. . . eyelids opening and returning to alertness. . .
8, 9	. . . alert and refreshed.
and 10	. . . Fully alert.

Do you feel alert? . . . Good."

(NOTE: assure that the subject reports alertness before proceeding with the Post-Hypnotic Scoring Inquiry.)

EHS Scoring Summary

Name: ______________________ Age: ______________________

Examiner: ______________________ Date: ______________________

1. Subjective Heaviness	Yes ____	No ____
2. Arm Immobilization	Yes ____	No ____
3. Subjective Lightness	Yes ____	No ____
4. Arm Levitation	Yes ____	No ____
5. Elbow Lift	Yes ____	No ____
6. Imagery	Yes ____	No ____
7. Dissociation	Yes ____	No ____
8. Faint Rose Smell	Yes ____	No ____
9. Distinct Rose Smell	Yes ____	No ____
10. Vague Hallucination	Yes ____	No ____
11. Clear Hallucination	Yes ____	No ____
12. Recalls One or Less Items	Yes ____	No ____

TOTAL SCALE SCORE ______________________

0–1	Very Low
2–3	Low
4–8	Middle
9–10	High
11–12	Very High

POST-HYPNOTIC INQUIRY AND SCORING FORM

Scoring the EHS is based upon both behavioral observation during administration and an understanding of the participant's subjective experience. The following post-hypnotic inquiry checklist can be used, as needed, to briefly review the participant's experience and clarify subjective experiences as needed to complete accurate scoring.

POST-HYPNOTIC AMNESIA SCORING INQUIRY

"I want to ask you a few questions about your experience. Please tell me what you can recall about what happened during our session today. What do you remember?"

(Record the subject's responses. Ask, "Anything else?" until the subject reaches an impasse.)

____

____

____

Post-Hypnotic Amnesia Scoring	
0	If the subject recalls 2 or more items
1	Score if the subject recalls 1 item or none

"Now, listen carefully to what I am going to say next. . . '*Now you can recall everything.*'

"What do you recall now?"

Record responses:

____

____

____

(continued)

ARM HEAVINESS/IMMOBILIZATION SCORING INQUIRY

"Earlier I suggested to you that your right arm and hand would feel heavy, and then I suggested that they would be too heavy to lift. I want to find out what your experience was."

Arm Heaviness/Immobilization	**Detail**
When I suggested that your right arm and hand would feel heavy, did you feel a sense of heaviness in your right arm and hand? Did they feel heavier? (Determine if subject experienced *any* feeling of heaviness.)	❑ Yes ❑ No
(If the hand/arm did *not* lift, ask) *Did you try to lift your hand and arm?* Determine if there was effort to lift the hand and arm. *Were they too heavy to lift? Did they feel stuck to the chair?*	❑ Yes ❑ No
Did the subject's hand and arm remain immobile and "stuck" to the chair? Review previous observations to determine if the subject's hand and arm remained on the chair with just minimal, temporary movements. Inquire as needed to determine if arm immobilization occurred. (NOTE: Small finger movements or *temporary* slight movements often occur with *successful* arm immobilization. Arm immobilization refers to an inability to lift the hand and arm.)	❑ Yes ❑ No

Arm Heaviness and Immobilization Scoring	
0	0, if no heaviness.
1	Score if the subject reports feeling a subjective sense of heaviness.
1	Score if beyond slight movements; the hand and arm did not lift. Arm immobilization occurred.

(continued)

ARM LEVITATION SCORING INQUIRY

"Earlier, I asked you to experience a very light and weightless feeling in your left arm and that the arm would lift all by itself."

Inquiry	
Did your arm feel lighter? Even if you arm did not lift; did it feel lighter?	
(If the arm lifted, ask) *Did it float up* all by itself *without any willful effort on your part?* (Inquire as needed to clarify the subject's experience. Determine if the subject experienced a sense of involuntary lifting.) *Could you feel it floating up all by itself or did you feel like you were lifting it? Did it feel like the balloons were pulling it up?*	
Arm Lightness/Levitation/Elbow Lift Scoring	
0	0 if the answer to the first question is no, whether or not the arm lifted; 0 if subjective description of lightness.
1	Score if the answer to the first question is yes, but the arm *did not lift out of its resting position.* (Score 1 if a *subjective sense of lightness is reported* and the hand did not lift.)
1	Score if the answer to the second question is yes, and the arm did lift out of its resting position. (Score if a subjective experience of lightness is described and there is some movement of the hand from the chair *with* a subjective description of an involuntary movement.)
1	Score if the answer to the second question is yes and the elbow lifted.

(continued)

IMAGERY INVOLVEMENT/DISSOCIATION SCORING INQUIRY

"Also, earlier, I asked you to experience going for a walk in a flower garden."

Imagery/Dissociation Inquiry	
1. *Were you able to experience what I suggested, or were you just listening to my voice?* (If no imagery or only vague imagery is reported, state*"Some people do not experience clear imagery.")*	
2. *Did you imagine being in the flower garden? Was the image clear? Could you really imagine being in a flower garden?* (Determine if the subject was able to imagine being in a garden. Determine if the image was clear or only vague [i.e., colors, etc., but no specific imagery of the flower garden].)	
Review the previous observations and the subject's verbal responses to the questions presented during the item. Determine if the subject's response to the questions, *"Where are you? What do you see around you?'* indicate that the subject may have experienced dissociation (i.e., felt that he or she was actually in the garden)? **3.** If the subject's responses suggested possible dissociation, ask: *Did you feel that, in a sense, you were no longer in this room, and instead you were actually in a flower garden, experiencing everything there?* (Determine if the subject experienced an alteration in perception in which he or she *felt* that he or she was no longer in the room and instead experienced being in a flower garden. Continue inquiry as necessary to distinguish between questions 2 and 3, i.e. *"Did it feel as if you were actually experiencing* [insert subjects report of sensations] *while you were* in the garden *or that you were here and imagining it?"*)	
Mental Imagery/Dissociation Scoring	
0	0 if the answer to the first question is no (no imagery or only vague imagery)
1	Score if the answer to the second question is yes (clear imagery but no dissociation).
1	Score if the answer to the third question is yes (clear imagery and dissociation).

(continued)

ROSE OLFACTORY HALLUCINATION SCORING INQUIRY

"Now, I also suggested to you that you could smell a rose."

Nquiry	
Did you smell the aroma of a rose? Did you actually smell it?	
0	0 if the answer is no. *Did not actually smell the rose* (even if it was imagined)
1	Score if the answer is yes and *smell was faint.*
1	Score if the answer is yes and *smell was also distinct.*
Establish the subjective rating of the intensity of the aroma. Check the subject's rating of the aroma: *How strong was the aroma? Please rate it as none, faint, or distinct.*	
❑ None ❑ Faint ❑ Distinct	

POSITIVE HALLUCINATION SCORING INQUIRY

"Also, earlier, I asked you to experience seeing a small block on the table in front of you."

Inquiry	
Did you see anything on the table? (NOTE: If response is "Nothing," repeat that "*Some people do not see anything.*")	
(If the subject reports *any* perception, inquire further) *Please describe what you saw. Did you see the block? Please describe it. Did you see anything on the table? If yes, please describe what you saw. Where was it?*	
Positive Hallucination Scoring	
0	0 if the subject answers negative to perception.
1	Score if there is any hallucinated perception. Scoring is lenient (i.e., score one if the subject reports perception color, shape, shadow etc.). Note if the subject reports a vague perception of any hallucination.
1	Score if the subject reports a clear perception of a block. The block is described with detail of color and shape. The block was clearly hallucinated.
Note Detail:	

"Very good. Thank you. Are there any questions or comments that you have before we stop?"

Debriefing includes allowing the subject to discuss any aspects of the experience he or she desires.

CHAPTER 11

Dealing With Resistance

Resistance, by definition, is an unconscious process that refers to a patient's difficulty in responding to hypnotic suggestion in spite of sufficient hypnotic ability and desire. Resistance is a psychological process in which there is some unconscious barrier to fully participating in the process of hypnotic induction or therapy, and can be expressed in a variety of ways. It is possible that the patient has difficulty "letting go" of conscious defenses, or may even find that the simple act of closing his eyes, when suggested, is uncomfortable at that moment. Resistance can sometimes take the form of avoidance. It is a feeling or a behavior that serves to work against the aims of therapy by either delaying or disrupting the process. The patient may experience frustration with his own resistance or may not even consciously recognize that he is resisting. Resistance is experienced to some degree by most patients; however, the degree of resistance can vary from patient to patient.

Resistance is experienced to some degree by most patients; however, the degree of resistance can vary from patient to patient.

One common way resistance can be expressed is when the patient has "just one more question," and then another question, and so on, before beginning a hypnotic induction. This may go on until time for the session has run out. Resistance can even occur through the patient "trying too hard" to follow suggestions, resulting in an impaired ability to experience a hypnotic state. It is important to keep in mind that this is something the patient is experiencing at a given moment. It does not mean that the patient is wrong, uncooperative, or "resistant." Additionally, it does not mean that the hypnotherapist is wrong or should be blamed. Resistance exists for a reason and at some level is serving an apparent function to protect, avoid, or reduce anxiety. When resistance occurs it needs to be acknowledged, understood, addressed, and respected.

RESISTANCE VS. DEFIANCE

The conscious nature of defiance distinguishes it from resistance.

Patients usually seek hypnotherapy because they are experiencing some problem or difficulty, and they have some belief that hypnotherapy can help them in some way. However, this is not always the case. It is important to distinguish between resistance and defiance. There are some instances where patients may be coerced into hypnotherapy and do not really want to engage in the therapy process. For example, one patient came self-referred for hypnotherapy for smoking cessation. However, it later became apparent that he was only coming for hypnotherapy at the insistence of his wife. He stated, "You can try to hypnotize me and make me stop smoking, but I don't think you can do it!" Of course he was right; *no one can be hypnotized against his or her will.*

The conscious nature of defiance distinguishes it from resistance. Defiant patients usually come for hypnotherapy at the urging of someone else. They are motivated to be seen for therapy, but they do not want to engage in therapy or a hypnotic induction unless they are convinced that it will not have any effect. A patient who worked as a prison guard was referred by his supervisor for treatment of acrophobia (fear of heights). His fear prevented him from climbing a high ladder to a lookout in the prison and instead he had been assigned to patrolling the outside of the prison on horseback (a more preferred job in Texas!). He expressed great interest in hypnotic relaxation therapy (HRT) to help him overcome his fear of heights. Hypnotic therapy was discussed and he participated in the initial induction, in which the Elkins Hypnotizability Scale (EHS) was administered. During the EHS, suggestions for arm levitation were given, to which he responded fully; however, he then abruptly opened his eyes and stated, "I'm not doing this, it might work and I hate climbing that ladder!" He refused to continue with hypnotherapy, preferring a "safer," less effective intervention.

SOURCES OF RESISTANCE

When patients experience resistance, it feels as if it is something that is happening outside their control.

When patients experience resistance, it feels as if it is happening outside their control. The patient is motivated to engage in hypnotherapy, but for some reason, he find that he is putting up barriers, pulling back from fully engaging in the hypnotic induction. There can be numerous reasons for resistance; some of the more common reasons are listed below.

FEAR OF FAILURE

This can occur in the highly motivated patient. The patient may be very distressed about a problem, and feel very hopeful about hypnotherapy. However, after a hypnotic induction is begun, the patient may interrupt the process, have questions, find they are "trying too hard to be hypnotized," or resist in some other way. The law of reversed effect can be used to teach the patient that, in regard to achieving a hypnotic state, "The harder one tries, the more one fails," and that acceptance of one's experience is as important as "trying to make something happen."

FEAR OF LOSS OF CONTROL

It has been stated that the goal of HRT is to empower the patient. However, the patient may be holding on to misconceptions about hypnotherapy. There is a widespread belief (largely promoted by popular media, in books and films for entertainment) that a hypnotherapist "can control the patent's mind" or that hypnosis represents a kind of "mind control." This can be addressed by reviewing previously provided information and again clarifying any misconceptions.

FAILURE TO ADEQUATELY ESTABLISH RAPPORT

> The interpersonal nature of hypnotic relaxation therapy is achieved when rapport is built and trust is established.

Resistance may also occur when the interpersonal relationship between the hypnotherapist and patient has not been adequately established. Given the interpersonal nature of HRT, the establishment of trust and rapport are critical. As the patient enters a trance state, conscious defenses are lowered and the patient allows his moment-by-moment experience to be guided by suggestions given by the hypnotherapist. This places the patient in a psychologically vulnerable position, and trust in the hypnotherapist is essential. Without it, resistance is almost certain.

INADEQUATE PREPARATION FOR HYPNOTIC INDUCTION

Before beginning a hypnotic relaxation induction, it is important to answer any questions the patient might have, as well as to convey: (1) the rationale for the hypnotic techniques, and (2) what to expect in regard to suggestions. It can be helpful to use the patient's own language where possible to enhance being "'in sync," and to make sure that ideas are communicated with mutual understanding. Additionally, it is very important to conduct a thorough case conceptualization and gather enough background information to adequately assess the patient and his problem. The hypnotic induction should never be rushed, and all questions and concerns should be addressed in an effort to sufficiently communicate the process of the hypnotic intervention.

AUTHORITY PROBLEMS

Resistance can come about due to transference issues in which the patient may react to the hypnotherapist as an authoritarian figure. If the patient has some issues with authority figures, this may lead to resistance and should be addressed or responded to before or during the HRT session. For example, a 43-year-old man was referred for HRT to better manage a chronic low-back-pain condition. He responded minimally to the initial hypnotic induction and later stated, "It's funny, every time you said my arm would feel lighter, it felt heavier . . . and every time you said it would be heavy, it started to feel light." He later revealed that he had a conflicted relationship with his older brother who was "always telling [him] what to do." The process of a directive hypnotic induction generated negative feelings for this patient, even though the feelings were initially unconscious and experienced by rebelling and responding in a manner that was opposite of what had been suggested. With insight, he was able to work through these issues, and a more permissive approach allowed him to respond to suggestions for pain management with greater ease.

INAPPROPRIATE TECHNIQUE

The suggestions given or technique used may also lead to resistance, such that the patient begins to lighten the trance state, experience anxiety, or have a negative response. It is important to remain aware that, in a hypnotic state, suggestions are often experienced in a literal manner due to the way the unconscious mind processes information. As an example of inappropriate technique, during a hypnotherapy workshop conducted by the author, a young physician was attending and was asked to complete a hypnotic induction with a volunteer subject (also attending the workshop). During his practice of hypnotic induction, he suggested that, within a deeply relaxed hypnotic state, the subject could see himself relaxing "sitting in a boat on a beautiful lake." The physician then went on to suggest that the subject would now "begin to sink deeper and deeper . . . sinking deeper and deeper . . . as you become more and more relaxed." The subject interpreted this technique as suggesting the boat was "sinking deeper and deeper," and he began to come out of trance during the session. It led to a good laugh at the workshop, but this incident illustrated the importance of attending to the specifics of language during hypnotic communication and assuring the technique is appropriate for the patient.

In a hypnotic state, suggestions are often experienced in a literal manner due to the way the unconscious mind processes information.

PRIMARY AND SECONDARY GAIN

In some cases, the presenting symptom may also serve a beneficial purpose for the patient. Primary gain refers to a condition in which the symptom itself serves to reduce anxiety, and removal of the symptom leads to greater anxiety and resistance. The primary gain from a symptom is likely to be unconscious and not recognized by the patient. For example, a 32-year-old woman was referred for HRT for weight loss. She had been obese for most of her life and related that she had a history of sexual abuse as a child. During hypnotherapy she experienced anxiety associated with suggestions to "see herself as slender and at her desired weight." After several hypnotherapy sessions, it became apparent that the obesity served a protective function; it kept her from dealing with sexual issues and dating.

Primary gain refers to a condition in which the symptom itself serves to reduce anxiety, and removal of the symptom leads to greater anxiety and resistance.

Secondary gain refers to benefit from a symptom that is externally provided. Examples of secondary gain include financial compensation, attention, support, sympathy, attention from others, or avoidance of responsibilities. Secondary gain can be conscious or unconscious for the patient. As one example of secondary gain interfering with treatment, it is often the case that patients who are actively involved in litigation achieve limited benefit until after the lawsuit has been resolved.

DEFENSE AGAINST PSYCHOPATHOLOGY

Patients should be screened for hypnotherapy, and the case conceptualization can help identify patients that may not be good candidates for HRT. Relative contraindications for HRT include: (1) borderline personality disorder; (2) active psychoses; and (3) paranoia. These are identified as relative contraindications because hypnotherapy can benefit such patients (Baker, 1981). However, in these cases, use of hypnotherapy must be approached with special care, as it may lead to increasing symptoms if the patient's defenses are not carefully managed. In my practice, a 23-year-old man was referred for HRT for "painful symptoms in both arms." When asked to describe the symptoms, he stated that he could "feel bugs crawling under [his] skin, causing [his] arms to itch." He was referred for a psychiatric consultation where he was diagnosed as schizophrenic. A hypnotic induction was not completed with this patient, but, had it been, would likely have led to resistance.

AVOIDANCE OF CONFRONTATION

During a hypnotic relaxation induction, there are normally fluctuations in depth of trance. At times, the patient is likely to be in a deeper hypnotic state and at other times lighter. It has been said that the depth of trance can be compared to the ebb and flow of ocean waves. However, depth of trance can sometimes be related to resistance. This is especially true when HRT is used to deal with emotional issues as in psychotherapy. For example, a patient may remain in a lighter hypnotic state to avoid uncovering unconscious

During a hypnotic relaxation induction, there are normally fluctuations in depth of trance.

material, or resistance may occur to avoid confronting a distressing memory, emotion, or behavior. It is important to keep in mind that the patient has a right to resist, and that the resistance itself provides important information. It is not that resistance is either good or bad; it can serve both functions. The important thing is that knowledge of the resistance is used to best work with the patient and to identify how the patient can best use HRT.

The patient has a right to resist, and the resistance itself provides important information.

MANAGING RESISTANCE

In many cases resistance can be resolved by providing information, clarifying misconceptions, or establishing a greater degree of trust and rapport before attempting a hypnotic induction. However, it is important to note that resistance in HRT does occur in some patients despite the therapist's attention to the areas identified above. This resistance should be differentiated from the patient's level of hypnotizability, as both resistance and hypnotizability can affect response to hypnotic suggestion, and hypnotic responsiveness is largely a reflection of the interaction of the two concepts. Therefore, both hypnotizability and resistance should be assessed, and the approach or style of hypnotherapy should be adjusted in response.

Both hypnotizability and resistance should be assessed, and the approach or style of hypnotherapy adjusted in response.

Table 11.1 provides an illustration of the "Resistance–Hypnotizability Matrix." There are four possibilities in the matrix and the approach to treatment varies depending on the interactions between hypnotizability and resistance.

Table 11.1
Resistance–Hypnotizability Matrix

	Resistance Is Low	Resistance Is High
Hypnotizability Is High	Directive Approach	Indirect/Permissive Approach
Hypnotizability Is Low	Multiple Session Directive Approach	Integrative-Limited Hypnotic Approach

If *hypnotizability is high and resistance is low*, then a directive approach is recommended. A directive approach is not an authoritarian approach. Rather, it refers to providing hypnotic suggestions in an unambiguous manner. Suggestions may utilize specific experiences, stories, metaphors, or preferences. Patients often prefer a directive approach, and this can be a most parsimonious way to achieve gains in HRT.

An indirect and permissive approach introduces some ambiguity and essentially means formulating hypnotic suggestions in a manner that emphasizes choices.

Alternatively, if *hypnotizability is high and resistance is also high*, then an indirect and permissive approach to providing hypnotic suggestions may be preferred. This is especially true when resistance is due to fear of failure, control issues, or authority problems. An indirect and permissive approach introduces some ambiguity and essentially means formulating hypnotic suggestions in a manner that emphasizes choices. Some examples of how to formulate permissive suggestions are given below.

In cases where *hypnotizability is low and resistance is also low*, a directive approach with multiple sessions may be most effective. If the patient is in the lower range of hypnotizability, it is still likely that he or she will be able to achieve treatment gains, but it may take more time or multiple sessions. It is important to keep in mind that low hypnotizability does not mean "no hypnotic ability." Hypnotizability can be thought of as a talent and a stable trait, and individuals in the lower range still have great potential to achieve their goals with HRT. Knowing that the patient is in the lower range of hypnotizability is not a reason to feel discouraged or doubt that he or she will benefit. Rather, it means that the patient (and hypnotherapist) should *not* be discouraged if progress is not immediate. It is an indication, especially if resistance is low, that, with continued compliance, practice, and hypnotherapy, progress will be achieved, albeit at a slower pace than with some other patients. This concept was illustrated in a study of HRT for pain management with cancer patients, (Elkins, Cheung, Marcus, Palamara, & Rajab, 2004). It was found that patients in the high range of hypnotizability significantly reduced pain after only one session, while those in the lower range of hypnotizability achieved comparable reduction in pain, but only after 3 to 4 weeks of HRT.

If *hypnotizability is low and resistance is high*, there are several alternatives that should be considered. It may be that the source of the resistance can be addressed through nonhypnotic means, such as dynamically oriented psychotherapy or a cognitive–behavioral approach. Then, once the resistance has been resolved, HRT can be utilized as needed.

Resistance should be respected and the goal is to best help the patient through whatever means may be of most benefit.

Alternatively, the clinician can recognize that these factors play a significant role, and can integrate HRT as a secondary, limited aspect of the patient's treatment. For example, the use of HRT may be limited to teaching relaxation skills, deep breathing, or increasing awareness of thoughts and feelings. As previously mentioned, resistance should be respected, and the goal is to best help the patient through whatever means may be of most benefit.

PERMISSIVE AND INDIRECT SUGGESTIONS

Permissive suggestions emphasize choices (i.e., "*You may notice a heavy feeling in your right hand, or perhaps in your left . . . I'm really not sure*") and indirect suggestions introduce ambiguity (i.e., "*You may wonder how you will experience hypnosis today . . . and not knowing can be accepted as you go deeper into a hypnotic state"*). Some examples of indirect and permissively worded phrases are: (Hammond, 1990).

- Allowing without trying . . .
- Can you notice . . . your breathing and whether it changes in some way?
- You may really wonder how deep you will go into hypnosis today . . .
- You really don't have to do anything . . . consciously . . .
- Perhaps you wouldn't mind allowing your thoughts to drift . . .
- Feelings of comfort can be experienced . . .
- It will be curious to find out which hand begins to drift upward as you drift deeper . . .
- Isn't it pleasant to find out how easily change can occur by letting go?
- Perhaps you would enjoy . . .
- Just noticing and allowing . . .
- As time passes. . . . becoming more and more aware . . .
- Changes in sensations naturally occur . . .
- Would you be willing to experience . . . today?
- Noticing . . . just really observing what happens next . . . as you experience a hypnotic state . . .
- Your breathing has already changed . . . has it not? . . . or has it started to change?
- It is possible to discover . . . a deeper understanding . . . and feeling . . . that is helpful . . .
- That's right . . . allowing whatever happens to occur . . . in ways that are best for you . . .
- Trusting your unconscious mind to take you where you need to go and experience . . .
- What you notice may be the most important thing to occur . . .
- It could be that there is something that needs to occur before you drift all the way into a deep hypnotic state . . .
- Would you rather go into a hypnotic state with your eyes open or closed . . . first . . . ?
- You really don't know . . . consciously . . . but your unconscious mind has an ability to . . .
- It can seem as though . . .
- You may be aware of the change occurring or maybe not . . . it really doesn't matter . . .

A SAMPLE INDUCTION FOR DEALING WITH RESISTANCE

Again, it is important that the clinician remember that resistance is an unconscious process that, with practice, can be effectively approached using the methods discussed in this chapter. The following illustrates how these techniques may be used when dealing with resistance. The clinician is encouraged to frequently refer back to the chapter contents as he or she reviews this sample induction and begins the work of effectively engaging patients who are experiencing resistance.

> "Now . . . as you begin the process of experiencing hypnotic relaxation . . . today . . . would it be acceptable to just allow your eyelids to close . . . whenever they want to close . . . and notice how pleasant that experience can be . . . to have a time . . . this time . . . as you experience hypnosis . . . when you don't have to do anything . . . nothing that you have to do . . . But it can be an interesting experience . . . to discover whatever you may notice today . . . and . . . allowing a positive experience . . . an experience that is beneficial in some way . . . some important way.
>
> "Just allowing those eyelids to close when they want to close . . . that's right . . . Very good . . . And as you do . . . I don't think you would mind at all for a sense of calmness to occur in a way that is very pleasant . . . and it is possible to notice calmness in so many ways . . . there can be a calm feeling in your left hand . . . or you may notice the calmness in your right hand . . . first . . . or last . . . But to observe the hand . . . to really notice the hand . . . the calm sensations in the hand . . . and how it can rest there . . . still . . . calm . . . a peaceful feeling . . . in the hand . . . and hand it to the hand . . . it knows what to do . . . some of the time . . . when to hold on . . . when to let go . . . when to relax . . . when it is OK . . . to rest for a time . . . And yet the hand is not alone . . . there is the arm . . . the elbow . . . the shoulder . . . and they all work together . . . they all are needed . . . And if the hand can relax . . . certainly it would be possible that the arm . . . the shoulders could relax . . . to be allowed some degree of comfort . . . certainly the hand would allow it . . . it could occur . . . without worry or concern.
>
> "Then there is the matter of the breathing . . . and as the hand considered a deeper relaxation . . . the patterns of your breathing may have shifted . . . a little slower . . . a little deeper . . . a little easier . . . without your having to do anything consciously . . . And that can be a pleasant experience . . . not having to . . . noticing and then wondering . . . as you can . . . notice your breathing . . . whether it would be possible . . . For calmness to become deeper . . . sometimes wondering can become noticing and sometimes we wonder what we will notice . . . Can it be possible for a pleasant relaxation to occur across your forehead? . . . into the neck and shoulders . . . Can it be

permitted? . . . Will the conscious and unconscious mind allow a certain degree of peacefulness? . . . a certain degree of relaxation? . . . a certain degree of letting go?

"I don't know how deeply you may drift into a hypnotic state . . . but your unconscious mind has the ability to drift . . . it has its own memories of comfort . . . And a part of your mind . . . remembers real comfort . . . there can be the comfort of sitting outside . . . looking up at the clouds . . . and just watching . . . observing . . . They float by . . . they drift and float by . . . There may have been a time when a thought came to your mind . . . of what it could be like to float like a cloud . . . to allow the time to pass as you drift across the sky . . . and what you might see . . . looking down from the clouds . . . drifting over a valley . . . a lake . . . whatever you would notice, looking and observing . . . And it could be pleasant to just observe and notice . . . not really knowing what you might see . . . what might be there.

"And yet . . . it is possible to have other experiences in a hypnotic state . . . Possible to observe the degree to which your back and shoulders have relaxed . . . back and stomach . . . and back to the comfort of breathing easily and comfortably . . . in a way that just seems to take you as deep into a hypnotic state as you need to go . . . to achieve what you want to accomplish today . . . Wouldn't that be pleasant?

"And I wonder if it would be alright for your legs to become as relaxed as the hands . . . I wonder if your right leg would be as relaxed as your right hand . . . or the left . . . and if it does . . . would that be experienced as a heavy feeling or a lightness?

"Deep hypnotic relaxation can be experienced in many ways . . . There can be the experience of letting go to such a degree that the body becomes as heavy as lead . . . no tension . . . heavy and limp . . . no tension . . . heavy and limp . . . And yet the deeper hypnotic state can change in experience . . . a heaviness can become a light feeling . . . floating like a feather in the wind . . . floating and drifting back and forth . . . back and forth . . . or other sensations . . . that can change . . . in other ways . . . expected . . . or unexpected ways . . . and how pleasant they can be . . . is something to discover.

"Just as you could discover where your mind may be willing to drift . . . thoughts do occur . . . memories do exist . . . And would they drift to that pleasant day? . . . near the beach . . . and listen . . . to the sounds . . . the ocean has its own sounds . . . the ocean has a particular sound of waves that come in on the beach . . . it can be fascinating to watch the waves . . . always changing . . . different sizes . . . different shapes . . . and the feeling of the breeze on the beach . . . one could discover all sorts of things walking along a beautiful beach . . . There could be sea shells . . . to be found . . . there could be a particularly beautiful part of the beach . . . I don't know if you would be there alone or if you might see someone else there . . . but everything could be . . . just right.

"As this experience with HRT today is your own experience . . . and within this experience . . . perhaps it would be acceptable to feel more at peace within yourself . . . more confident in your abilities . . . a feeling that everything is going to be alright . . . that you are strong and worthy . . . that you deserve good things . . . that you can notice the feeling of the warm sunshine on a beautiful day . . . that you can notice a beautiful sky . . . and a beautiful sunset.

"Returning to conscious alertness is something that can happen when you wish for it to occur . . . Finding whatever you need from this experience of HRT today . . . And when you do return to conscious alertness . . . it is . . . at your own time . . . in your own way . . . that is right for you . . . that you choose . . . and returning to conscious alertness . . . That's right . . . Good . . . What are you most aware of now?"

In addition to effectively dealing with resistance, the hypnotherapist should also develop knowledge and skill toward refining the process of hypnotic inductions and interventions. This is a critical part of becoming a skilled hypnotherapist. The details of this process are covered in Chapter 12.

CHAPTER 12

Refining Hypnotic Inductions and Interventions

This chapter provides information on how to refine hypnotic inductions over the course of therapy. Additional methods for facilitating hypnotic communication, trance management, ideomotor responses, metaphors, and ego strengthening will be presented and illustrated. Developing a high level of skill in HRT takes practice, and in addition to reading and studying, it is recommended that the clinician attend workshops and seek feedback on how to refine inductions and interventions.

VARIATION IN VOICE QUALITY AND INTENSITY

It is important to keep in mind that the unconscious mind is experiential, holistic, and emotionally oriented. Therefore, hypnotic suggestions are likely to have greater influence when delivered in a manner that evokes an emotional response—at least to some degree. The hypnotherapist should be mindful that voice quality and intensity, as a form of hypnotic suggestion, is just as important as the content of the suggestion. That is, both the content and process of hypnotic suggestions are very important.

Hypnotic suggestions are likely to have greater influence when delivered in a manner that evokes an emotional response—at least to some degree.

It is helpful to think of the specific wording or content of hypnotic suggestions as a road map of where you want to go, and the process of delivery as the gasoline in the engine. The hypnotherapist should vary the delivery of hypnotic suggestions depending upon the goal or intent of those specific suggestions, and the "monotone voice" or "whisper" should be avoided. For example, if the intent is to facilitate a calm and relaxed feeling, the suggestion should be delivered with a calm and relaxed voice. On the other hand, if the intent is to intensify awareness of an issue or feeling (e.g., increasing confidence or developing hypnotic phenomena such as analgesia), then the hypnotherapist should intensify his or her voice. Voice intensity and quality should fluctuate across the HRT session as various experiences, feelings, and goals are addressed.

VERBAL AND NONVERBAL HYPNOTIC SUGGESTION

The HRT practitioner should also be mindful of the fact that hypnotic suggestions can be provided through verbal and nonverbal means. The interpersonal process during hypnotherapy includes both verbal and nonverbal behaviors, and it is important to remember that nonverbal behaviors do convey suggestions. Additionally, as has been noted, the unconscious mind processes hypnotic suggestions in a holistic manner and is more crudely differentiated and integrated such that nonverbal communication takes on greater importance during a hypnotic state. Therefore, hypnotherapists should be aware of nonverbal cues that they may provide, and they should utilize their own nonverbal behavior to enhance the therapeutic interaction in HRT. Nonverbal behaviors from the hypnotherapist can include facial expressions, sighs, taking a deep breath following a hypnotic suggestion, or using touch.

The interpersonal process during hypnotherapy includes both verbal and nonverbal behaviors, and it is important to remember that nonverbal behaviors do convey suggestions.

Examples of using touch include a handshake before or after hypnotic induction, gently lifting a patient's wrist to facilitate arm levitation, or touching the patient's shoulder to provide a nonverbal cue for deepening trance. The use of touch should be cautiously approached with respect to and in consideration of the patient's background and culture. Additionally, it is good practice to ask permission from the patient before using touch as a nonverbal suggestion. Inappropriate touch should always be carefully avoided.

USE OF HYPNOTIC PHENOMENA

In refining and developing greater skill in hypnotic inductions and interventions, use of increasing numbers of hypnotic phenomena can have a very positive effect in some cases. The term *hypnotic phenomena* refers to suggested effects that the patient can experience during the session. As discussed in Chapter 3, hypnotic phenomena include suggested effects such as arm levitation, glove analgesia (suggestions that a hand can become numb), age regression, as well as suggested relaxation and imagery. These can be especially powerful suggestions since, for the unconscious mind, "experience is believing." HRT can be thought of as a method that provides the patient with "healing experiences" through hypnotic phenomena. Hypnotic suggestions are provided, and, ideally, the patient has a positive or helpful experience as a result of the suggestions.

Because the unconscious mind is outcome-oriented, the use of hypnotic phenomena during the HRT session can provide tangible evidence of an outcome.

Because the unconscious mind is outcome-oriented, the use of hypnotic phenomena during the HRT session can provide tangible evidence of an outcome. The hypnotic induction encourages the patient to suspend critical judgment and to allow experiences to occur. As outcomes and experiences are created, the patient can experience increased confidence, openness to later hypnotic interventions, and willingness to comply with suggestions and even homework assignments between HRT sessions.

TARGETING HYPNOTIC SUGGESTIONS FOR DESIRED EFFECT

Targeting hypnotic suggestions has been shown to be relevant in a range of areas such as reduction of pain (Patterson & Jensen, 2003), treatment of dermatological disorders (Shenefelt, 2000; Rucklidge & Saunders, 2002), removal of warts (Spanos, Stenstrom, & Johnson, 1988), and reduction of hot flashes (Elkins, Fisher, & Johnson, 2012). Evidence also supports the assertion that hypnotic relaxation therapy (HRT) is a means to achieve a trance state in which suggestions connected to a therapeutic purpose can be more likely to have their desired effects. A creative study by Barabasz & McGeorge (1978) compared four groups with the desired effect being to increase hand temperature: (1) biofeedback; (2) false biofeedback; (3) relaxation; and (4) hypnotically suggested hand warming, with biofeedback. While all four groups achieved some increase in hand temperature, only the hypnosis group achieved increases that were significantly greater than any of the other three.

> When targeting hypnotic suggestions for desired effect, it is important to remember that the unconscious mind encodes reality in concrete images.

The hypnotherapist's knowledge and understanding of the dynamics and physiology of a disorder can be helpful in determining how to best formulate suggestions, and these suggestions will vary depending on the desired outcome. When targeting hypnotic suggestions for a desired effect, it is important to remember that the unconscious mind encodes reality in concrete images. When these images are created, an associated physiological response is more likely to follow. Therefore, suggestions should be targeted to achieve the desired effect. For example, if the physiological response of salivation is desired, then suggestions (hypnotic or nonhypnotic) for imagining eating a very sour lemon or a favorite food is more likely to bring about salivation than imagining a block of wood.

TRANCE MANAGEMENT

It is important that the therapist carefully observe the patient during a hypnotic induction in order to direct hypnotic suggestions. The depth of trance does not remain the same

> The depth of trance does not remain the same throughout a session, but varies; at times, it may be important that the patient be in a deeper hypnotic state.

throughout a session, but varies; at times, it may be important that the patient be in a deeper hypnotic state. At other times, a lighter trance may be more appropriate. The term *trance management* is used to signify the degree to which the hypnotherapist is aware of this and gives suggestions to either deepen or lighten the hypnotic state as needed.

The treatment of post-traumatic stress disorder (PTSD) provides an illustration of how trance management is important. When HRT is used in the treatment of PTSD, treatment likely involves some aspect of guided exposure to deal with the traumatic events in the person's past. During imaginable exposure, it is important that the patient re-experience some aspect of the trauma, but it is also important that the patient not be overwhelmed. Trance management means observing the patient, monitoring his or her emotional responses, and providing suggestions to vary the depth of trance. This serves to achieve an ideal level of imaginable exposure while protecting the patient from being retraumatized.

USE OF IDEOMOTOR RESPONSES

Ideomotor responses refer to motor movements that arise from the unconscious mind. Everyday examples of ideomotor responses are automatic head nods while talking, jittery movements when anxious, or a clenched jaw when a person is tense. Ideomotor responses can be utilized in hypnotherapy to provide a means for communication with the unconscious/experiential system. This is typically done through suggestions for finger movements in response to questions that are directed toward the unconscious.

After completing a hypnotic induction and determining that the patient is capable of a sufficient depth of trance to allow unconscious responses, a finger is identified to represent a "yes" response and another finger to represent a "no" response. The reason for using finger signals is convenience. Finger movements are easy to observe and can be established through direct suggestion. Given that the unconscious is somewhat crudely integrated and organized in part by emotional complexes, it is recommended that finger signals be established in a more simplistic manner. For example, in most cases, simply establishing a yes and a no finger is enough and preferred over a more complex approach using multiple fingers. If a complex number of fingers are involved (i.e., a finger for yes, a finger for no, a finger for I don't know, a finger for I don't want to answer, a finger for perhaps . . .), then the concern exists that the responses will actually be consciously directed rather than emerging from the unconscious.

Ideomotor movements that answer questions during a hypnotic state feels involuntary to the patient. Finger movements are typically small, jerky, or slow. The patient may or may not be consciously aware that the movement has occurred. The feeling of an ideomotor response is comparable to a circumstance such as riding in a car as a passenger and seeing a tricycle role into the street in front of the car. Although there is no brake pedal on the passenger side of the car, and pushing one's foot into the floorboard serves no useful purpose, the passenger may find that his or her foot does want to make the motion of stepping on the brake pedal, and will, if allowed. In the same way, ideomotor responses occur involuntarily and the phrasing to allow the finger to rise "all by itself" is useful to suggest to the patient that this movement will be involuntary. While they can be consciously suppressed by the patient, these responses, if allowed, can provide an insight into unconscious beliefs, understandings, and perceptions.

Use of suggestions for an ideomotor response is one of the main tools in hypnotherapy. An ideomotor response can give an indication of the patient's internal experience with a suggestion, such as, "The yes finger can rise all by itself as you drift into an even deeper hypnotic state and begin to notice a floating feeling . . ." Also, ideomotor responses can be used to explore unconscious perceptions or ideas, with suggestions such as, "Would it be alright to begin to understand and know the cause of this anxiety?" Unconscious exploration will be further discussed in Chapter 18.

USE OF THERAPEUTIC METAPHORS

In most cultures, metaphors have been used for ages and have an enduring quality when skillfully communicated. Parables and stories have also been used for centuries among major religions (i.e., Christianity, Buddhism, and Confucianism) to convey ideas in a powerful manner. Within HRT, therapeutic metaphors can be used to convey hypnotic suggestions, facilitate insights, reframe problems, introduce solutions, and confront issues, and the use of metaphors is an essential aspect of hypnotic communication. Metaphors can be defined as ". . . a way of speaking in which one thing is expressed in terms of another, thereby bringing this together throws a new light on the character of what is being described" (Kopp, 1971). The unconscious mind tends to encode reality in terms of concrete images, metaphors, and narratives. Therefore, stories, ideas expressed in symbolism, parables, and descriptive imagery may be most meaningful, and have the greatest impact, at an unconscious level. It is usually the case that an idea is communicated twice when metaphors are used; once in rational language (explaining an idea in logical or rational terms, examining evidence, etc., as is done in cognitive therapy) and then again in symbolic form. Either one may come first, as each is directed toward a different level of information processing; however, HRT intervention is most often directed toward the experiential system. For example, the hypnotherapist may utilize "truisms" to illustrate ideas that are inherently true, or as a way to

> The hypnotherapist may utilize "truisms" to illustrate ideas that are inherently true, or as a way to convey an idea.

> Within HRT, therapeutic metaphors can be used to convey hypnotic suggestions, facilitate insights, reframe problems, introduce solutions, and confront issues.

convey an idea. He or she may refer to anger as "a wound" that needs healing or convey the idea that there can be more than one solution to a problem.

Metaphors can also involve more formal stories or narratives. Formal metaphors are narratives that are developed to address the patient's concerns or symptoms through a story made up of characters and situations that are related to the patient's difficulties. A formal metaphor can be introduced by simply saying, *"During your hypnotic relaxation therapy session today, after completing a hypnotic induction, I would like to tell a story that may convey some meaning to you at either a conscious or unconscious level of awareness."* Formal metaphors should not begin with, "Once upon a time," as that may seem condescending to some patients. The preparation for the formal metaphor is important, as it creates appropriate expectancy. Formal metaphors may be intuitive, drawn from popular literature, or created for a particular situation. For example, the fable of "The Frog and the Scorpion" can be adapted to address issues of codependency, failure to acknowledge the reality of a destructive relationship, or as a way to deal with feelings or change self-defeating behavior.

FORMAL METAPHOR TO OVERCOME CODEPENDENCY

> "As you remain deeply relaxed, I would like to relate a story to you . . . a story that may be meaningful in some way . . . It is a story that is symbolic . . . of some relationships . . . and by seeing in your mind . . . these events . . . involving a frog and a scorpion . . . you may find meaning that becomes apparent to you now . . . or later . . . at a conscious level, or understood within your unconscious mind.
>
> "The story involves a frog . . . and one day the frog was sitting outside near a beautiful pond . . . and feeling the warm sunshine . . . you could just imagine the pond and the frog there . . . and yet, the frog was lonely.
>
> "A scorpion came nearby, and the scorpion said to the frog . . . 'I need your help . . . I need to get across the pond . . . carry me across the pond . . . and you won't be lonely because we will be together' . . . But the frog had a feeling this was not quite right . . . that the scorpion would sting her . . . but the scorpion said, 'No, I would not sting you because that would only hurt us both' . . . and so the frog agreed . . . and they began to go across the pond with the scorpion on the frog's back.
>
> "Then, as you might guess . . . the scorpion stung the frog . . . and as he did, she felt so much pain . . . she thought she might die . . . but she did not die . . . The frog somehow made it across the pond . . . and survived. . . . The scorpion fell upon a leaf and drifted away . . . unharmed . . . and unchanged.

"Time passed . . . and eventually the pain became less and the frog's intense hurt began to fade . . . so that after some time had passed . . . that frog was again sitting near the beautiful pond . . . and feeling the warm sunshine . . . and noticing all of the good things around her . . . But the frog was lonely . . . And then that same scorpion came nearby . . . and the scorpion said, 'I am so sorry about what happened before . . . I don't know how that could have happened . . . I did not mean to hurt you . . . and I need you . . . to help me . . . get across the pond . . . please . . . only you . . . only you . . . can help me get across the pond.'

"And you can well imagine what happened next . . . (*pause*) . . . the frog looked at the scorpion and blinked her eyes . . . and without saying a word . . . slipped into the water . . . and swam away to the other side of the pond . . . where . . . she met another frog . . . and it was good. . . . and after a time . . . she really never even thought very much about the scorpion at all."

EGO-STRENGTHENING SUGGESTIONS

Ego-strengthening suggestions are designed to enhance the patient's self-esteem and self-efficacy. The concept of ego-strengthening was introduced by John Hartland (1965). The goals of ego-strengthening include: (1) to increase self-image and self-esteem; (2) learn the ability to cope with difficulties: (3) build self-confidence; and, ultimately, (4) achieve self-efficacy.

> Ego-strengthening suggestions are designed to enhance the patient's self-esteem and self-efficacy.

Ego-strengthening suggestions may include general suggestions, or suggestions very specific to a particular task or issue within the individual. General ego-strengthening suggestions are those that are broadly applicable, can be applied to many situations and patients, and can be included in many hypnotic inductions. General ego-strengthening suggestions may be formulations with ideas such as:

"Each time you practice self-hypnosis you will find that you feel more at ease and more confident . . . every day . . . in some way, that becomes apparent to you . . . feeling better and better . . . able to cope with stress . . . and handle difficulties . . . with greater confidence and greater self-esteem . . . a positive feeling . . . that becomes more a part of you."

Ego-strengthening suggestions can also be presented in a more specific or individualized manner. In this use of ego-strengthening, suggestions are directed toward a particular situation, time, or behavior.

> "Now, there has been a particular issue at your workplace where you have needed to express your feelings . . . with confidence . . . and as you practice self-hypnosis you will find that you will be able to deal with this situation in a more effective manner. There has been this situation with your coworker where you have needed to confront and express your feelings . . . and you now know just what to say and just how to do it . . . now . . . you may see this happening . . . in your mind . . . or it may just occur spontaneously . . . you will have the confidence you need to express your feelings at work . . . in an appropriate and assertive manner . . . with confidence . . . as you deal with this issue."

Ego-strengthening suggestions can be thought of as a way to focus upon developing greater self-efficacy. Although he did practice hypnotherapy, Albert Bandura (1982) identified the concept of self-efficacy as being a powerful mediator and one of the most effective predictors of behavioral change. Self-efficacy can be defined as the belief that one can successfully execute a behavior required to produce a particular, and expected, outcome. It relates to the individual's sense of personal mastery and outcome expectations. It is influenced by the magnitude, generality, and strength of efficacy expectations. Each of these components can be addressed in hypnotic suggestions for ego-strengthening. Bandura identified four ways that self-efficacy can change.

Self-efficacy can be enhanced through emotional arousal.

First, self-efficacy can be changed through *verbal persuasion*. In HRT, this can be suggested through general or specific ego-strengthening suggestions, such as:

> "Day by day, you will find that you are in fact more confident . . . just as you hear these words . . . now . . . in the future you will be . . . more confident in your ability to do the things that you really wish to do . . . As you can imagine them . . . so you will be able to do them . . . and they will have a wonderful outcome for you."

Self-efficacy can be defined as the belief that one can successfully execute a behavior required to produce a particular, and expected, outcome.

Second, self-efficacy can be enhanced through *emotional arousal*. This is a way to associate an emotion with suggestions for the desired change. Examples would include suggestions for relaxation, changes in perceived breathing patterns, or associated tension. For example:

> "Now, knowing these events are going to occur, you will be able to do them, and as a way of acknowledging that these events are going to occur . . . that you will be able to do them with confidence and

effectiveness . . . I would like you to focus your attention on your right hand. In a few moments this hand will begin to form into a strong fist . . . and as it does, as this fist forms, you will feel the strength in that fist . . . now . . . and being filled with a feeling of confidence and strength . . . now . . . a feeling of security . . . more confident than you have been in a long time . . . Your unconscious mind acknowledging you will be able to do the things you wish to do . . . and they will have a wonderful outcome . . . Your confidence becomes stronger and stronger as the fist becomes stronger . . . and when your confidence is where it needs to be . . . and you have a strong belief in yourself . . . then the fist can relax . . . with confidence . . . it relaxes."

Third, self-efficacy can be enhanced through *vicarious experience*. This refers to experience that is observed through modeling; visualization; or in a meaningful, symbolic manner. As the unconscious mind responds to images, imagined experiences, and "vibes," this can be a powerful use of HRT and ego-strengthening. Age-progression suggestions may be utilized in this regard, such as:

Now, as you are sitting in a comfortable chair . . . there is a television in front of you . . . and on this television you can view some events that will be very important and very significant to you . . . as if some events in the future had been recorded and can be viewed on this television. In a few moments, viewing a time in the future where you are accomplishing a great deal of what you wish to accomplish. When you are ready . . . turn on the television . . . and as you begin to see these events in the future, seeing yourself there, and you are doing the things you wish to do [the hypnotherapist may interject visualization toward goal achievement] . . . and also notice what you are doing. Notice how confidently you are accomplishing this . . . really see it. . . . [again, the hypnotherapist may interject whatever behaviors are desired toward goal achievement]"

Post-hypnotic suggestions are used to indirectly influence self-efficacy.

The fourth way self-efficacy can be influenced is through *performance accomplishments*. For example, the patient can achieve reduction of stress responses during a hypnotic relaxation induction, thereby strengthening self-efficacy. In addition, post-hypnotic suggestions can be given such that the suggested accomplishments occur outside the hypnotherapy sessions. In this case, post-hypnotic suggestions are used to indirectly influence self-efficacy. Post-hypnotic suggestions for this purpose could include:

"You have accomplished a great deal today . . . and you will feel a sense of pride and confidence in the future . . . and you will be able to do the things you have seen today on the television . . . just as you have seen yourself doing them . . . so you will do them . . . Just as they have been visualized . . . they will now occur in real life . . . and as they do your confidence and belief in yourself will grow even stronger . . . And now you can relax . . . relax deeply."

Suggestions for ego-strengthening and self-efficacy enhancement can be productively integrated in a wide variety of HRT interventions. As skills in HRT are refined, the clinician will gain greater use of ego-strengthening suggestions and creative ways to enhance the patient's self-efficacy expectations.

CHAPTER 13

Pain Management

Hypnotic relaxation therapy (HRT) for pain management typically involves a hypnotic induction consisting of suggestions for relaxation, changes in perception, and improved coping as well as instruction in self-hypnosis. In addition, post-hypnotic suggestions may be useful for the continued management of pain once the session ends. This chapter will discuss both assessment of patients presenting with primary complaints of pain, as well as hypnotic strategies for pain management. These methods will then be illustrated through a case example and transcript of a hypnotic relaxation intervention for pain management.

Hypnotherapy has been shown to be effective in treating a number of different types of chronic pain.

Hypnotherapy has been shown to be effective in treating a number of different types of chronic pain (Elkins, Fisher, Johnson,2012). Evidence supports the efficacy of hypnotherapy for the treatment in chronic low back pain (McCauley, Thelen, Frank, Willard, & Callen, 1983; Spinhoven & Linssen, 1989; Jenson, et al., 2009), as well as pain associated with cancer (Spiegel & Bloom, 1983; Elkins, Cheung, Marcus, Palamara, & Rajab, 2004), osteoarthritis (Gay, Philippot, & Luminet, 2002), sickle cell disease (Dinges, et al., 1997), temporomandibular disorder (Drangsholt & LeResche et al., 1990; Winocur, Gavish, Emodi-Perlman, Halachmi, & Eli, 2002; Abrahamsen, Zachariae, & Svensson, 2009), and fibromyalgia (Haanen et al., 1991; Castel, Pérez, Sala, Padrol, & Rull, 2007). Hypnotherapy has also been effectively utilized to address non-cardiac chest pain (Jones, Cooper, Miller, Brooks, Whorwell, 2006), and disability-related chronic pain (Jensen, Abresch, Carter, & McDonald, 2005; Jensen, et al., 2011). Importantly, the treatment of chronic pain with HRT requires assessment and consideration of biological, psychological, and interpersonal factors in case conceptualization and planning.

PATIENT ASSESSMENT FOR PAIN MANAGEMENT

Patients who are referred for HRT for pain management may be in considerable emotional or physical distress. They may be frustrated with the lack of pain relief from traditional measures. In addition, they may have developed lifestyle issues that can impact the chronic nature of their pain. During the assessment process, several key areas should be addressed as a part of the case conceptualization. These include: (1) hypnotizability; (2) biopsychosocial factors; (3) perception of pain; (4) suffering; (5) emotional distress; and (6) goals.

HYPNOTIZABILITY

In working with individuals with chronic pain, it can be especially useful to assess the patient's hypnotizability according to the Elkins Hypnotizability Scale (EHS). This is because the patient may have moderate to severe pain, and knowing if the patient is in at least an average range of hypnotic ability can help in treatment planning and conceptualizing the role of hypnotizability versus resistance. The clinical version of the EHS (see Chapter 10) can be used in the first hypnotherapy session, as the processes of intervention and assessment can be integrated.

Pain is a complex problem involving physical, emotional, cognitive, and interpersonal aspects.

BIOPSYCHOSOCIAL FACTORS

Pain is a complex problem involving physical, emotional, cognitive, and interpersonal aspects. In treating patients with chronic pain, the case conceptualization should include a history of the onset and progression of symptoms as well as any known physical causes. Medical tests and prior interventions should be considered and ongoing pathology should be ruled out. In addition, a thorough psychosocial history is needed. The clinician should obtain sufficient history to evaluate depression, anxiety, somatization, physical or sexual abuse, drug abuse/dependence, and any associated family problems. In regard to possible complicating psychological factors, Sternbach's 6 *D*'s (Sternbach, 1968) of chronic pain assessment serve as a useful check list:

- *Dramatization of complaints.* (Is the patient's description of pain emotionally dramatic? This may indicate catastrophizing or attention-seeking.)
- *Drug misuse.* (Has the patient developed drug dependency? If so, this may need to be addressed in conjunction with HRT for pain management.)
- *Dysfunction/disuse.* (Has the patient withdrawn from activities or become inactive, unsuccessfully relying on devices for pain relief?)
- *Dependency.* (Are there indications of emotional dependency on family or friends due to pain complaints?)

- *Depression.* (Do the mental status examination and history indicate the patient is experiencing clinical depression? Depression itself can contribute to the perception of pain.)
- *Disability.* (Is the patient receiving financial compensation or involved in any lawsuits related to pain complaints?)

PERCEPTION OF PAIN

Information on the location of pain can be useful in understanding the patient's perception of his or her symptoms and in planning hypnotic relaxation suggestions. In addition, it is important to determine what factors cause, intensify, or alleviate the pain. For example, relaxation (either suggested or pharmaceutically induced) may decrease musculoskeletal pain. The clinician should gather information regarding the patient's description of pain in terms of intensity and severity. Additionally, any adjectives that the patient uses to describe the pain (i.e., burning, itching, throbbing, radiating) should be attended to. A visual analog scale or numeric rating can provide useful information on the patient's perception of the severity and intensity of pain. It is also very useful to engage the patient in some discussion of symbolic representations of the pain. Determining how the patient symbolically conceptualizes the pain provides useful information in forming hypnotic relaxation suggestions. For example, the patient may imagine the pain as having a color, brightness, certain size, character (like a "monster" or a tiger, etc.), or emotion (anger, sadness, etc.).

Determining how the patient symbolically conceptualizes the pain provides useful information in forming hypnotic relaxation suggestions.

SUFFERING

It is also important to make a distinction between pain and suffering. The patient may give very different ratings of pain and the degree to which he or she suffers from the pain. A visual analog or numeric rating of suffering should be obtained to both gain greater insight into the patient's experience and also to help the patient to begin to make this distinction. In relation to suffering, the clinician should gather information on how pain impacts the patient's quality of life (such as sleep, leisure activities, work, etc.)

EMOTIONAL DISTRESS

The therapist should attend to the patient's level of emotional distress. Pain is an emotional experience as well as a physical and cognitive one. The patient may be experiencing emotions ranging from anger to depression or guilt. Identifying emotions and their intensity can be helpful in planning HRT interventions.

GOALS

Most certainly, one goal for patients with chronic pain is to reduce the frequency, severity, and intensity of pain and suffering. However, in addition to pain reduction, goals for pain management may include: (1) improved coping skills to deal with pain; (2) increased physical activity; (3) improved sleep; (4) decreased reliance on pain medications; (5) reduced muscle tension; and (6) increased awareness of emotions related to pain.

QUESTIONS TO ASK ABOUT PAIN DESCRIPTION

- Where do you most experience pain?
- What things make the pain worse?
- What things make the pain ease?
- On a 0 to 10 scale, with 0 being "none" and 10 representing "as bad as it could be," how would you rate your pain: at its worst; at its least; on average; and right now?
- I also want to ask you about the degree to which you suffer from pain. On a 0 to 10 scale, with 0 being "no suffering" and 10 representing "the worst suffering possible," how would you rate your level of suffering at its worst; at its least; and right now?
- How is the pain affecting your life at the present time? In what way does it affect your sleep, mood, activities, family relationships, or other areas?
- What kinds of words can you use to describe your pain? Various terms can be used to describe pain, such as: throbbing, pounding, shooting, pricking, boring, stabbing, lancinating, sharp, cutting, lacerating, pressing, cramping, crushing, pulling, pinching, stinging, burning, splitting, penetrating, piercing, squeezing, and dull aching, etc. (Note, the McGill Pain Questionnaire [Melzack, 1975] can be used to identify adjectives to describe pain.)
- Can you think of your pain in a symbolic way? Does it seem to have a shape or a color? What do you imagine represents the intensity of your pain? Can you think of the pain as being like an animal or in another way?
- How do you feel emotionally right now? Does the pain get worse when you are angry, depressed, nervous, etc.?
- In addition to having less pain, what other goals do you have? Would it help you to sleep better, use fewer pain pills, exercise more, feel calmer, or cope better with the pain?

HYPNOTIC TECHNIQUES FOR TREATING PAIN

> Physical and emotional relaxation can lead to decreased pain.

HRT uses a variety of techniques for pain management. Suggestions for relaxation, comfort, and alteration of pain perception can be used to help the patient reduce pain and better cope. Suggestions also may be directed toward reducing suffering and other symptoms associated with the pain. Post-hypnotic suggestions and self-hypnosis also can be useful in empowering the patient to achieve greater pain management.

RELAXATION AND PAIN REDUCTION

Physical and emotional relaxation can lead to decreased pain. The following illustrates how relaxation—and therefore, decreased pain—can be achieved by utilizing HRT.

> "Relaxation can be experienced in many different ways . . . There is of course the experience of physical relaxation . . . the experience of muscles that are allowed to experience a deep sense of calmness and comfort . . . And today finding that as you enter a deeper and more relaxed state . . . the pain becomes less and less. There is the matter of the pain–tension cycle . . . pain leading to tension . . . and tension leading to pain . . . but within a deeply relaxed state . . . the pain–tension cycle starts to fade . . . until soon . . . for a time . . . all that remains is the experience of becoming deeper and deeper relaxed . . . And so . . . you do that now . . . as a wave of relaxation comes to you . . . spreading across your forehead . . . your neck, your shoulders, your face, deeper and deeper relaxed . . . letting all the tension go . . . deeper relaxed whereever you need more comfort . . . that wave of relaxation now . . . spreading into your shoulders . . . your upper back and your lower back . . . back and stomach . . . Relax . . . notice your breathing as it . . . becomes more relaxed . . . no tension, no stress . . . the relaxation now can spread further . . . deeper . . . more complete . . . letting all the tension go . . . as the legs relax . . . deeply relax . . . legs and feet . . . relaxed . . . no tension. . . . and the deeper the relaxation, the better the response; the deeper the relaxation, the better the response . . . And just as there can be a physical relaxation . . . a good physical relaxation . . . so there can be an emotional relaxation . . . to feel calm . . . to feel at ease . . . at peace within yourself . . . at peace . . . calm . . . at ease . . . as if you were looking out across a calm lake in evening time . . . watching the sun setting . . . seeing the calm water . . . feeling calm . . . no tension, no stress . . . As you see the water is calm . . . so you feel calm . . . The deeper the relaxation, the better the response . . . to finding comfort . . . comfort in the hands . . . comfort in the breathing . . . comfort in the back . . . comfort in looking out across that beautiful lake [or wherever the patient may prefer] . . . Calm and comfortable . . . good comfort . . . that lasts a long time . . . And notice if there are other good . . . calm . . . sensations . . . safe and secure . . . calm . . . no bother, no stress . . . emotionally relaxed . . . physically relaxed . . . and comfortable. . . ."

DISSOCIATION FROM PAIN EXPERIENCE

Dissociation refers to an alteration in consciousness such that the patient can become so deeply absorbed in the suggested experience that there is a feeling of being in another place. It is as if the patient has left his or her body and the present time and has gone to another place and time where pain is much less. Suggestions are given for mental imagery, then dissociation to another place, and then feeling detached from present pain experience. For example:

> "And there is a part of your mind . . . that still remembers comfort . . . a part of your mind . . . that remembers a feeling . . . of comfort in your back, your shoulders, your legs . . . as you drift into a deeper hypnotic state . . . today . . . it will be possible to re-experience such feelings . . . Again . . .
>
> ". . . hearing my voice and knowing you are here . . . with a part of your mind . . . and yet . . . able to experience being in another place . . . and time . . . where you find comfort . . .
>
> "Now . . . just going into a deeper hypnotic state . . . letting go more and more . . . so that the relaxation becomes more complete . . . Arms, neck, shoulders, back, and chest . . . relaxed . . . deeper and deeper . . . And there is a memory that you have . . . where you enjoyed going sailing . . . that part of your mind . . . knows all about sailing . . . And soon you can see a beautiful sailboat . . . and you might really enjoy going sailing today . . . One part of your mind can be here and responding to each hypnotic suggestion I give you today . . . and yet . . . as you are soon at the boat dock . . . walking to the sailboat . . . once you reach the boat . . . you will be there . . . you will be on the boat . . . experiencing everything there . . . It is about 6 steps to the boat . . . and then going sailing . . . as I count from 6 to 1 . . . 6 . . . 5 . . . 4 . . . 3 . . . 2 . . . 1 . . .
>
> "Now . . . you are there . . . you are on the sailboat . . . and it is a beautiful day . . . today . . . the sky is clear . . . and there is a strong breeze . . . You can see the sail is up. . . . and you are gliding through the water . . . Look at how beautiful the water is . . . and as you move the sail . . . as you steer the boat . . . there is just the comfort . . . feeling the breeze in the air . . . there are some sea birds . . . and notice if there are any other boats that you can see . . . Steering the sailboat . . . to where you want to go . . . today . . . there is just the comfort when you are there . . . on the sailboat . . . gliding through the water. . . ."

It can be quite useful to suggest alterations in the patient's symbolic representations of pain.

ALTERATION IN PAIN SENSATION

Direct suggestions can be given for alterations in pain so that sensations such as a numbness, warmth, or tingling occur as pain lessens. It can be quite useful to suggest alterations in the patient's symbolic representations of pain.

For example, the therapist may suggest that the patient imagine the pain as a bright light that can be turned down to become a dimmer, less intense, and softer light as pain becomes less intense, as illustrated below.

> "There has been this matter of pain . . . pain in your left arm . . . and you have experienced the pain . . . and you have observed the pain . . . It changes in sensations . . . sometimes more and sometimes less intense . . . as you go into a much deeper hypnotic state . . . the pain can change . . . more and more . . . as you drift deeper . . . going deep enough . . . so deeply relaxed . . . that you do begin to notice changes in sensations . . . Certainly with the deepest levels of relaxation . . . there can be a heaviness . . . the arms become heavier and heavier . . . so very heavy . . . they would be hard to lift . . . they are so very heavy . . . and as that occurs . . . as you go deeper . . . other changes can be observed . . . perhaps a tingly feeling . . . at times . . . or a numbness . . . and pain can become less . . . At times the pain has been like a loud noise . . . too loud . . . like a rushing of noise . . . loud and annoying . . . but the sound can change . . . As you drift into a deeper hypnotic state . . . it begins to change . . . becoming softer and gentler . . . like the sound of a small brook . . . cold, clear water, that you can hear as it trickles over the rocks and stones . . . the sound goes from 10 . . . to a lower number . . . less intense . . . calmer . . . and more comfortable . . . The pain becomes less and less . . . you experience a calmness in the sound . . . it becomes the sound of a small brook . . . cool and calm and . . . as it does . . . there can be a tingly sensation . . . a numbness . . . or other ways of feeling more comfort . . . as the sound becomes so much softer . . . 10 . . . 9 . . . 8 . . . 7 . . . 6 . . . 5 . . . 4 . . . 3 . . . 2 . . . 1 . . . and the changes in sensations occur."

DECREASE SUFFERING

It is sometimes helpful to include suggestions for the patient to be able to distinguish between pain and suffering. This can be directly suggested as is illustrated in the following example.

> "There is a distinction between the pain and suffering from the pain . . . now . . . today . . . soon going into a sufficiently deep hypnotic state . . . that the pain can be observed . . . You could give the pain a number . . . and that number could change . . . pain could become less . . . And then there is the matter of suffering from the pain . . . and that number is . . . to a certain extent . . . within your control . . . Pain can be ignored at times . . . it is possible for the pain to exist . . . but for it to not bother you all that much . . . for a time . . . Because in spite of the pain . . . there is the matter of quality

of life . . . the degree to which you can find happiness . . . enjoy a good day . . . sleep well . . . enjoy laughter . . . at times . . . just forget about the pain . . . suffering can become less and less . . . You might be aware that the level of suffering . . . can become small at times . . . the experience of recognizing the pain exists . . . but suffering is another matter. . . . just now knowing the things that need to occur . . . so that the amount of suffering is minimal."

SELF-HYPNOSIS SUGGESTIONS FOR COPING WITH PAIN

Suggestions to increase the patient's ability to practice and experience hypnotic relaxation–associated reduction in pain contribute to the patient's increased control. This can be seen in the following example.

"Each time you practice self-hypnosis you will be able to enter a very deep state of relaxation . . . physical and emotional relaxation . . . And within this practice of self-hypnosis, you will find that you are able to enter an adequately deep hypnotic state . . . you will be able to become deeply relaxed and comfortable . . . and you will be able to become so absorbed in the suggestions that pain will become less and less bothersome . . . You will feel more in control . . . as you find greater comfort . . . time and time again during your practice of self-hypnosis."

HYPNOANALGESIA FOR PAIN MANAGEMENT

The goal of suggestions for hypnoanalgesia is to alter pain sensations and perception, leading to the reduction of pain. It is recommended that an assessment of hypnotizability be completed in order to estimate the patient's ability to achieve a hypnoanalgesic response. Incorporating suggestions for hypnoanalgesia is illustrated in the following example.

"Now, as you drift into a deeper hypnotic state . . . it is possible to achieve a reduction in pain . . . This hand . . . this right hand . . . will soon become numb . . . thick . . . and rubbery . . . It will be as though a thick glove is being placed around that hand . . . and the hand becomes . . . more and more numb . . . numb and rubbery . . . Now . . . as I touch this hand . . . it becomes more and more numb . . . numb and rubbery . . . so numb . . . able to feel pressure but no pain . . . pressure but no pain . . . This is a hypnoanalgesia . . . and the hand is numb . . . Remaining in a deep hypnotic state . . . you can open your eyes . . . take your left hand and test this numbness . . . pinch the hand . . . and notice it is so numb and thick . . . rubbery . . . Very good . . . Now as your eyelids close again . . . going into an even deeper state of hypnotic relaxation . . . the relaxation becomes very deep . . . and taking that thick . . . rubbery . . . numb hand . . . and placing it wherever you need more comfort . . . As you place that hand now . . . on your shoulder . . . the numbness spreads . . . into the shoulder . . . numb and comfortable . . . more and more numbness in the shoulder . . . And as that occurs . . . bringing the right hand down to rest . . . on the arm of the chair . . . normal sensation returns to the hand . . . as I touch the hand . . . now . . . normal sensation returns . . . but the comfort and numbness remains in the shoulder . . . in a way that is acceptable . . . helpful . . . and appropriate for you . . . More and more comfort . . . each time you experience hypnoanalgesia."

POST-HYPNOTIC SUGGESTIONS FOR PAIN MANAGEMENT

Post-hypnotic suggestions are especially useful in pain management, because it is desirable for pain reduction and benefit to continue beyond the HRT session. Post-hypnotic suggestions can also be given for feelings and behaviors that are consistent with the patient's goals. For example:

> "Each time you experience hypnotic relaxation . . . the benefits will last longer and longer . . . the reduction in pain . . . you experience . . . in a deeply relaxed hypnotic state . . . will . . . over time . . . last longer and longer . . . Even when you return to conscious alertness . . . the comfort will remain . . . longer and longer . . . and can be reinforced . . . as you practice self-hypnosis . . . Learning more and more about how to control the pain . . . your sleep will improve . . . suffering will become less . . . and you will feel more at peace . . . happier . . . every day . . . And as you find that you are in greater control of the pain . . . you will remember to take good care of yourself . . . you won't overdo things . . . you will protect your body . . . in ways that are best for you."

CASE EXAMPLE: TRANSCRIPT OF HRT WITH A CHRONIC PAIN PATIENT

The following transcript is from a post-treatment interview with Deborah, a 53-year-old woman with a history of chronic back pain who was referred for HRT. She obtained a score of 9 on the EHS, indicating she was highly hypnotizable. After completion of five sessions, she met with the therapist to provide information about her experience with HRT.

> **Therapist:** *How did you get hurt?*
>
> **Patient:** *Well, I was working in the emergency room and we were in the process of transferring a patient back to the nursing home and . . . the driver and I were going to load the stretcher into the back of the ambulance and . . . it didn't release . . . when I started*

up with the bar, for some reason it didn't release and I wasn't expecting it, you know, because it always had, and . . . I felt, I don't know, basically when I blew the disc, but I know I had a real bad burning pain . . . but then I worked for three days.

Therapist: *Let me ask you a few questions about the pain, itself, that you've had. What does it feel like? How would you describe it?*

Patient: *My pain, the way I see it is . . . it's maybe like a hard ball* (puts hands into a fist) *and it has shoots off of it, you know, like maybe something exploded, it's just got bright red is the way I visualize it, the shoots. And that's basically when I'm in real bad pain, intense pain.*

Therapist: *So you can picture that.*

Patient: *Oh yeah, mmm hmmm. It's a deep pain to me, but I imagine that it comes to the surface, you know, and it's just right there. I try to picture warmth.*

Therapist: *And do you see a color change? You said bright red. Does it seem to change color?*

Patient: (nodding) *Uh huh, yeah. I do . . . I guess I hadn't really thought about it changing colors. I know it's not red anymore; it seems to blend more with me.*

Therapist: *Kind of a blending, a spreading.*

Patient: (nodding) *Uh huh.*

Therapist: *More diffuse.*

Patient: (nodding) *Uh huh.*

Therapist: *And . . . when it's at its worst, the bright red, what number would you give that, say 10 is the worst and 0 is no pain; what number* (moves hands like a scale)*?*

Patient: *Oh a 10 plus.*

Therapist: *OK a 10? And . . . in hypnosis, what number are you able to reduce that to?*

Patient: *Um, basically almost all the way down.*

Therapist: *OK.*

Patient: *Not at first, not at first, because I was a doubting Thomas, you know . . . Maybe not completely to a zero, but almost there.*

Therapist: *And where are you right now?*

Patient: *As far as my pain level?*

Therapist: *Yes*

Patient: *The weather is bad, you know? I'm probably maybe a 4, a 3.*

Therapist: *OK, so let's begin with hypnotic relaxation therapy. . . . Please settle back into the chair . . . allow your head to be supported . . . and focus your attention on a spot . . . It begins to fade into the background . . . and as it does . . . take a deep breath of air . . . hold it and as you exhale . . . allow your eyelids to close . . .* (In a slow, soothing tone) *Very good . . . are you beginning to relax? Deeper and deeper relaxed. That's right . . . you might notice your breathing becoming more comfortable in some way . . . perhaps noticing the scents . . . that's right, a spreading relaxation, letting tension go . . . achieving a greater sense of control, through hypnosis . . . through a kind of special relaxation . . . And with a part of your mind, you can listen to my voice . . . and yet at the same time knowing that you are in control . . . and you can do whatever it is that you need to do to achieve comfort . . . because that's what is really important . . . a greater sense of comfort and relaxation . . . That's right . . . really letting the tension go now in your forehead . . . neck, shoulders, relax . . . arms, back . . . and legs . . . and in some way, as you relax deeper and deeper, you may come back to that picture of pain . . . and I don't know what color it is now, how close the pain is to the surface . . . how spread out it is, but you know . . . That's right . . . it can change, coming closer to the surface . . . spreading out more . . . going down as though the numbers were going down from 4, then you reach the number 3, just nodding your head yes . . . Very good . . . perhaps even going further . . . finding that you may notice a tingling or a relaxation . . . a comfort, wherever you need to feel that, and it's possible to allow your mind to drift . . . perhaps drifting somewhere else, somewhere pleasant . . . leaving your body behind, leaving this place behind . . . while you can hear my voice, but going somewhere else . . . as though you had gone to a beautiful field, a meadow, green, lovely . . . And when you're there, nodding your head yes, you've found that place . . . very good . . . and enjoy being there . . . feelings of comfort that have been experienced in the past can be re-experienced again, it's possible to go back . . . and find a sense of comfort that can be enjoyed . . . and that comfort can last a long, long time . . . hours and hours, perhaps even days . . . And you don't need to consciously be concerned with that, because your unconscious mind has a great deal of control and ability . . . unconcerned . . . as though you might imagine that the pain becomes less and less . . . drifts toward the surface and it's spreading out . . . As though the signals that turn discomfort on were turned off . . . like a dimmer switch that you could turn down . . . bright red, then dimmer . . . and dimmer, and dimmer . . . and dimmer . . . And when it's where it needs to be, simply letting it remain there, knowing that it'll last a* *long time . . . that you can enjoy that special place . . . that green meadow . . . that you can be successful in your use of hypnosis, that whenever you feel discomfort you can know, "I can relax." . . . You will be able to suggest to yourself and remind yourself that you have a control within your own mind . . . and your own body . . . you will be able to recall comfort . . . It's not necessary to reduce all pain to be successful . . . the numbers may be reduced to 3, or 2, or 1 . . . perhaps even zero . . . and all of those will be successes . . . It's good to feel successful . . . and in control . . . and as you are aware of that, perhaps you can allow yourself to drift further . . . to that meadow, and I don't know if it's a warm summer day, but would it be alright to feel a greater sense of warmth? . . . would that be OK? . . . If it would, just nod your head yes . . .*

Patient: (nods head yes)

Therapist: *Very good . . . Allowing that warmth to begin to spread, wherever you need it . . . perhaps your lower back, your shoulders . . . because the sunshine can be a very special kind of warmth . . . warming your skin . . . your muscles . . . And all these muscles relax . . . spread out . . . let go . . . and you can notice that the numbers have gone down even further, 3, 2 . . . just wherever they've gone . . . and that feels so good . . . that comfort is going to stay with you a long, long time . . . and yet, you will find that you will be wise in being gentle with your body . . . you will not overdo . . . you will have a kind of gentleness and respect for your body . . . and your body will respect you with more comfort . . . a surprising amount of comfort, as you are gentle with yourself by not overdoing . . . by taking the time to reinforce . . . to practice hypnosis . . . and by being aware of the things that are truly important for you to do . . . Taking good care of yourself every day . . . finding the things that give you enjoyment of life, and giving yourself permission to pursue those things . . . as far as you are capable . . . and know that you can achieve so much . . . knowing that you already know this . . . and you will be able to remember and remind yourself of it frequently . . . And in a moment with a sense of comfort . . . returning to conscious alertness . . . in your own time . . . in your own speed, letting your eyes open . . . fully alert, as you are ready to . . . no hurry, but gently alerting yourself.*

Patient: (opens eyes after a few moments, breathes deeply) *Good morning* (laughs).

Therapist: *Hi. How do you feel? What do you notice now?*

Patient: (sighs) *It feels good. A person just wants to stay there when there is no pain. It just feels so good.*

Therapist: *Do you find that sort of happens?*

Patient: (nods) *Uh huh. Yeah.*

Therapist: *In that state of hypnotic relaxation, the pain goes down and you really notice how good that is to have more control.*

Patient: *It's so relaxing, it just really is. And I'm just so hyper, I'm normally such a hyper person . . . and it feels good.*

Therapist: *OK. What number is the pain at right now?*

Patient: *Oh my goodness, I'm just . . . I'm so relaxed; it's a zero right now.*

Therapist: *And what special place did you go to?*

Patient: *I don't know. I was floating on an air mattress. And it was just . . . I don't know where I was. It was a lot deeper than I can do myself. Ah, it felt great.*

Therapist: *OK, well, thank you. I think we'll stop here for today and schedule your next appointment.*

Patient: *OK.*

This case illustrates the effectiveness of HRT for chronic pain. It also demonstrates the integration of the patient's perception of pain and associated symptoms into the hypnotic relaxation intervention. Deborah was seen for two additional sessions in which she continued to make progress.

CHAPTER 14

Smoking Cessation

The purpose of this chapter is to provide guidelines for hypnotic relaxation therapy (HRT) for smoking cessation. A brief literature review reveals that, in general, the research on hypnosis for smoking cessation has been quite variable. For example, in one study, biologically verified (expired carbon monoxide) smoking cessation rates of 60% at 12 weeks follow-up and 40% at 26 weeks follow-up were achieved using HRT (Elkins, Marcus, Bates, Rajab, & Cook, 2006). However, this rate of smoking cessation is based upon HRT as an intensive approach to smoking cessation, involving multiple sessions, individualized contact, and attention to assessment in treatment planning. In contrast, minimal approaches involving only one or two sessions have reported cessation rates of only around 20% (Spiegel, 1970; Berkowitz, Ross-Townsend, & Kohberger, 1979; Cornwell, Burrows, & McMurray, 1981; Hyman, Stanley, Burrows, & Horne, 1986; Javel, 1980; Neufeld & Lynn, 1988; Pederson, Scrimgeour, & Lefcoe, 1975; Rabkin, Boyko, Shane, & Kaufert, 1984; Spanos, Mondoux, & Burgess, 1995; Spanos, Sims, deFaye, Mondoux, & Gabora, 1992; Spiegel, Frischholz, Fleiss, & Spiegel, 1993; Stanton, 1978; Williams, & Hall, 1988). In a comprehensive review of hypnosis for smoking cessation, Green and Lynn (2000) also concluded that group hypnosis intervention and minimal, individual hypnotic interventions (involving one or two sessions) achieve smoking cessation rates of only around 20% or less when verified by physiological measures.

The success of hypnotic intervention for smoking cessation may be increased by a more intensive approach (Holroyd, 1980; Niaura & Abrams, 2002; Fiore, et al., 2000). Such an approach is characterized by multiple sessions, individualized hypnotic suggestions, and a positive interpersonal relationship between the therapist and patient. Using an intensive, five-session, individual hypnotherapy intervention, Crasilneck (1990) reported smoking cessation rates of up to 81% at 12-month follow-up. However, the data were based solely on self-reports and are therefore possibly inflated. Similarly, Johnson and Karkut (1994) reported a cessation rate of 87% at 3 months post-treatment, following multiple hypnotherapy sessions and self-hypnosis practice outside the sessions. Again, the results were based entirely on self-reports.

ASSESSMENT FOR SMOKING CESSATION

A complete clinical interview that considers the patient's problem from a biopsychosocial perspective should be completed before initiating HRT for smoking cessation. During the clinical interview, the clinician should gather information on the patient's history of smoking, including prior attempts at cessation, motivation, social support, expectations, and smoking-related beliefs. In addition, the clinical interview should include a mental status examination and a thorough review of medical and psychiatric history for the purpose of case conceptualization. Depression, stress, substance abuse, and family/work environment can all have an impact on smoking cessation. In addition, assessment of hypnotizability may be considered. Specific questions may include:

The clinician should gather information on the patient's history of smoking, including prior attempts at cessation, motivation, social support, expectations, and smoking-related beliefs.

- When did you first start smoking? How old were you?
- Have you tried to stop in the past? What was your experience?
- What methods did you use in the past to try to stop smoking?
- Were you able to stop smoking for any length of time?
- Did you experience any withdrawal symptoms?
- What caused you to resume smoking (i.e., stress, cravings, social factors)?
- Does anyone else in your household/workplace smoke?
- How supportive are others (i.e., spouse or friends) for you to stop smoking?
- Have you ever been treated for depression or anxiety?
- How motivated are you to stop smoking at this time?
- What makes you want to stop smoking?
- Are you ready to set a date to stop smoking?
- Are you experiencing medical problems related to smoking?
- Is there someone or something that is important enough to you to increase your desire to stop smoking?

In addition to the clinical interview, there are several questionnaires that can be used to determine the severity of nicotine dependency, smoking-related beliefs, and readiness to stop smoking. The Fagerstrom Test of Nicotine Dependency (Heatherton, Kozlowski, Fecker, & Fagerstrom, 1991) is a 6-item questionnaire that provides an estimate of nicotine dependency and is easy to administer as a part of the clinical interview. The Contemplation Ladder (Biener & Abrams, 1991) is a useful tool to estimate a patient's readiness to stop smoking. The instrument, which consists of a picture of a ladder, is based on Prochaska and DiClemente's motivational theory (1983), which postulates that the process of change ranges from pre-contemplation to action and to maintenance. The patient is instructed to circle a number at each rung of the ladder to represent his perception of where he is in the process of stopping smoking.

In addition to the clinical interview, there are several questionnaires that can be used to determine the severity of nicotine dependency, smoking-related beliefs, and readiness to stop smoking.

GENERAL GUIDELINES FOR HRT FOR SMOKING CESSATION

In addition to assessment, the clinical interview also helps to prepare the patient for HRT and to set a date to stop smoking. HRT can be an effective treatment for nicotine dependency; however, it is essential that the therapy process be clearly explained to the patient and that the patient "do his part" by setting a date to stop smoking and making a commitment to that date. The patient needs to do several things to prepare to stop smoking, including:

It is . . . important that the patient understand that the cravings will always pass, and that, with time, they will become less severe and less frequent.

1. Make a clear decision to *go through the withdrawal phase* of smoking cessation. The patient must understand that he will experience withdrawal symptoms such as irritability, disrupted sleep, and cravings. It is also important the patient understand that the cravings will always pass, and that, with time, they will become less severe and less frequent.
2. *Inform others* that he is stopping smoking, *destroying all tobacco products* including cigarettes, cigars, lighters, ashtrays, and *discarding everything connected with smoking.*
3. *Identify some event, person, or circumstance* that means more than cigarettes. The emotion attached to this event, person, or circumstance should be strong and will be used by the therapist to give power to the hypnotic suggestions.
4. Make a *commitment to continue treatment until he stops smoking completely.* Any failure is only a learning experience and is used to increase success in setting the next stop date. Persistence pays off, and if the patient will not "give up," he will be successful.

It is also important to remember that the basic goals that underlie this hypnosis intervention are to empower the patient and to foster the patient's sense of mastery and control of smoking habits. Hypnosis represents a tool that the patient can use to become a nonsmoker. Remember, hypnosis is not something that is done to the patient; rather, it is something the patient learns to utilize and practice.

The patient should practice self-hypnosis (with and without the CD recording) on a daily basis. This takes time and commitment, but it is essential. If the patient does not practice self-hypnosis, then the hypnotic inductions during sessions should cease until the patient begins to fully participate in this most important aspect of therapy.

Hypnosis represents a tool that the patient can use to become a nonsmoker.

Patients should also understand that the most common reason for relapse after stopping smoking is stress. People associate smoking with relaxation, and the pleasant feeling associated with smoking results in dependency. This is true of smoking, alcohol, and drugs. The patient's conscious commitment to stop smoking, even during times of stress, is key to using self-hypnosis for relaxation and to control stress. Once the patient accepts that smoking is no longer an option, his desire for hypnosis becomes stronger and more integrated into daily life.

Smoking cessation is a lifestyle change, and the patient must understand that his old patterns of associating with people who are smokers must change. This involves developing a new level of self-respect, and learning to love and protect oneself from nicotine. He may ask others not to smoke around him and develop new patterns, interests, and a lifestyle that does not include smoking. For some, this is the most difficult part.

As with any other hypnotic intervention, the power of the therapeutic alliance should never be underestimated. Within the trust and collaboration of the hypnotherapeutic relationship, the patient should collaborate with the therapist to identify and overcome any problems or issues.

As with any other hypnotic intervention, the power of the therapeutic alliance should never be underestimated.

It is important to identify the emotional association with smoking cessation and individualize suggestions to target the patient's difficulties (such as stress, sleep, or coping with withdrawal symptoms such as irritability or lifestyle change). The therapist should always keep the *law of dominant affect* in mind; that is, "a stronger emotion replaces a weaker emotion." Additionally, as mentioned, it is essential that the therapist identify something that means more to the patient than a cigarette and use this information to individualize and give power to hypnotic suggestions to become and remain a nonsmoker. The more powerful the emotion, the more powerful the hypnotic suggestion.

It is important to identify the emotional association with smoking cessation and individualize suggestions to target the patient's difficulties.

HYPNOTIC SUGGESTIONS FOR SMOKING CESSATION

Examples of hypnotic suggestions for smoking cessation are provided in this section. However, it is important to remember that the intervention can be individualized depending upon the clinical interview and the patient's experience with hypnotherapy as treatment progresses.

Relaxation

"As you enter a hypnotic state . . . becoming more and more relaxed . . . And this is especially important to achieve . . . because you may have relied on cigarettes as a way to relax . . . but now finding that you can enter an even deeper level of relaxation . . . and this will provide a means of control . . . At any time you experience excessive craving you will be able to enter a deeply relaxed hypnotic state . . . and this will be a source of empowerment . . . a source of control . . . As your eyelids remain closed . . . a feeling of relaxation can come to you . . . spreading across your forehead . . . your face . . . your neck and shoulders . . . Every muscle . . . every fiber of your body becoming more and more relaxed . . . letting go of any tension . . . drifting deeper and deeper . . . so that there is soon a feeling that the relaxation is becoming complete . . . your back, your chest, legs, and feet [*relaxation suggestions are continued until the patient indicates a feeling of deep relaxation*]."

Comfort

"And with the relaxation . . . comes a feeling of comfort . . . a peaceful, calm feeling . . . that is so necessary. . . . calm and at ease . . . so very calm and relaxed . . . as you drift into an even deeper state of hypnotic relaxation . . . just as deep as you need to go to accomplish what you wish to accomplish today."

Commitment for smoking cessation

"And there is the matter of becoming free from cigarettes . . . a decision that has been recognized by both your conscious and your unconscious mind. . . . Today . . . as you drift into a very deep hypnotic state . . . an experience occurs . . . that provides the commitment and the strength to remain a nonsmoker . . . You will not smoke again . . . not even a puff. . . . Each time you experience hypnotic relaxation . . . this commitment will become stronger and stronger . . . you will not smoke again . . . not even a puff . . . And there is a reason for this commitment . . . something you care about . . . that is greater than a cigarette . . . the love of a child . . . the commitment to a spouse . . . the respect of your body . . . as these things come to mind (*suggestions should be linked to concepts of most relevance to the patient*) . . . the commitment to remain free . . . from cigarettes . . . becomes stronger and stronger . . . You will not smoke again . . . not even a puff . . . Each time you enter a state of hypnotic relaxation . . . these things will come to your mind . . . just as they do . . . now . . ."

Dissociation from cravings

"Within a hypnotic state . . . your mind will function in such a way as to block from conscious awareness . . . any excessive craving for nicotine . . . Any withdrawal symptoms that occur . . . you will be able to tolerate . . . and they will always pass . . . As you listen to my voice . . . with another part of your mind . . . drifting to another place . . . a pleasant place . . . [*include individual suggestions for dissociation and experiencing a pleasant place*] . . . you may be near a lovely field . . . beautiful flowers . . . or another place . . . as if you were just drifting into such a deep hypnotic state that at times it can seem as if you were in that pleasant place . . . experiencing all of the good feelings that are there . . . perhaps a floating feeling . . . Certainly in that place . . . you will not be bothered by any excessive craving . . . feeling calm and in control . . . any excessive cravings are blocked from conscious awareness . . . as you are there . . ."

Post-hypnotic suggestions

"Each day that passes . . . you will find it easier and easier to remain free from cigarettes . . . free from a substance that can cause so much damage . . . free from a substance that could hurt you or someone you love . . . And as you remain free . . . from cigarettes . . . you will have a sense of satisfaction and accomplishment . . . you will find that you are able to use hypnotic relaxation to sleep very well . . . your sense of smell will improve . . . your sense of taste will improve . . . as you become and as you remain . . . more relaxed . . . Every day . . . you will find an appropriate amount of food to be satisfying . . . you will not overeat . . . you will feel more in control . . . more calm . . . than you have felt in a long time . . . now drifting, more deeply relaxed . . ."

Self-hypnosis

"Your practice of self-hypnosis . . . will be necessary and effective . . . each time you practice self-hypnosis . . . you will be able to enter a very deep state of hypnotic relaxation . . . Notice how relaxed you have become . . . and this will occur again . . . and again . . . as you experience self-hypnosis . . . And within this state of hypnotic relaxation . . . you will find a feeling of control . . . you will be able to drift . . . within your experience . . . to a most pleasant place . . . and while you are there . . . dissociated from any excessive cravings or withdrawal symptoms . . . any excessive craving will just remain outside of conscious awareness and will not bother you . . . The deeper you drift into hypnotic relaxation . . . the less the bother . . . and as you experience self-hypnosis . . . your commitment to remain . . . free . . . from cigarettes will become even stronger. . . . You will find the practice of self-hypnosis to be effective . . . and very satisfying."

Positive imagery for benefits of smoking cessation

"Now . . . you have done very well . . . and now you can see a time in the future . . . a picture comes to your mind . . . soon . . . seeing yourself as a nonsmoker . . . It's a time from now . . . you have remained free from cigarettes . . . you are a nonsmoker . . . you do not smoke cigarettes . . . Notice how you look . . . notice how you are feeling . . . [*here, individualized imagery is introduced, depending on the patient's motivation and perceived benefits*] . . . In the future you will not smoke . . . no matter if times become stressful or difficult . . . you will be able to remain calm . . . use self-hypnosis to maintain control . . . And as you see this time in the future . . . you are a nonsmoker . . . so it will occur."

CASE EXAMPLE

Norma, a 62-year-old woman, was referred by her family practice physician for smoking cessation. She was well-prepared for the visit and had a positive expectancy for hypnotherapy. Her physician had discussed the process of hypnotherapy and encouraged her to set a date to stop smoking. During the clinical interview, the patient revealed that she had smoked for almost 40 years. She initially began smoking because her husband smoked and estimated that she smoked about one pack of cigarettes per day. She had been a widow for 5 years after her husband died of a heart attack, and she lived alone. She described a very close and supportive relationship with her son, daughter-in-law, and grandchildren, who lived in the same town. She stated that her primary reasons for wanting to stop smoking were due to health concerns and to "be around for my family." She described her primary health concern as shortness of breath. She denied previous attempts to stop smoking, and offered that she tended to smoke more when feeling stressed. She denied any particular stresses or pressures in her life, aside from dealing with the loss of her husband. She had no history of treatment for any psychiatric disorders and was in generally good health.

The patient obtained a score of 10 on the Fagerstrom Test of Nicotine Dependency, indicating at least moderate dependency. Her responses to the Contemplation Ladder showed that she was between the conceptual and action phases of readiness to change. Her score on the EHS was 7, indicating a moderate, or average, hypnotic ability.

The patient possessed several strengths that were indicative of a positive prognosis. She was able to identify clear and relevant reasons for stopping smoking. She had good social support from her family and physician. They were in agreement with her plan and strongly wanted her to stop smoking. No one else in her family smoked, so this was also a source of encouragement. She appeared ready to begin making some changes to become a nonsmoker, and her EHS score was in the average range. However, several factors that could potentially influence a negative outcome also had to be considered. These included a chronic history of smoking (40-plus years), a lack of previous quit attempts, and at least a moderate level of dependency, suggesting that she would likely experience withdrawal symptoms upon cessation.

These issues were discussed with the patient, who appeared to have good insight. She set a date to stop smoking at the next appointment. While discussing the process of HRT and specific hypnotic suggestions that would be utilized during therapy, the patient was asked to identify "the most important thing in [her] life at this time." It was discussed that this was important in order to individualize hypnotic suggestions to help her stop smoking. She quickly stated that her great-grandchildren were very important to her. In fact, she stated that they were 6 and 7 years old (a boy and a girl), that they came by every day after school, and that she looked forward to those visits very much. We discussed that this could be very relevant for her efforts to stop smoking. Additionally, the law of dominant affect was explained to her. During this initial session, the patient also agreed that, after she stopped smoking, she would see the great-grandchildren every day . . . unless she smoked a cigarette. To make this commitment emotionally powerful, it was discussed that, if she smoked, she could imagine the words: "Grandma can't see you today . . . because Grandma would rather sit in the house alone and smoke her cigarettes than see the two of you." As she repeated these words, tears began to fall from her eyes. She had truly identified something more important to her than cigarettes, and this could be individualized to increase the impact of hypnotic suggestions to remain a nonsmoker.

This patient did very well. She stopped smoking at the next appointment and discarded all remaining cigarettes, lighters, and ashtrays. She attended eight sessions of HRT and was very compliant with her self-hypnosis practice. At a 6-month follow-up, she had remained abstinent from cigarettes and was very satisfied with her accomplishment and treatment. She stated that she continued to use self-hypnosis to manage stress and to help her go to sleep at night.

CHAPTER 15

Post-Menopausal and Hot Flash Symptoms

There is an accumulating body of research to support the efficacy of hypnotic relaxation therapy (HRT) in the treatment of post-menopausal hot flashes and associated symptoms. This chapter will review the research on HRT for hot flashes. In addition, the clinical application of HRT will be outlined and illustrated with a case study.

EVIDENCE FOR HRT FOR HOT FLASHES

Research from the Mind–Body Medicine Research Laboratory at Baylor University has provided evidence that HRT can reduce both the frequency and severity of hot flashes (Elkins, Fisher, & Johnson, 2012). In addition, there is evidence that HRT is safe and effective, can reduce the interference of hot flashes in daily life, and improve sleep quality.

There is evidence that HRT is safe and effective, can reduce the interference of hot flashes in daily life, and improve sleep quality.

In an initial study, 16 breast cancer survivors were given individual weekly sessions of HRT targeting a decrease in hot flashes. Women in the clinical study recorded hot flashes using daily diaries that provided reports of both the frequency and severity of hot flashes. Hot flash scores, a measure of severity and frequency, were determined by multiplying the daily frequency of hot flashes by their average severity. The results indicated a 70% decrease in hot flash scores at the end of treatment (Elkins, Marcus, Stearns, & Rajab, 2007).

A randomized trial was conducted that compared HRT with a wait-list control in reducing hot flashes and improving sleep quality (Elkins et al., 2008). The participants in the HRT group received five weekly sessions and were instructed in the use of self-hypnosis. The primary outcomes were hot flash scores, sleep quality as measured by the Pittsburg Sleep Quality Index (Buysse, Reynolds, Monk, Berman, & Kupfer, 1989), and ratings of interference with ten different aspects of participants' lives, (i.e., work, social activities, leisure activities, sleep, mood, concentration, relations with others, sexuality, enjoyment of life, overall quality of life) using the Hot Flash Daily Interference Scale (Carpenter, 2001). At the end of treatment, hot flash scores decreased by 68% among the women who received HRT. In addition, HRT resulted in significantly improved sleep quality and reduction in the degree to which hot flashes interfered with daily activities.

HRT resulted in significantly improved sleep quality and reduction in the degree to which hot flashes interfered with daily activities.

More recently, a large clinical trial involving 187 post-menopausal women with moderate to severe hot flashes was conducted. Participants were randomized to five weekly sessions of either clinical hypnosis or structured-attention control. Primary outcomes were hot flash frequency (subjectively and physiologically recorded) and hot flash scores assessed by daily diaries at weeks 2 through 6 and week 12. Secondary outcomes included measures of hot flash–related daily interference, sleep quality, and treatment satisfaction.

In a modified intent-to-treat analysis that included all randomized participants that provided data, reported subjective hot flash frequency from baseline to week 12 showed a mean reduction of 74% for the HRT intervention versus 17% for the control. Mean reduction in the hot flash score was 80.32% for the HRT intervention as compared to 15.38% for the control. At 12-week follow-up, the mean reduction in physiologically monitored hot flashes was 56.86% for HRT and 10% for the control. Secondary outcomes of hot flash–related interference sleep quality and treatment satisfaction were significantly improved compared to control at 12-week follow-up.

GENERAL TREATMENT GUIDELINES

It is important to emphasize that providing HRT for reduction of hot flashes is a process that involves giving the patient information about the intervention, completing an initial hypnotic relaxation induction, individualizing hypnotic suggestions, teaching self-hypnosis, monitoring progress, trouble-shooting as necessary, and targeting efforts at relapse prevention. The clinical interview, case conceptualization, and assessment of hypnotizability can help to guide specifics of treatment as well. The hypnotherapist should be well-trained both in general principles of HRT as well as the specific treatment of hot flashes using HRT. Knowledge of menopause symptoms and hot flashes is recommended. The intervention is not achieved by simply reading a hypnotic induction transcript to the patient.

The patient's practice of self-hypnosis is most important.

The patient's practice of self-hypnosis is most important. Instructions in self-hypnosis are provided, and the patient should be provided

Considerable attention should be given to individualization of hypnotic suggestions to achieve ideal gains.

with a CD recording of hypnotic relaxation induction for reduction of hot flashes (contact the author for ordering information). The patient's compliance and daily practice is necessary. In addition, considerable attention should be given to individualization of hypnotic suggestions to achieve ideal gains. Experience has shown that most women can reduce hot flashes by 40% to 50% in the first three weeks of treatment, and reduction continues during weeks 5, 6, and even 12 with regular practice of self-hypnosis.

INDIVIDUALIZATION OF HYPNOTIC SUGGESTIONS FOR HOT FLASHES

The clinician can gather information about the types of suggestions for coolness that the patient prefers by simply asking about what types of sensations or experiences she believes are associated with coolness and relief from hot flashes. This may include such things as opening a refrigerator door, coolness of walking through snow, sitting under a cold shower, floating on a cloud, or dissociating from the body and walking through a garden where it is cool and comfortable. The following questions/prompts may be helpful in gathering this information and individualizing suggestions:

- What experiences have been helpful in feeling cool?
- In finding comfort, do you prefer coolness, a tingly sensation, or numbness?
- Can you imagine the hot flashes flowing out of your body?
- Can you imagine the hot flash being less intense or reduced by visualizing a light that changes in color or becomes dimmer?
- Can you imagine floating outside your body and going for a walk (in the mountains, in a garden etc.)?
- Would it be alright with you to go back in time, within your mind, to another day and time, when you felt cool and comfortable? When would that time be?
- What type of suggestions help you feel most cool and relaxed?
- Does comfort help you sleep better, do more things, exercise, or improve your quality of life? In what ways?

As information is gathered, the therapist may use this information in giving more individualized suggestions at appropriate times during the following process. The induction begins with eye focus, followed by suggestions for:

- relaxation
- dissociation and deepening
- safe-place imagery and comfort
- reduction in the frequency and intensity of hot flashes
- improved sleep and activities
- practice of self-hypnosis

RECORDING HOT FLASHES

It is also important to monitor the patient's progress. It is recommended that patients keep a diary of the frequency and severity of hot flashes for at least one week before initiating treatment, and then throughout the 5 or more weeks of HRT. The Hot Flash Daily Diary (Figure 15.1) is a well-validated measure, and the hypnotherapist should facilitate a discussion about the patient's experiences with hot flashes through inquiry. This is introduced in a straightforward manner by simply asking questions such as: "How many hot flashes did you have yesterday/last week?" or "How severe were your hot flashes yesterday/last week?" A sample hot flash diary is provided below.

The Hot Flash Daily Diary is a well-validated measure, and the hypnotherapist should facilitate a discussion about the patient's experiences with hot flashes through inquiry.

HOT FLASH DAILY DIARY					
Name:					Date:__________
Date (month/day/ year)	Number of hot flashes today	For each day, write the number of hot flashes that were mild, moderate, severe, or very severe			
		Mild	Moderate	Severe	Very severe
Day 1: / /					
Day 2: / /					
Day 3: / /					
Day 4: / /					
Day 5: / /					
Day 6: / /					
Day 7: / /					
Total number of hot flashes					

Figure 15.1

(continued)

(continued)

Severity Descriptions
MILD: Sensation of heat without sweating.
MODERATE: Sensation of heat with sweating that does not cause you to stop your current activity.
SEVERE: Sensation of intense heat with extreme sweating that causes you to stop your current activity.
VERY SEVERE: Sensation of very extreme heat (boiling eruption), rolling perspiration, and behavioral disturbance.

Figure 15.1

Hot Flash Diary (Adapted from Sloan, et al., 2001)

HYPNOTIC SUGGESTIONS FOR TREATMENT OF HOT FLASHES

The following are standardized hypnotic suggestions that represent an initial transcript following assessment and a hypnotic induction.

Relaxation

"And with each breath, let go of all of the tension and drift so deeply relaxed . . . every muscle and every fiber of your body becoming so deeply relaxed . . . More and more noticing a feeling of "letting go" and becoming so deeply relaxed . . . your thoughts and feelings can become deeper and deeper relaxed with each suggestion that I give you . . . and finding more and more comfort and calm feelings . . . Going so deeply relaxed that it would take too much effort to even try to open your eyelids . . . This is a good feeling that allows you to relax even deeper . . . and as you go deeper relaxed you're drifting into an even deeper level of hypnosis."

Mental imagery and suggestions for coolness

"Now in a moment I am going to ask you to notice some images in your mind . . . You can hear my voice with one part of your mind and with another part of your mind going to a pleasant, peaceful place where you notice and experience everything that is there, every sound, every sight, every sensation of coolness . . . images and scenes that allow you to experience even more comfort and control . . . Going to a place where you find the comfort that you need . . . learning to use hypnosis to remain more comfortable and relaxed . . . every day . . . and here finding a coolness and comfort . . . Now going to a place where it is cool and so comfortable . . . finding that you are in the mountains [*Note: individualized mental imagery for relaxation and coolness may be inserted here and used instead of mountain imagery depending on the patient preference. However, the same phrases for coolness should be used*] . . . it is cool here, in fact there is snow all around . . . the air is very cool and it is pleasant to notice the white snow on the trees and on the ground . . . You might want to take a deep breath of the crisp, cool air . . . and feeling cool waves of comfort flowing over you and through you . . . and feel more refreshed . . . It is the kind of day when the cool air and the cold snow feels very good . . . this is a very beautiful place and perhaps you can see a lake in the distance . . . there is a path before you and you might enjoy walking down that mountain path . . . with every step you take feeling the cool air, the fresh cool . . . feeling the air on your face, your forehead, and a gentle breeze across your ears.

"It is just so pleasant there and just notice the coolness while standing at the top of this snow-covered mountain . . . cool waves of comfort flowing over you and through you . . . And while you are there it is possible that your mind could drift to other times when you have felt such a coolness and comfort . . . perhaps the coolness of standing in front of an air conditioner . . . feeling the cold air . . . or the coolness one could experience when opening a refrigerator or having a cool drink of ice water when one is really thirsty, and feeling the cool water that is clear and clean and so refreshing."

Deepening the hypnotic state and dissociation from hot flashes

"Now it is possible to enter an even deeper state of hypnosis . . . deeper and deeper relaxed . . . now letting all the tension go . . . and as you do, beginning to enter an even deeper level of hypnosis . . . Now as this occurs you may notice a change in sensations . . . this may be a floating sensation . . . a drifting sensation and perhaps just less aware of your body . . . just floating in space . . . your body floating in a feeling of comfort . . . and just so aware of being in that pleasant place where you find coolness and a sense of well-being . . . just noticing a detached feeling . . . floating within feelings of coolness and comfort . . . drifting and floating . . . more and more . . . as your body floats, finding even more comfort. Now as this occurs, finding that it is so natural that your mind blocks from conscious awareness any excessive discomfort . . . and it is possible that you can feel more detached from your body . . . feeling the coolness . . . as you become more relaxed."

Post-hypnotic suggestions

"And as you become more comfortable . . . you will find a sense of being more in control . . . and as this occurs you will find that, more and more, you are able to sleep very well, your feelings of well-being will improve, and your quality of life will improve . . . You will not be bothered by any excessive anxiety, and any hot flashes will become less and less frequent and less severe . . . As time passes, you simply will be less bothered by hot flashes . . . more calm and relaxed and comfortable . . . every day."

Self-hypnosis

"Each time you practice self-hypnosis, you will be able to enter a very deep state of relaxation, just as deep as you are today . . . and within this relaxed state, you will find a feeling of control . . . You will be able to become so deeply relaxed that you will become very comfortable, and within this relaxed state, you will be able to experience coolness . . . coolness and comfort flowing over you and through you . . . you will find a kind of strength from your practice of self-hypnosis."

Positive imagery for the future

"Now, seeing yourself in the future in a way and a place where you experience that coolness and calm feelings so that you can just imagine a time in the future when you are no longer bothered by hot flashes . . . No matter if times become stressful or difficult . . . you will be able to remain calm and relaxed, both now and in the future."

CASE EXAMPLE

The patient, Natasha, was a 42-year-old female. She was married and had a 6-year-old daughter. Diagnosed with breast cancer at age 40, she subsequently went through the course of treatment that included a lumpectomy, lymph node removal, chemotherapy, and radiation. During this time, she was started on tamoxifen and began having hot flashes. After she completed five sessions of HRT, she agreed to return for an additional appointment to discuss her experiences and complete an additional session. During this follow-up visit, she was asked to describe her hot flashes when they first began.

Patient: *They were at first really, really bad . . . you know, sweats and things along those lines. They tapered off, but they still woke me up two, three, four times a night depending on severity. I'd have to do everything from getting up, walking around the house, getting a cold glass of water, to the worst-case scenario, getting undressed and getting in the shower. That was only a couple of times, thankfully, but most of the time when I'd have a hot flash, I'd have to completely uncover from the bed and sometimes get undressed.*

Therapist: *So we rate those hot flashes from mild, to moderate, to severe.*

Patient: *That would be a moderate to severe. And in the past 6 months, I would rate them moderate on your scale. I've been averaging the last 6 months three to four a night, waking up every hour-and-a-half, two hours. And wearing very little, if anything, to bed just because I know I'll have to uncover and get cooled off. During the day, they don't bother me nearly as much. I don't notice them. I think it's because I'm so busy with my job and what I'm doing. The fact that my building is very cold helps the fact, but the biggest problem was the nighttime because it disturbed my sleep and I just didn't get enough sleep.*

Therapist: *So they were really pretty bad . . .*

Patient: (nods) *Right.*

Therapist: *On the scale, we ask you to rate how much the hot flashes interfere with your life, and I guess, at that point, you would have rated them as interfering a good bit.*

Patient: (nods) *A good bit. It's when you have your full-time job and a 6-year old and your household and your marriage to keep up, if you don't get enough sleep I think it goes down the tubes pretty quickly. So, yeah, irritability was high, and I just couldn't get enough sleep, enough of a long period of sleep and rest. I had an appointment with my oncologist and explained to him that I had a problem with my hot flashes and I wanted to know what I could do with them. Well, because my tumor was estrogen- and progesterone-positive, hormones are out of the question, so my other options were a low-dose antidepressant or this hypnosis. And so I was referred to the hypnotic relaxation therapy and got to see you.*

Therapist: *OK, so let's talk a little bit about what your experience has been. Could you just sort of describe how it went for you and what you found helpful, and just talk a little bit about it?*

Patient: *The first session, um, we talked about* [*severity*] *and how many I was having, night and day, and I did a week-long diary on that. And it kind of surprised me to realize how many I* [*was*] *having because I really didn't think about them throughout the day; it was mainly the ones through the night . . . and when I sat down and thought about and counted how many I was having throughout the day, I didn't realize how many I was having. The first session was, like I said, kind of an enlightenment, because it was so much like the mental imaging, just a different slant. That was actually quite nice and enjoyable. I came out of the session quite relaxed and wished I didn't have to drive home, but that's just how that one goes* (laughs). *The CD and the headphones that you gave me were extremely helpful. I did it every night after my child was in bed, and hopefully, if my husband wasn't snoring too loud, I would lay in bed and run through the tape and then go to sleep immediately afterward. And*

I did it every night. Occasionally, I was interrupted. As you know, "mommy radar" can be on, and if your daughter calls out for you, I had to get up and go take care of her. But 9 times out of 10 I made it all the way through the CD without any interruptions.

Therapist: *That's good.*

Patient: *I didn't really see a reduction, or at least I didn't really notice a big reduction in severity and in numbers, until probably the second or third week. I still have them, but they aren't very noticeable. For a lack of a better description, I might wake up one or two times in a night, but it's hard to tell whether it's because I was having a hot flash or whether I just needed to go to the bathroom.*

Therapist: *So that's a good change.*

Patient: *Yes, it is.*

Therapist: *Let's talk a little bit about the mental imagery part, because I know we've used a variety of suggestions. Would you please talk a little bit about what you found effective, for you personally? What kind of imagery or what kinds of suggestions did you find that have helped?*

Patient: *Personally, for myself, it is a combination of things. I look back to a very good memory where I was in a quiet, calm situation. In my case, it was the lake in Michigan, with my family around me, the grass, the breeze coming in off the lake. Something that I can see vividly in my mind because it's something that's reinforced every year because we go up there every year. That and watching my daughter play in the water is very relaxing and very cool. And that was one of them. Of course, the other is a more severe image—the 5-foot high snow drift on the window . . . in Michigan, and, of course, that is very, very cold. But there again, the sparkling snow, the ice on the lake, the kids playing in a snowball fight, building a snowman, you know, that's all . . . it's not only a scene of cold, it's a scene of happiness and enjoyment and contentedness . . . but I tend to focus on the one with the water.*

Therapist: *What makes this stand out to you?*

Patient: *Well, it's something that I have a very strong memory of, that when I close my eyes, I can picture myself sitting in that lounge, watching my daughter play in the water. And I can almost feel the cool breeze wafting across the lake . . . and the trees, the maple leaves, the quiet, that, to me, worked really well.*

Therapist: *It's the best of mind–body medicine when you can relate to it personally in that way and find it comforting.*

Patient: *Especially something that you have experienced.*

Therapist: *Yes.*

Patient: *It's a little harder to do something that's a bit more abstract, I think.*

Therapist: *And I think you'd like the specific imagery . . . of being at the lake, a particular place.*

Patient: *Yes, that reinforces and focuses my memory and works.*

Therapist: *Very good. Well, you've done very well. Just sort of get comfortable in the chair, and we'll go through an induction.*

Patient: (leans back in chair) *OK.*

Therapist: *It won't be quite as long as what we've done before, but we're going to follow the same types of suggestions.*

Patient: *OK.*

Therapist: *If you would, just begin as you would at home or during a session by focusing your attention on a spot on the wall or the ceiling. Just setting everything else aside and concentrate so intently that other things begin to fade into the background. Good. Now, if you would just take a deep breath of air, hold as you exhale, allow your eyelids to close.*

Patient: (eyelids close)

Therapist: *Very good . . . and allow your body to relax. Just noticing more and more a feeling of drifting . . . into a deep . . . and comfortable . . . relaxed state. And now just taking another deep breath of air . . . hold it . . . and as you exhale this time, going into a very deep state of relaxation . . . so that each time you breathe out, drifting deeper and deeper relaxed . . . letting all the tension go . . . every muscle, every fiber of your body becoming completely calm and relaxed . . . And as this occurs within yourself, finding a feeling of coolness and comfort . . . feeling safe and secure . . . a calm, peaceful feeling, in which nothing bothers and nothing interferes as you drift into a deeper level of hypnosis. From time to time you may notice a drifting or floating sensation . . . drifting and floating . . . as if you were floating on a cloud . . . and becoming more and more relaxed . . . As you hear my voice, count from the number 1 to 10 . . . with each number, finding yourself drifting into a deeper . . . a more relaxed state . . . so that you can hear my voice with a part of your mind . . . and with another part of your mind becoming completely absorbed in that place where you feel safe, cool, and comfortable . . . And as you do, that wave of relaxation can spread . . . a wave of relaxation spreading from the top of your head to your feet and drifting into a deeper level of hypnosis . . . 1 . . . Number 1 . . . deeper and deeper relaxed. Letting all the tension go from your forehead, face, neck, and shoulders. Nothing bothers; nothing interferes with this relaxed feeling . . . 2 . . . More deeply relaxed now . . . your neck can go limp,* *jaw can go slack, as all the tension drifts away . . . 3 . . . Deeply calm . . . perhaps noticing special colors associated with coolness and calmness . . . blue, soft pastel colors, just noticing . . . perhaps the sight of glistening white snow . . . or sounds, sounds like the rustle of cool wind . . . just a gentle breeze, or a cool fountain . . . perhaps the sound of music, your favorite music, that allows you to relax deeper and define coolness and comfort as all the tension just drifts away . . . flowing out through your arms, down into the hands, out the fingertips . . . 4 . . . your upper back, and lower back, relaxed . . . filled with comfort . . . and letting that become more complete with every breath of air, relaxed . . . 5 . . . Halfway there. . . . deeper and deeper relaxed . . . all the tension drifts away . . . and more at peace, more at peace within yourself . . . and more at peace with everyone and everything around you . . . every day . . . 6 . . . even more calm, back and chest, stomach and legs, relax . . . letting all the tension go . . . and going deeper within yourself to find more comfort . . . 7 . . . Arms, legs, and feet become so deeply relaxed, as that wave of relaxation spreads down into your legs and feet . . . a cool, relaxed feeling . . . a pleasant feeling . . . and with this comes a sense of control and comfort, deeper and deeper relaxed . . . 8 . . . even more calm and at ease. Nothing bothers, nothing disturbs . . . 9 . . . Almost there . . . just letting any tension that's remained . . . letting it go now . . . 10 . . . All the way there, deeply, comfortably relaxed. And now, in a moment, I'm going to ask you to have some experiences of coolness and comfort so that as you can hear my voice with a part of your mind, with another part of your mind going to a place where you experience the sensations of coolness . . . images and scenes, that allow you to experience control . . . so that your hot flashes will become less and less . . . less frequent . . . less and less severe . . . seeing a door in front of you, a special door, that will lead you to a place where you would really like to be . . . Today as you walk through that door, you will find, as you can hear my voice with a part of your mind, that you will be at a beautiful lake in Michigan . . . it will be just the kind of day you would like to experience . . . Able to see that beautiful lake now . . . as you walk through that special door, finding that you are near that beautiful lake . . . And as you walk down toward the lake, there is a cool breeze that just flows around you and through you, filling you with comfort and coolness and feelings of control. I don't know if you have shoes on, but the grass is soft and cool . . . and up ahead, there is a chaise lounge, a chair, and soon finding that you're sitting in that chair . . . and it's the most pleasant place to be . . . As you look out across the lake, you might notice that the water is crystal clear, very peaceful. . . . you might see an island out in the lake . . . and the water is so still and peaceful. It's very blue . . . and the trees are reflected like a mirror around the lake . . . you might want to take a deep breath of that cool, crisp air and feel more refreshed and calm. And it's the kind of day when the coolness, even the cold air, feels very good. And there are sounds there today, perhaps the sounds of people that you love talking to . . . children playing. Just noticing all the wonderful and pleasant things that are there and feeling the cool fresh air, the cool feeling of the air across your face and forehead, a gentle breeze, across your ears, just pleasant to be there . . . just noticing, watching, seeing everything that's there, every feeling of comfort and it's the kind of place a person could spend quite a bit of time . . . you might even enjoy watching a sunset from that place . . . You might have a cool drink sitting beside you with ice . . . it tastes so good and you feel really thirsty and it's just the right thing to have, very refreshing. And now, just drifting a little deeper relaxed . . . going into such a deep hypnotic state that as you practice hypnosis, perhaps already noticing your sense of well-being improves . . . as you practice hypnosis more and more, you will be able to sleep very well . . . you will not be bothered by any excessive anxiety, any hot flashes will become less and less frequent, less severe . . . As time passes, you simply will be less bothered by hot flashes . . . and more calm and more relaxed and more comfortable every day and every night . . . Each time you practice self-hypnosis you will be able to enter a very deep relaxed state . . . within this relaxed state, you will find feelings of control . . . you will become so deeply relaxed that you will become quite comfortable . . . and in this relaxed state, you will be able to experience coolness . . . waves of coolness and comfort, flowing over you and through you . . . feeling so cool and comfortable each time you practice self-hypnosis . . . and you will find a kind of strength from your practice of self-hypnosis . . . Now, just noticing everything that is there . . . that beautiful lake in Michigan, and it is a place you may return to time and time again . . . and finding all of the comfort and knowledge, everything that you need in that place . . . so that in a few moments with comfort and coolness and confidence, beginning to return back to this place in the present time. In a few moments, returning to conscious alertness, in your own time, at your own pace, in your own way . . . in a way that just feels about right for you today . . . feeling good and normal, good normal sensations in every way, as you return to conscious alertness . . . And returning to conscious alertness as I count from the numbers 4 to 1. Returning in a way that just feels good for you, as I count, 4, beginning to return to conscious alertness . . . 3, 2 . . . and coming all the way back . . . just in a way that is comfortable and gentle and at ease . . . letting your eyelids open . . . 1 . . . that's right.*

Patient: (slowly opens eyes)

Therapist: *Take your time.*

Patient: *I could stay here and go to sleep right now.*

Therapist: *It's a good feeling, isn't it?*

Patient: *An excellent feeling.*

Therapist: *Good. Were you able to experience going to the lake?*

Patient: *Oh yes, this time the texture of the grass was really . . . I really discerned it . . . and like some of the grasses we have here in Texas, it's very fine . . . it'll almost tickle your feet when you walk over it.*

Therapist: *Yeah.*

Patient: *Yeah. It's not hard to slip back to that place because it's just a really nice place to be.*

Therapist: *And I think as you've practiced this you're able to get back to that fairly quickly.*

Patient: (nods) *Uh huh.*

Therapist: *You know just what you're doing and you know just how to do it.*

CHAPTER 16

Anxiety Management

Anxiety disorders are highly prevalent, affecting approximately 40 million adults in the United States (Kessler, Chiu, Demler, & Walters, 2005). The average age of onset is 11 years old, and women are 60% more likely than men to experience an anxiety disorder at some time in their lifetime (Kessler, et al., 2005). Anxiety is characterized by feelings of fearfulness, tension, uncertainty, and the irrational perception of threat. Physical symptoms may include racing heart rate, dizziness, sweaty palms, jitteriness, muscle tightness, elevated blood pressure, or nausea. Anxiety can emerge as a chronic condition, and can take many forms. Thus, treatment will vary depending upon the patient's symptoms and experience of anxiety. It should come as no surprise that hypnotic relaxation therapy (HRT) is beneficial in the treatment of anxiety. Most effective interventions for anxiety management, whether they are psychological or pharmacological, induce a state of relaxation as a core mediator of their effectiveness. HRT can be used to teach patients relaxation, reinforce coping skills, and provide therapeutic experiences at the unconscious/experiential level of awareness. Hypnotic relaxation can be integrated with cognitive-behavioral approaches, facilitate mental imagery, and, at times, it can effectively provide a brief intervention for anxiety. Along with a transcript, a case example of a patient with a dental phobia that was effectively treated for anxiety management will be given at the end of this chapter.

It should come as no surprise that HRT is beneficial in the treatment of anxiety.

HRT can be used to teach patients relaxation, reinforce coping skills, and provide therapeutic experiences at the unconscious/experiential level of awareness.

ASSESSMENT AND CASE CONCEPTUALIZATION OF ANXIETY PROBLEMS

The case conceptualization should include differential diagnosis and consideration of physical, social, and psychological factors that may be contributing to the patient's anxiety. Social factors may include social supports or any particular stresses related to social interactions. Physical factors that warrant review include any evidence of thyroid problems, transient ischemic attacks, hyperventilation, Vitamin B2 deficiency, or hypoglycemia. Psychological factors include the patient's beliefs and cognitions related to his or her fear and symptoms. Attention should be given to history, key events related to the anxiety disorder, and factors that may be contributing to maintaining the fear. Interview questions that may be helpful in this regard are:

- Would you please tell me about when you first began to notice the anxiety?
- Has the anxiety gotten better or worse over time?
- What kinds of thoughts go through your mind when you feel anxious?
- What do you do when you feel anxious?
- Do you avoid any situations because of the anxiety?
- What things do you do to try to reduce anxiety?
- How easy is it for you to relax?
- What symptoms do you have that indicate you have a problem with anxiety?

CONSCIOUS/RATIONAL VERSUS UNCONSCIOUS/EXPERIENTIAL PROCESSING OF THREAT

It is also recommended that the patient's experiential representations of anxiety be explored. Anxiety is closely related to the perception of threat. The threat may be consciously perceived, or it may be symbolic. For example, a man developed a fear of driving across bridges and began to avoid them. Not surprisingly, he had to drive much longer distances to avoid them. He described feeling intense anxiety, feeling closed in, and as if "something bad were going to happen" when driving across the bridge. However, he had no previous history of any anxiety disorder and there had not been any traumatic event on the bridge. During the clinical interview, he revealed that his first episode of anxiety occurred when he had to drive across a long bridge on his way to talk with his divorce attorney. He stated that the divorce was very difficult and involved numerous areas of conflict. It became clear that within this patient's unconscious, the bridge represented several things to him, such as: "heading into conflict" and "crossing over from peace to trouble." It was important that these representations of the bridge, whether rational or not, were addressed in treatment.

HYPNOTIZABILITY AND ANXIETY

Assessment of the patient's hypnotizability can be helpful, and evidence suggests that some patients who develop anxiety disorders may be more hypnotizable. For example, Frankel and Orne (1976) found that patients with phobias were significantly more hypnotizable than a control group, and those with multiple phobias generally scored higher on standard measures of hypnotizability compared to those with a single phobia. These findings have been replicated, adding to the confidence in this association (Foenander, Burrows, Gerschman, & Horne, 1980; Gerschman, Burrows, & Reade, 1987; Gerschman, Burrows, Reade, & Foeander, 1979; John, Hollander, & Perry, 1983; Kelly, 1984).

HYPNOTIC RELAXATION AND COGNITIVE–BEHAVIORAL THERAPY

There is considerable evidence in favor of cognitive-behavioral therapy (CBT) for treatment of anxiety disorders (Barlow, 2002; Chambless & Ollendick, 2001). For example, several meta-analysis studies have pointed to the superiority of CBT for treatment of generalized anxiety disorder (Borkovec & Whisman, 1996; Gould, Otto, Pollack, & Yap, 1997; Weston & Morrison, 2001). In addition, CBT interventions have been shown to be effective in treatment of social phobia (Federoff & Taylor, 2001; Feske & Chambless, 1995) and panic attacks (Deacon & Abramovitz, 2004).

The methods used in CBT, namely changing underlying cognitions, relaxation-based interventions, imagery, and exposure therapy, are very complementary with HRT. The primary objective of therapy according to HRT is to produce positive changes in the experiential system. There are three basic ways this can be accomplished (Epstein, 1994). First, the rational system can be used to influence the experiential system, as is done in cognitive restructuring and disputing irrational (conscious) beliefs. Second, real-life experiences (e.g., exposure therapy) within a therapeutic relationship can alter unconscious/experiential processing. Third, the experiential system can be positively changed by communication that uses its own language (e.g., fantasy, imagery, narrative), as is done in imaginable exposure, hypnotic suggestion, and hypnotic relaxation induction.

The primary objective of therapy according to HRT is to produce positive changes in the experiential system.

HYPNOTIC SUGGESTIONS FOR ANXIETY MANAGEMENT

One study has provided evidence that integrating hypnotic induction and suggestions can enhance CBT. Schoenberger, Kirsch, Gearan, Montgomery, and Pastyrnak (1997) randomized individuals with public speaking anxiety to one of three conditions: (1) CBT involving cognitive restructuring, exposure, and relaxation training; (2) CBT (identical) but with hypnotic induction and suggestions; or (3) no treatment. Both active treatments were found to be more effective than no treatment; however, those that receive CBT in conjunction with hypnotherapy had a reduction in anxiety more quickly than those who received CBT alone. Examples of HRT and hypnotic suggestions are provided below.

Cognitive restructuring

"As you enter a deeper hypnotic state, it can occur to you that there are different ways of knowing. You know, in an objective manner, that your anxiety in social situations and public speaking has been related to the irrational belief that it would be awful to be judged negatively, and fearing being judged has only led to more anxiety . . . And you know . . . consciously . . . that being judged has no real threat . . . you can stand it . . . it can be accepted . . . it is OK to not have the approval of everyone . . . But today, coming to an understanding and knowing . . . that you *feel* in your heart . . . because if the heart is at peace . . . then the emotions are calm . . . There was young a boy . . . who was afraid . . . he was on a baseball team . . . but he was afraid to go up to bat . . . he thought, 'everyone is looking at me' . . . 'they will laugh at me' . . . 'this is awful' . . . In fact, when he went to bat he could hear the other team taunting him . . . judging him . . . he thought 'I have to be perfect . . . I have to hit a home run every time . . . or I can't bat' . . . and of course he knew he could not hit a home run every time . . . He was anxious . . . you could feel for him . . . but there was a solution . . . he had to accept being judged . . . and accept being taunted . . . and accept even swinging and missing . . . while taking his turn at bat . . . and every time . . . getting better and better . . . And soon he knew by feeling it was true . . . that the best thing was to have fun . . . and being judged was OK . . . and as you can see this . . . the same is true for you . . . Take your turn at bat . . . let them judge . . . it is OK . . . in fact . . . it is part of the game . . . of life . . . not just baseball."

Deepening relaxation

"As you experience relaxation . . . a deep state of hypnotic relaxation . . . you are learning through this experience . . . just how deeply relaxed you can become . . . physically relaxed . . . mentally relaxed . . . And in the future you will be able to go just as deeply relaxed as you choose . . . at that time . . . you will need only to find a place and time . . . where you can become absorbed in the feelings of calmness . . . sit comfortably . . . take a deep breath of air . . . and as you close your eyes . . . the feelings of relaxation will begin to occur . . . Notice these feelings . . . of relaxation . . . now . . . as they are important to you . . . you are learning a kind of self-control . . . able to become deeply relaxed . . . when it is important for you . . . and this will be a source of positive control . . . giving you greater control of your feelings."

Visualization and exposure therapy

"The fear of public speaking is something you have decided to overcome . . . and this will occur . . . by doing the very thing you have avoided . . . in the past . . . but not now . . . public speaking . . . Today,

I will soon ask you to visualize speaking to a group of people . . . to engage in this fantasy . . . as I suggest it to you . . . deeply engaged . . . so much that it will be just as if you were giving the speech . . . the effect will be the same . . . and you will give the speech while you are calm, relaxed, and at ease . . . So identifying the topic of your speech . . . when you know it, nodding your head, yes . . . very good . . . Now you can see the podium at the front of the classroom . . . do you see it? . . . good . . . Now look at the room . . . about how many people are there in the audience? . . . about 20 . . . very good . . . Now walking up to the podium . . . very calm . . . deeply relaxed . . . let the relaxation become a little more complete . . . as you are soon at the podium . . . Calmly . . . take your time to spread out your notes . . . look at the audience . . . you might want to smile . . . this is going to be fun . . . And soon you are speaking . . . I am going to be silent for a few moments . . . as you give your speech . . . It is a short speech . . . but it is a good one . . . *(pause)* and now there is the applause . . . it is good . . . .soon someone will be shaking your hand . . . walking to the side of the room . . . job well done . . . each time you speak in public . . . it will become easier and easier . . ."

Mindfulness suggestions

"Within this hypnotic state . . . it is possible to relate to your thoughts in a different way . . . observing them . . . without judging them . . . without struggling . . . or trying to change them . . . they are just thoughts . . . As you are deeply relaxed . . . you can observe the thoughts . . . and just watch them float on by . . . Even if it is a negative thought . . . it can be observed . . . the way you could imagine a river . . . and there are some leaves on the surface of the river . . . they float on by . . . one of the leaves . . . may have the thought . . . 'I have to be perfect' . . . watch it just float on by . . . it is just a thought . . . or 'I can't stand rejection' . . . if it is written on one of the leaves . . . it floats on by . . . floats away . . . accepting each thought . . . for what it is . . . They are thoughts . . . but they are not you . . . you can observe them . . . no need to struggle with them . . . thoughts always pass . . . if we allow them."

Post-hypnotic suggestion

Remaining deeply relaxed . . . and notice just how calm and relaxed you have become . . . and it will be possible to return to this deeply relaxed state . . . quickly and easily . . . an association can be made . . . a cue . . . that signals . . . a response . . . to feel . . . calmness . . . Now, in the future . . . a simple gesture . . . of placing your right hand . . . your thumb and first finger . . . together on your right earlobe . . . this will serve as a cue . . . to experience calmness . . . this feeling and action . . . will occur together . . . Now take your right hand . . . the thumb and first finger . . . and touch the earlobe . . . and as you do . . . let all the tension go . . . Very good . . . relaxing deeply . . . so calm . . . and as you feel the calmness . . . the hand can return to the arm of the chair . . . easily and relaxed . . . a cue for calmness . . . and as relaxed as you need to be . . . Now and in the future . . . you will find . . . that you are more confident . . . more accepting of yourself . . . really liking . . . you . . . The experience of hypnotic relaxation . . . will have a greater and greater impact . . . on how you feel . . . everyday . . . You will be calmer and more at ease . . . in social situations . . . public speaking . . . more calm and more confident . . . with each day that passes . . . and each experience with your cognitive therapy and hypnotic relaxation therapy . . . these things will happen . . . more and more."

CASE EXAMPLE: DENTAL ANXIETY

The following transcript is of an HRT session with Rebekah, a 27-year-old married woman with a history of dental anxiety. The patient's anxiety had been severe, and she had avoided going to a dentist for many years. However, she now needed to have some dental work done and was motivated to overcome her fear. She scored 9 on the EHS and was seen for four sessions. She enjoyed snorkeling and had a pleasant memory of a vacation in Cozumel, and this was used as the bases for imagery and suggestions for relaxation and control. The following is the second session.

Therapist: *You need to overcome the dental anxiety, to be calm and in control when going to the dentist.*

Patient: *Yes . . . I agree.* (nodding) *I have just always been so anxious.*

Therapist: *Well, I want to review with you what we will do today to help you reduce the anxiety.*

Patient: *OK.*

Therapist: *What I thought I would do is just begin with an induction by having you focus on a spot, as we've done before; then suggestions for relaxation, and heaviness. Just a heavy feeling. So I might say, "As you notice this heavy feeling, nod your head yes."*

Patient: *OK.*

Therapist: *Then we would go on and I will give you a suggestion for arm levitation. And your arm floats up. OK. And then, what I would talk about is that you are going to have some dental work done . . . cleaning your teeth, and as that's being done, you can just become absorbed in going to Cozumel. And you're going to go snorkeling while you're there. And just become very absorbed in that. Sound OK so far?*

Patient: *Uh huh* (nodding).

Therapist: *Then I'll give you some suggestions that whenever you feel any sensations related to cleaning your teeth, this will feel comfortable, and this will symbolize and mean that you are taking good care of yourself. And these will be good feelings.*

Patient: *OK.*

Therapist: *In other words, you know, a person feels something . . . what does it mean? OK . . . it can now mean something very good and calming . . . and positive.*

Patient: *OK, that sounds great.*

Therapist: *And then from there, we'll go on to some more relaxation and I'll give you a post-hypnotic suggestion for self-hypnosis, in which I'll just say, "In the future you'll be able to practice self-hypnosis. You need only to roll your eyes upward, focus on a spot, take a deep breath, eyelids closed, relax, and go back to Cozumel."*

Patient: *Cool, that's fine with me.* (nodding)

Therapist: *Anything you want to change, or you know . . .*

Patient: *Makes sense to me. I mean. . . .* (laughing) *I'm just going. . . .* (shrugs shoulders)

Therapist: *That sounds alright?* (both laughing)

Patient: *I'm ready.*

Therapist: *Now this chair you're in . . . this is a recliner. Would you be more comfortable just really reclining?*

Patient: *Sure* (adjusts chair to reclined position).

Therapist: *Great. Go ahead and just push back in the chair, and that's just wonderful. And what I would like for you to do then is . . . do you like to have your glasses on, or would you like to take them off?*

Patient: *It doesn't matter.*

Therapist: *Would you probably have them on when you go to the dentist, or . . .*

Patient: *Probably.*

Therapist: *Let's leave them on then. Alright, if you would just go ahead and roll your eyes upward . . . that's just perfect. And I'd like for you to concentrate on keeping your eyes in that rolled-up position as you focus your attention. Good. Concentrate so that other things begin to fade into the background . . . and as they do, as you notice that occurring, just taking a deep, deep, deep* *breath of air . . . hold the air . . . hold. . . . hold . . . hold . . . and as you exhale, allowing a heaviness to come over the eyelids, the eyelids begin to close . . . close . . . and just allow the eyelids to close . . . deeply relaxed . . . So that somehow, with each breath of air you breathe out, drifting into a very deep level of relaxation as if there were a kind of wave of relaxation spreading over you . . . across your forehead . . . These muscles begin to relax across your face . . . your neck . . . deeper and deeper relaxed . . . this wave of relaxation spreads down into your shoulders, your jaw and your shoulders . . . your teeth may become slightly parted as your jaw hangs like a hinge . . . and this feeling of deep relaxation spreads into your shoulders and your arms . . . perhaps already you've noticed that your breathing has become a little slower . . . a little deeper. Just a very good feeling; a deep relaxation . . . a very good feeling that everything's alright, and that everything's going to be alright . . . Calm and relaxed . . . and as you become . . . and as you remain . . . deeply relaxed, so drifting into a deeper level of trance . . . in which you will be able to experience and accomplish all of the things that you would like to experience . . . and accomplish with a feeling of control . . . Drifting deeper now . . . even more deeply relaxed as that wave of relaxation spreads through . . . across the muscles of your back. . . . your chest, your stomach . . . legs and feet . . . and sinking way down into the cushions of the chair . . . And as you do, noticing a heaviness . . . a heavy feeling in your right leg . . . as you notice this heavy feeling in your right leg, just nodding your head yes.*

Patient: (nods yes)

Therapist: *That's right . . . this heavy feeling is a feeling of relaxation and it is a good feeling and drifting even further . . . more completely and soundly relaxed . . . In a moment, I'm going to touch the wrist of your left hand, and as I do, a light feeling, a weightless feeling can come over this hand . . . the hand can become light and weightless so that it just begins to float . . . drifting and floating, the way a helium-filled balloon just floats and drifts . . . and you really don't have to do anything consciously . . . just drifting even more relaxed. That wave of relaxation and calmness across your head . . . and shoulders . . . neck . . . back . . . and legs . . . deeper . . . and deeper relaxed . . . and as I touch this wrist, it begins to float up . . . up . . . up . . . That's right . . . and just letting it float wherever it wants to go . . . calm and relaxed . . . so that in a moment, as I touch this hand . . . this wrist, again, a heaviness begins to come over it, and as the hand begins to become heavy, it begins to drift back down toward the arm of the chair . . . coming to rest comfortably as it drifts down, so you begin to drift into an even deeper level of trance. Touching the wrist . . . the hand now;*

it floats down, heavier and heavier . . . and just placing it in that comfortable place . . . and that comfort that is experienced in the hand can be experienced in the arm . . . and the comfort in the arm can be experienced in every part of your body . . . your chest . . . your neck . . . your throat . . . your mouth . . . arms and legs . . . back and shoulders. Because there is this matter of taking care of yourself . . . going to the dentist, and sitting in the dental chair and resting and feeling comfortable . . . of having the necessary and important dental work, the examination and cleaning of your teeth, and experiencing this in a comfortable way so that you can just feel soooo relaxed as that occurs . . . very comfortable . . . a positive, good experience because this is a part of taking good care of yourself, knowing that you deserve to take good care of yourself . . . so that as with one part of your mind, able to just see yourself, knowing the feeling of sitting in the dental chair, that your dentist will be with you soon; able to have the examination procedure, a good cleaning of your teeth done . . . As with another part of your mind, going back to Cozumel, seeing everything that you see there, and experiencing everything there . . . because going to Cozumel is a time and place where you just feel very good, and very relaxed, and very happy . . . and it is the kind of day where it is warm, and feeling the sunshine feels good . . . and able to breathe fresh sea air, and look along the sandy beach . . . and today, you're going to go snorkeling . . . something that you've looked forward to and something that you enjoy so much . . . and whenever you're there . . . whenever you can just really feel the warmth of the sunshine, and are able to see all the things that are there in Cozamel, just nodding your head yes, so that I'll know that you are there.

Patient: (nodding yes)

Therapist: *Good. And as you're ready to go snorkeling . . . just getting into the water and placing the mouthpiece in your mouth . . . Pretty soon you're going to be seeing all the fish . . . all the different colors and the coral . . . and as you begin snorkeling, just becoming absorbed, and enjoying going snorkeling and looking at the different colors . . . the coral . . . the different fish . . . there are some interesting things, aren't there? . . . surprising things, the sea discovered . . . and so much fun . . . just to be able to have such a wonderful experience . . . And as you are there in Cozumel and going snorkeling, you really don't have to pay very much attention at all to what's happening as your dentist begins the examination of your teeth . . . you can just feel sooo relaxed . . . and become even more relaxed and seeing everything, going snorkeling in Cozumel . . . so much fun, because everything's alright . . . And even as you begin to feel the sensations as your teeth . . . are getting clean, this is just such a good thing of taking care of yourself . . . each time you feel* *any of these sensations, they will mean that you are taking good care of yourself, good care of your teeth, in a healthy way . . . in a positive way . . . These sensations will mean that you are healthy and that you have a sense of caring about yourself . . . enough to take good care of yourself . . . As you become more absorbed in seeing everything before you, the different colors . . . as you are snorkeling, you may even notice a kind of numbness around your gums and your teeth. Not an extreme numbness . . . but a comfortable numbness . . . able to block from conscious awareness any unnecessary or unpleasant sensations and drifting even deeper . . . more profoundly and more completely relaxed . . . and so drifting even more relaxed now. All the tension going from your forehead . . . your neck and your shoulders . . . arms and legs . . . muscles of your jaw, tongue, and neck . . . your legs and feet . . . deeply, deeply relaxed . . . deeper and deeper with every comfortable breath of air . . . That's right . . . just breathe out . . . comfortable and at ease . . . and you will find the dental visit, the dental exam and procedures . . . the cleaning of your teeth to be a wonderful and good experience . . . You will find a positive experience . . . You will feel comfortable and more in control than you have felt in quite a long time . . . You're just going to enjoy everything that happens as you go back to Cozumel, so that in the future, each time you wish to have this feeling of control and calmness, you will be able to practice self-hypnosis. You will be able to practice self-hypnosis . . . as I give you this post-hypnotic suggestion, in the future, each time you wish to practice self-hypnosis, you'll need only to roll your eyes upward and focus on a point . . . become absorbed in where you are looking, take a deep breath of air, and as you exhale, eyelids close . . . and drifting deeply relaxed with each breath of air . . . and then, with a part of your mind, becoming very absorbed in going snorkeling in Cozumel . . . And you will find a kind of strength, and a control in this. You will each time be able to return to conscious alertness . . . comfortably, in your own time, your own pace and your own way, just by counting the numbers 1 to 4 . . . But for now . . . drifting deeper . . . more deeply relaxed . . . drifting way. . . . way. . . . deeper . . . into an even deeper level of trance. Calm . . . and peaceful . . . at ease . . . and these are the feelings that you will have when you see your dentist at the examination, throughout the cleaning of your teeth . . . calm and peaceful. In practicing self-hypnosis, you'll need only to roll your eyes upward, focus, take a deep breath of air . . . eyelids close, drift . . . deeply relaxed, and go back to Cozumel. In just a moment, returning to conscious alertness . . . as I count from the numbers 1 to 4 . . . 1 . . . 2 . . . gently in your own time . . . your own pace . . . returning to conscious alertness. . . . 3 . . . that's right . . . and 4 . . . yes . . . take your time.*

Patient: (opens eyes)

Therapist: *What are you most aware of right now?*

Patient: *Uhhh . . . how heavy my hands feel* (laughs lightly)

Therapist: *How are you feeling emotionally, and just within yourself right now?*

Patient: *Ummm. . . . fine. Relaxed.*

Therapist: *Good. What did you see at Cozumel?*

Patient: *The place at the hotel where we stayed. They have jet skis right along the beach, and they have, uh. . . . the beach chairs and things.*

Therapist: *Oh, that sounds wonderful.*

Patient: *And the water's so blue.*

Therapist: *You could see the blue water today?*

Patient: *Yeah . . . when I saw it, it was like being there. I think I can do this when I go to the dentist. The session today was kinda weird, but it's a good feeling. You know, like if something were to, you know. . . . be really be stressing you, it would be a good way to take yourself away from it . . . just be in Cozumel.*

Therapist: *Yeah . . . that's right. That's right. I know you're going to have just a really good experience, going to your dentist.*

Patient: *Probably . . . I will!*

Therapist: *Everything's going to go really smoothly. You have the control . . . the ability to do this, and you've already had so much success; and it's just going to continue to just go wonderfully for you. Use the CD recording of today's session.*

Patient: *It's been an interesting learning experience.*

Therapist: *Yeah?*

Patient: (nodding yes) *Thank you.*

On follow-up, Rebekah reported she was able to complete her needed dental work with minimal anxiety.

CHAPTER 17

Insomnia

Many patients experience insomnia. It is estimated that 20% of all adults and 40% to 50% of older adults report problematic insomnia (Morin, 1993). This chapter will review causes of insomnia as well as research on behavioral interventions such as sleep hygiene, stimulus control, and sleep restriction therapy. The advantages of integrating hypnotic relaxation therapy (HRT) in an overall treatment strategy will also be discussed. In addition, guidelines for assessment and HRT will be presented. This includes a transcript of HRT for insomnia. A case example will be utilized to illustrate this approach.

It is estimated that 20% of all adults and 40% to 50% of older adults report problematic insomnia.

DEFINITION OF INSOMNIA

Insomnia is defined as a disturbance of sleep and may consist of several features: (1) difficulty initiating sleep; (2) difficulty maintaining sleep; (3) early awakening; or (4) poor sleep quality. One or all four characteristics may be present for a given patient. Difficulty initiating sleep is more common in younger individuals, while difficulty maintaining sleep is more common among older adults (American Psychiatric Association, 2000).

Chronic insomnia occurs when complaints of poor sleep have persisted for 6 months or more. An important aspect of chronic insomnia is the powerful impact it has on a person's life and daytime functioning. In contrast, acute insomnia is experienced by most people at some time in their lives and refers to a short-term episode of poor sleep, most commonly related to stress or physical conditions.

It is also important to distinguish between primary insomnia and secondary insomnia. Primary insomnia is sometimes referred to as *psychophysiological insomnia,* or learned insomnia. It is a sleep disorder that arises from poor sleep habits, unrealistic expectations for sleep, and association of arousal with bedtime cues (pillow, bed, etc.), leading to wakefulness at times when sleep is desired (American Psychiatric Association, 1994).

Secondary insomnia is caused by another primary factor such as depression, pain, anxiety, medications, or physical illness. Depression is associated with poor sleep maintenance and early awakenings. Anxiety and post-traumatic stress disorder (PTSD) are more likely to be associated with difficulty initiating sleep, awakenings, and sometimes parasomnias or disturbing dreams (American Psychiatric Association, 2000).

ASSESSMENT

Diagnostic criteria for insomnia have been provided by both the American Psychiatric Association (1994) and the American Sleep Disorders Association (1990). Morin (1993) presented a listing of diagnostic considerations that incorporates information found in the *Diagnostic and Statistical Manual of Mental Disorders* (1994) and the *International Classification of Sleep Disorders* (1990) criteria for insomnia:

- Subjective complaints of poor sleep onset or maintenance
- Sleep-onset latency or middle-of-the-night awakenings must be greater than 30 minutes
- Sleep efficiency (the percentage of time that is spent in bed and asleep) must be lower than 85%
- Sleep difficulties occur three or more nights per week
- Sleep difficulties persist for at least 6 months
- Subjective complaints such as fatigue, performance impairment, or mood disturbance that are attributed to poor sleep
- Sleep difficulties cause significant impairment in social or occupational functioning or cause marked distress

The case conceptualization should include a review of the patient's sleep environment, stresses, sleep habits, medications, any substance use, and sleep history.

The case conceptualization should include a review of the patient's sleep environment, stresses, sleep habits, medications, any substance use, and sleep history. Additionally, other sleep disorders such as obstructive sleep apnea, restless leg syndrome, sleep walking, and nightmare disorder should be ruled out.

SLEEP STAGES AND AGE

The identification of sleep stages and the study of sleep have been advanced by the use of electroencephalography that allows for identification of brain waves during sleep. There are five relatively well-defined sleep stages.

Stage 1 is the beginning of the sleep cycle. It is not true sleep. Rather, it is the transition from wakefulness to sleep and is characterized by drowsiness. During this stage, there is an increase in theta waves and a decrease in muscle tone. Stage 1 normally lasts only a brief period of time (5 to 10 minutes) and comprises only about 5% of sleep.

Stage 2 is the onset of true sleep. Brain waves change, and there are bursts of rapid, rhythmic brain activity known as *sleep spindles*. Body temperature decreases, and heart rate slows. Awareness of the external environment also decreases. This stage occupies 45% of total sleep in adults.

Stage 3 sleep is characterized by the presence of deep, slow brain waves known as *delta waves*. Stage 3 is the transition between light and very deep sleep. Parasomnias such as sleep walking or night terrors are most likely to occur during Stage 3 or 4. Approximately 12% of sleep is Stage 3.

Stage 4 is sometimes referred to as *delta sleep* because of the preponderance of delta waves that occur at this stage. This is a deep and satisfying sleep stage that usually lasts 30 minutes at a time and comprises approximately 13% of total sleep time.

Total sleep time and sleep architecture changes with age.

Stage 5 is referred to as rapid eye movement, or *REM*, sleep. REM sleep is identified by rapid eye movements, rapid low-voltage brain waves, and increased respiration rate. It is also characterized by greatly decreased muscle tone referred to as *atonia*. Dreaming occurs in this stage. REM sleep accounts for 25% of total sleep time in adults.

These sleep stages are repeated several times during the night. Sleep begins with Stage 1 and progresses to the other stages. Once an REM sleep stage is over, the body usually returns to Stage 2 and then progresses to the other stages. Sleep cycles through these various stages about four or five times during a night's sleep.

Total sleep time and sleep architecture changes with age. This is important to consider in regard to realistic expectations for normal sleep at various ages. In general, less sleep is required with advancing age. Total sleep time for a newborn is 16 to 18 hours per day; however, by age 10, total sleep time decreases to 10 to 11 hours. A healthy adult sleeps 7 to 8 hours per night. After age 65, total sleep requirement decreases to about 6.5 hours per night, and there is also a decrease in Stages 3 and 4 sleep.

MEDICATIONS FOR INSOMNIA

Benzodiazepine receptor agonists have been approved by the U.S. Food and Drug Administration (FDA) for treatment of insomnia. These medications fall into two broad categories of prescription hypnotics: benzodiazepines (e.g., estazolam, flurazepam, quazepam, temazepam, and trizolam), and agents that act similarly but have a nonbenzodiazepine structure (e.g., zaleplon, zolpidem, and eszopicine). The newer nonbenzodiazepines such as zolpidem and zaleplon are generally preferred because they have a shorter half-life and cause minimal daytime sleepiness. These medications are appropriate for the short-term management of insomnia. However, the long-term use of these prescription medications can be problematic due to dependency, rebound insomnia when the medication is discontinued, and habituation. Because of this, these medications are only indicated for short-term use, such as when poor sleep is due to a stressful event or concurrent with a medical condition. Only one medication (eszopiclone) has been approved for long-term use; other medications for sleep have been approved by the FDA for limited use (35 days or less) in treating insomnia.

It is also noteworthy that, outside of prescription medication, the most common treatments used by people with chronic insomnia are over-the-counter (OTC) antihistamines and alcohol (Walsh & Schweitzer, 1999). Antihistamines (such as diphenhydramine) have a sedative effect and can facilitate sleep onset. They can be used long-term but can have some adverse side effects such as daytime sedation, diminished cognitive function, dry mouth, blurred vision, urinary retention, constipation, and increased risk of intraocular pressure.

Alcohol consumption does reduce sleep latency, however regular drinking and larger amounts result in poorer sleep. Excessive alcohol use is associated with disturbing dreams and middle insomnia, the inability to fall back asleep once awakened in the night.

BEHAVIORAL TREATMENTS FOR INSOMNIA

Because of the adverse side effects associated with pharmacological treatments, behavioral interventions are very often considered for chronic and primary insomnia. The most commonly used approaches are discussed below, as they may be used in conjunction with HRT.

SLEEP HYGIENE

Recommendations that contribute to good sleep habits can be helpful in some cases. Habits such as drinking coffee in the evening or leaving the television on in the bedroom can contribute to sleep problems. Educating the patient in good sleep hygiene can be accomplished by reviewing the patient's routine at night and before going to bed. Sleep hygiene recommendations are summarized in Table 17.1.

STIMULUS CONTROL INSTRUCTIONS

Stimulus control instructions (Bootzin, Epstein, & Wood, 1991) have been shown to be effective in improving insomnia. These are instructions to the patient to associate the bed and bedroom with sleep as opposed to other

Table 17.1
Sleep Hygiene Recommendations

1.	Go to bed only when drowsy.
2.	Get up at approximately the same time each morning, including weekends.
3.	Avoid naps during the day.
4.	Avoid alcohol prior to bedtime.
5.	Do not consume caffeine within six hours prior to bedtime.
6.	Exercise regularly, but avoid strenuous exercise just prior to bedtime.
7.	Do not smoke for several hours before bedtime.
8.	Have a light snack before bedtime.
9.	Maintain a cool temperature in the bedroom.
10.	The sleep environment should be dark.
11.	Reduce or eliminate any distracting noise.
12.	Maintain a "wind-down" period before bedtime by engaging in a relaxing activity.

activities such as reading, watching television, or "tossing and turning" during the night. Patients are told to reserve the bed for sleep and sex. They are told to avoid watching television, reading, or talking on the phone, etcetera, in bed. They are also instructed to get out of bed if not asleep within 15 to 20 minutes of turning off the lights and attempting to go to sleep. If this happens, they should get out of bed and stay up until feeling drowsy and then repeat the cycle as needed. Stimulus control instructions are provided in Table 17.2.

Table 17.2
Stimulus Control Instructions for Improving Sleep

1.	Use your bed and bedroom only for sleep or sex. Do not read, eat, or watch television in bed.
2.	Establish a regular pre-sleep routine before going to bed.
3.	If you do not fall asleep within 20 minutes, get up and go into another room. Engage in a boring activity. Do not eat, listen to music, or watch television. You may read material if you find it boring.
4.	Return to bed when you feel sleepy. If you do not fall asleep within 20 minutes repeat with step 3.

SLEEP RESTRICTION THERAPY

Sleep restriction therapy (Spielman, Saskin, & Thorpy, 1987) is somewhat similar to stimulus control instructions. With sleep restriction therapy, the patient is instructed to limit the time in bed so that the cues in the bedroom are associated with tiredness and sleep, and sleep curtailment ultimately results in sleep improvement. Sleep time is initially restricted to the number of hours the patient is already getting. This is defined as the "sleep window." The patient uses a sleep diary for one week to determine a baseline. Once the patient's number of actual sleep hours is known, the patient is instructed to establish a set time to go to bed and to wake up, while maintaining the amount of sleep determined at baseline. Patients are instructed to keep a record of the amount of sleep they actually get each night. When they are sleeping at least 85% of the time during the designated sleep window, they are then to increase the sleep window by moving the bedtime back by 20 minutes. This continues until the patient is getting a satisfactory amount of sleep.

Hypnotic relaxation therapy is utilized to improve sleep through absorption, mental and physical relaxation, and suggestion.

HRT FOR INSOMNIA

HRT is utilized to improve sleep through absorption, mental and physical relaxation, and suggestion. It is recommended that the patient follow the instructions for good sleep hygiene and have a regular bedtime and time to get up each morning. Generally, daytime naps are avoided, unless they do not interfere with nighttime sleep. Nightly practice of self-hypnosis, usually CD assisted, is strongly recommended. Many patients experience significant reduction in insomnia with HRT as the primary intervention. Compliance is usually very good as the patient experiences improvement. However, HRT can be integrated with either sleep restriction therapy or stimulus control instructions if necessary. As the patient makes progress in improving sleep, sleep medications can be tapered as appropriate. The following transcript provides a hypnotic relaxation induction for sleep. It can also be used for anxiety reduction and pain management. The transcript does not make any specific reference to sleep, beyond referring to a "stairway to sleep." This is because going to sleep is an involuntary process, and "trying to go to sleep" can have the opposite effect. Since the goal in this case is sleep, the hypnotic induction should be provided with a very soft, slow, and somewhat monotone voice.

HYPNOTIC RELAXATION INDUCTION FOR IMPROVING SLEEP

> "You can begin the process of deep hypnotic relaxation now by settling into the chair and just taking a moment to get very, very relaxed . . . Keep your eyelids open for the moment . . . and pick a point on the wall or ceiling and focus your attention on that point. . . . concentrate on that point so intensely that you allow other things to drift into the background . . . so that you are mainly aware of my voice and that point that you are looking at . . . Focus on that point more and more, and as you do, allow the tension to begin to drift out of your body . . . just becoming very, very relaxed . . . allow your arms and

hands to become more heavy as they relax, and as you focus on that point, notice your breathing . . . each time you exhale and breathe out becoming a little more relaxed . . . allow your eyelids to feel heavy and take a deep, deep breath of air . . . now hold the air . . . hold . . . and as you exhale, let your eyelids close . . . For the next few moments think the word "relax" silently to yourself . . . each time you breathe out think the word "relax" and allow your body to respond to this word . . . relax . . . and just allow a drifting, relaxing, floating feeling to develop, letting all the tension flow out of your muscles. . . . For the next few moments the most important thing you have to do is relax . . . any worries or concerns can be set aside for the moment . . . the most important thing is to achieve a state of calm relaxation . . . and you may notice a wave of relaxation that spreads from the top of your head eventually down to your feet . . . concentrate on that relaxed feeling, gently and easily as I describe it . . . Feeling that wave of relaxation spread from the top of your head, across your forehead . . . allow the muscles of your forehead to unwind and relax . . . like a rubber band that has been twisted and knotted very tight . . . and then as you exhale, is allowed to unwind, letting all the tension go out of that rubber band as it unwinds, loose and relaxed . . . Let that wave of relaxation now spread across your face and neck . . . Allow the muscles of your face to smooth out and let the tension go from your jaw . . . allow your teeth to become slightly parted as your jaw hangs like a hinge and your neck is becoming limp and relaxed . . . and as your neck goes limp, allow your head to rest on the pillow, or if you are sitting up, your chin may drift down toward your chest . . . allow your body to be supported completely as you become as limp as a rag doll . . . allow that wave of relaxation now to spread across your shoulders . . . down across your shoulders and down into your hands . . . perhaps you can concentrate on your right hand first and give yourself the suggestion, 'My right hand is heavy and relaxed. . . .' Allow that right hand to become so limp that it simply lies there like a very heavy piece of lead . . . very . . . very heavy . . . heavy . . . warm . . . And concentrate now on your left hand . . . allow your left hand to become even heavier than your right . . . so very heavy that there is simply no tension left in your left hand . . . allow it to relax . . . heavy and warm . . . and take a deep, deep, deep breath of air, and as you exhale, relax twice as much . . . any tension that remains—allow it to go now . . . relax. . . .

"Deeply . . . deeply . . . deeply . . . relaxed . . . and notice that wave of relaxation as it does spread across your shoulders and lower back . . . Notice the warmth across your back . . . you may notice the pressure of your back against the cushions and notice the warmest part of your back . . . Feel the warmth as it penetrates into your skin and muscle, into the cartilage and bone, warming . . . and relaxing . . . more and more warming and relaxing . . . allow that warmth to spread across your chest . . . and as you take another deep breath and exhale, that warmth spreads into your stomach . . . warming, calm, relaxed . . . allow the muscles of your stomach to relax as your legs become very, very heavy . . . There's no need to maintain any tension now . . . letting go because relaxation is a process of letting go . . . letting go of any worry, letting go of any stress, letting go of any strain . . . and for the next few moments as I am silent, simply, gently, pleasantly . . . think the word 'relax' as you exhale, normally and calmly . . . and allow yourself to feel pleased with how relaxed you are becoming . . . And perhaps it would be alright to get even more deeply relaxed by imagining that you are standing at the top of a flight of 20 stairs . . . the staircase of sleep . . . the stairs are covered with a very thick, plush, red carpet and there is a heavy oak rail on each side of the stairs, and you can hold on to that rail and feel secure and safe . . . and with each step you take going down, down the stairs, each step will serve as a cue to relax even more . . . and it's very important to take that first step and in your own mind . . . in your imagination, take that first step now. And as you do, respond to the word 'relax' . . . Step number 20. . . . 19, Step 19 . . . going down the stairs . . . 18 . . . more relaxed . . . 18 . . . Step 18 . . . and notice whether you made that step first with your right or left foot . . . 17 . . . Step 17 . . . go all the way down now to step number 16, relaxed . . . 16 . . . and notice how far you've come . . . notice how much you've achieved . . . 15 . . . more relaxed at 15 . . . 14 . . . just as calm and relaxed as if you were resting on a recliner near a lake on a warm summer day, near a lake . . . A warm summer day and the sky is so blue, and the sunshine is warm . . . and it's early enough in the day that perhaps it would be alright to be alone and notice the quiet around you . . . and notice how still and peaceful the water is . . . there is not a ripple on the water . . . the trees are reflected on the surface of the water like a mirror . . . so peaceful . . . so serene and calm . . . and you can have that same serene, quiet feeling inside now. Step number 14 . . . and go even deeper to step number 13, down the stairs . . . 12. . . . step number 12 . . . 11 . . . Step eleven . . . ten. Halfway there. Twice as relaxed and take a very, very deep breath of air and let go of all the tension that remains now. Limp . . . limp, relaxed, all the way down . . . 9 . . . step number 9 . . . 8 . . . step number 8 . . . 7 . . . 6 . . . relax . . . 5 . . . 4 . . . almost there . . . 4 . . . 3 . . . 2 . . . and 1 . . . all the way down. So completely relaxed. Now you're standing in a room . . . there's a large over-stuffed chair there . . . and in front of the chair is a fireplace. Notice, as you walk across the room, that you are standing in front of the chair. As you sink down into it, the cushions are very . . . very soft, and the chair supports you and surrounds you . . . the chair and the cushions have been warmed by the fireplace, and although it may be cool outside, it's very . . . very warm where you are and you enjoy that warmth . . . and as you gaze into the fireplace, allow your mind to drift to some very pleasant memory. A time in your life when you felt so safe . . . so very secure, so very happy . . . and that time may have been a day ago . . . a week ago . . . a year ago . . . many years ago . . . perhaps in your childhood . . . but there was a time in your life when you felt relaxed . . . a time when you felt secure . . . a time when you felt happy . . . enjoy that time, that memory and relax even deeper . . . Perhaps that can be a favorite place, a secure place to go, and a happy time . . . and as you rest in front of the fireplace and gaze toward the fire, each and every breath will serve as a cue to relax more and more . . . and with that comes a feeling of accomplishment and self-confidence that grows stronger and stronger with each day that passes . . . and you can continue relaxing there, perhaps drifting into sleep . . . perhaps maintaining that same relaxed feeling whenever you open your eyes, alert and refreshed . . . but yet calm and self-assured . . . calm and quiet, and relaxed . . . As I begin counting now from the number 3 to 1 you can return to a state of conscious, relaxed, alertness . . . or perhaps drift even deeper relaxed and to deeper sleep . . . whatever is best for you . . . 3 . . . 2 . . . and 1."

CASE EXAMPLE

A 76-year-old widow, Emmaline, was referred by her family physician due to chronic insomnia. She stated that she had problems with her sleep since her husband died of a heart attack 15 years prior. However, during her initial session, she denied any symptoms or problems with depression, unresolved grief, or anxiety. She was in good health and denied any breathing or pain problems. She lived alone, but had good support from her daughter, church, and friends. She was financially secure and denied any persistent stresses.

She had been taking 10 mg of zolpidem (Ambien) per night for the past 12 years. There was a concern about her use of the medication, as it had become less effective over time. Her physician was urging her to taper down her use.

Emmaline's sleep habits were reviewed. She stated that she usually got in bed at 8:00 p.m. and watched television until she felt sleepy. She also stated that she would usually take the Ambien at 8:30 p.m. and then turn off the lights to go to sleep at about 9:30 p.m. She would go to sleep but then wake up around 3:00 a.m. She would typically stay in bed and "try to go back to sleep" until 7:30 a.m. When asked about daytime naps, Emmaline indicated that she would usually take a 45-minute nap around noon most days. She felt she could not go to sleep at night without taking Ambien, and she was concerned about waking up so early.

The process of HRT was discussed, and Emmaline was also provided with sleep hygiene instructions. This included a discussion of realistic expectations for sleep. She was informed about the relationship between sleep time and age, and that 6.5 to 7 hours sleep would be reasonable for her and should be sufficient to avoid daytime drowsiness. It was recommended that she establish a new routine consistent with this expectation. She was instructed to move the television out of the bedroom, and, in addition, she was instructed not to get into bed before 12:30 a.m. while maintaining her regular routine of getting out of bed at 7:30 a.m. Finally, she was to discontinue daytime naps.

The EHS: C was administered, and Emmaline obtained a score of 7. The hypnotic relaxation induction for improving sleep was completed. The session was recorded and Emmaline was provided with a CD recording and instructed to listen to the recording in bed when she was ready to go to sleep. She used a portable CD player and ear buds. During the first week, she was to take the Ambien at 12:30 a.m. when she was ready to go to sleep, but not earlier. It was also discussed that she would eventually be able to taper her use of the medication once she had established good sleep patterns.

The patient was seen for five sessions over a period of two months. She made excellent progress. Within 3 weeks, she had discontinued daytime naps (she initially resisted this instruction). She used the CD recording nightly, and changed her bedtime as recommended. She was not having any problem with daytime sleepiness. She then agreed to a schedule to decrease her use of Ambien. Initially, she reduced it by half (.5 mg) every other night. After 2 weeks of that schedule, she reduced her dosage further to .5 mg nightly. This tapering process continued until she was taking only .5 mg once per week or less. Both she and her physician were pleased with this level of use, and she continued her use of HRT, although she stated, "I never make it to the stairs before going to sleep."

CHAPTER 18

Hypnotic Relaxation Therapy to Facilitate Insight

This chapter will discuss the use of hypnotic relaxation therapy (HRT) to facilitate insight during the course of psychotherapy. Methods of hypnotic suggestion to identify unconscious perceptions and emotions, use of hypnoprojective methods, and post-hypnotic suggestion to facilitate insight will be discussed. In addition, HRT to facilitate insight will be illustrated by a case example drawn from the author's clinical practice. The case presentation includes a transcript of the intervention and a discussion of the later outcome.

There are two ways of knowing—from beliefs and perceptions that are formed in the rational conscious system, and from those that exist within the experiential unconscious system.

THE EXPERIENTIAL SYSTEM AND INSIGHT:

There are two ways of knowing—from beliefs and perceptions that are formed in the rational/conscious system, and from those that exist within the experiential/unconscious system. When there is a consistency between these two systems, the patient has insight.

Both the rational system and experiential system attempt to understand the self and the world.

Both the rational system and experiential system attempt to understand the self and the world. The experiential system automatically constructs an implicit understanding or "theory of reality" (Epstein & Pacini, 1999) that is derived from emotionally significant experiences. It functions rapidly and effortlessly and is a source of intuition and creativity. It is more crudely organized than the rational system and represents events concretely and in metaphors, associations, feelings, narratives, and generalizations (Epstein & Pacini, 1999; Epstein, 1994). The experiential system is powerful, and the images, expectations, and beliefs contained therein can affect behavior and physiology.

Perceptions, feelings, and beliefs in the experiential system may not be consciously perceived for several reasons. First, the experiential system serves as a "bank" of memories of past events and associated emotions (Epstein, 1994). It is naturalfor these associations to remain at a pre-conscious or unconscious level of awareness much of the time, as it allows the rational system to process information in its own, more logical way. Second, information that cannot be easily processed, such as traumatic experiences, may be dissociated until it can be assimilated. In this case, healing experiences or new information may pave the way for conscious assimilation to occur at a later time. It is for this reason that establishing relaxation and "safe place" imagery is very important in using hypnotic relaxation for further insight. Third, events and perceptions that are anxiety-provoking may be disguised by the experiential system. Such perceptions or beliefs may be held in the experiential system in a symbolic manner and be revealed to the rational system indirectly, such as through dreams, impressions, and meaningful symbolism.

Perceptions, feelings, and beliefs in the experiential system may not be consciously perceived for several reasons.

TRANCE MANAGEMENT AND ABREACTIONS

The goal of using HRT to facilitate insight is to increase conscious awareness of material in the experiential system so that it can be processed by the rational system. The material may be very anxiety-provoking, have strong associations with past events, or cause internal conflict. This is not always the case, but because the possibility exists, the hypnotherapist should provide as much support as needed and proceed in a careful manner so as to not overwhelm the patient. Abreactions can occur and should be carefully monitored and moderated based upon professional judgment. The goal is not to bring about abreactions, but they can occur in some cases due to the emotional content of associations. If the patient appears to have an overly difficult time with emerging insight, then trance should be managed accordingly. This can be done by reassuring the patient that feelings can be brought to conscious awareness as slowly as needed and over multiple sessions if needed. Trance management can also be achieved by using suggestions to lighten the hypnotic state and to return to feelings and images of safety.

The hypnotherapist should provide as much support as needed and proceed in a careful manner so as to not overwhelm the patient.

When unconscious perceptions and associations with past events are brought forward, the patient in a hypnotic state may experience memories in an intense manner. However, it is important to keep in mind that, while a patient can have emotionally meaningful experiences during hypnotherapy, there is a large body of evidence to point to the fact that actual physical age regression (such as to childhood, past events, or "past lives") does not exist (Nash, 1988). In a hypnotic state, critical judgment can be suspended, more primitive modes of mental functioning can occur, and fantasy can be experienced as reality. These are important and useful processes when managed properly.

Throughout sessions to facilitate insight, the patient's emotional reactions should be carefully monitored. Observation of the patient and post-hypnotic inquiry are of key importance. Any unintended suggested effects should be removed by corrective suggestions, and sessions should end with time to assure the patient's well-being and feelings of control. The following are several methods to facilitate insight.

IDEOMOTOR RESPONSES TO FACILITATE INSIGHT

Ideomotor signaling involves informing the patient that it is possible for him or her to allow the unconscious mind to respond to questions.

In order to communicate with the unconscious/experiential system, it is necessary to establish a method or "vehicle" for communication to occur. This can be done through imagery, sensory alterations, or the motor system. Ideomotor response suggestions were initially described by Dr. David Cheek (1962) as a method for patients to answer questions in a hypnotic state. Ideomotor signaling involves informing the patient that it is possible for him or her to allow the unconscious mind to respond to questions. The responses can occur by a feeling in one finger that represents "yes" and a feeling in another finger that represents "no." The feeling can cause the finger to gently lift to indicate a response. The responses should occur effortlessly and not be consciously directed.

Suggestions for a "safe place" and relaxation should be given prior to suggested ideomotor responses and questions.

In utilizing ideomotor signaling, it is important to first establish a sufficient depth of trance so that involuntary, ideomotor movements can occur. In this regard, prior assessment of hypnotizability can be valuable to determine the patient's hypnotic ability. Suggestions for a "safe place" and relaxation should be given prior to suggested ideomotor responses and questions. Once ideomotor responses are established, the subsequent questioning should be simple, direct, respectful, nonleading, and exploratory. An outline of the use of ideomotor signaling to facilitate insight follows:

1. Complete a hypnotic relaxation induction with appropriate deepening of the hypnotic state.
2. Establish mental imagery and suggestions for "a place of safety."
3. Establish an ideomotor response mode.
4. Use progressive questioning with a careful and respectful, nonleading approach.
5. Return to place of safety.
6. Use permissive post-hypnotic suggestions for recall or amnesia (e.g.,"as you return to conscious alertness, thinking about all or only a part of this . . . whatever is best for you").

7. Remove all suggested effects (e.g., normal sensations return to your fingers).
8. Alert to conscious awareness.

An example of verbalization used for ideomotor signaling of responses follows. The example represents verbalization that may be used after the hypnotic relaxation induction and establishment of a "place of safety."

> "Would it be alright for your unconscious mind to respond to some questions, allowing this to occur, without any conscious effort on your part? If the answer to this is 'yes,' then one of your fingers can have a light feeling and begin to rise. This is your 'yes' finger. Good. If the answer to a question is 'no,' another finger or thumb can experience that light feeling and rise. [*Ask a false question*]. Allow the 'no' finger to feel light and rise . . . good. Allow your unconscious mind to respond. Would it be alright to better understand this symptom? [*if yes, proceed*]. Does this symptom relate to some emotion? Does this symptom relate to some events? Would it be alright to become more aware of that emotion? What feeling are you aware of now? [*Ask for a conscious, verbal response*]."

Continue to explore the symptom, feeling, or events as directed by the ideomotor responses.

HYPNOPROJECTIVE METHODS

Projective techniques are characterized by the creative use of imagery or ideomotor expressions to gain greater insight into a particular behavior, symptom, or relationship problem. In a hypnotic state, a patient may be asked to visualize clouds or pictures that take on shapes or images that are associated with a problem or issue. The projective imagery provides a means to communicate with the experiential system in its own language and to allow expression of unconscious perceptions. Hypnoprojective methods involve: (1) providing a somewhat ambiguous stimulus; and (2) suggestions for the unconscious to project perceptions and images onto the stimulus while the patient is in a hypnotic state.

Projective techniques are characterized by the creative use of imagery or ideomotor expressions to gain greater insight into a particular behavior, symptom, or relationship problem.

As with ideomotor signaling techniques, it is important to determine that the patient is capable of a moderate hypnotic state and to introduce suggestions for relaxation and feelings of safety. Once these suggestions have been achieved, projective imagery can be introduced. The suggestions for visualization should be responded to in an involuntary manner and should not result from the patient attempting to imagine a particular thing. This is important, because the point of a hypnoprojective intervention is to allow unconscious expression.

For example, one hypnoprojective technique is that of visualizing an old trunk (or box) in which some items reside that have particular meaning. Verbalization for use of the Old Trunk Technique, leading to insight, may include:

> "Now, as you continue walking down this path . . . up ahead you can see an old trunk . . . a kind of box . . . and somehow knowing that inside this trunk is something . . . that is important . . . something that is related to this problem . . . this symptom . . . that you have dealt with for so long . . . walking closer . . . so that now you are there . . . at the very base of this old trunk . . . not knowing what you will see . . . but ready to find out . . . And so . . . as you begin to open the trunk lid . . . as you are ready . . . looking into the trunk and finding what is there . . . it may be a picture . . . an old picture from the past . . . a remnant of clothing . . . a piece of paper upon which something is written . . . a recording upon which is a voice . . . or other sounds that have a particular meaning . . . But today . . . finding what is in the trunk . . . facing it . . . and it will bring greater understanding . . . greater conscious insight . . . to this problem . . . this symptom . . . as you see into the trunk . . . and are aware of what you have found there . . . nodding your head yes . . . very good . . . What is in the trunk? . . . you can answer me verbally."

Hypnoprojective techniques are highly interactive and the patient's experience and visualization guides further exploration of the response. The specific ambiguous stimulus (i.e., trunk, cloud, picture, television) is less important than the manner of presentation and exploration. This is further illustrated in the case example presented at the end of this chapter.

AFFECT BRIDGE

The *affect bridge* was developed by Dr. John Watkins (Watkins, 1971) and is a useful technique to explore emotions. The technique can be utilized following several steps. First, the patient is asked to identify a particular emotion while in a hypnotic state. The emotion may be related to a symptom or problem. Second, once the emotion has been identified, it is suggested that the patient experience the emotion and that the feeling is amplified. Once the emotion is more intensely experienced, it is used as a bridge to the past. Third, suggestions are then given for the patient to follow the emotion to times in the past. For example, "The emotion becomes a bridge to the past . . . to times in the past when you have experienced this emotion . . . ." Fourth, suggestions are given for the patient to experience and describe the events or situations associated with the emotion. The emotion then serves as a way to identify past memories that may be

The affect bridge was developed by Dr. John Watkins and is a useful technique to explore emotions.

relevant to current symptoms or problems. Verbalization such as the following may be used:

> "Now following this emotion back in terms of time and space. Following the emotion back to where it begins. Going back in terms of time and space to that time, that place. Everything you saw then, you see now. Everything that you felt then, you feel now. Everything you heard then, you hear now. Following that emotion and becoming aware of where it leads you . . . so that you will be able to better understand these symptoms, and when you are there, just nod your head 'yes' so that I will know you are there. Your unconscious mind takes you back as I count from one to ten . . . 1, 2, 3, 4, 5, 6, 7, 8, 9, 10. Where are you? What do you see or hear?"

POST-HYPNOTIC SUGGESTION

The creative use of post-hypnotic suggestions can be especially useful to facilitate insight. Post-hypnotic suggestions can be given for the patient to have an experience at a later time that will serve to bring about greater insight into a symptom or problem. For example, suggestions can be provided that the patient will have a dream time that will stand out and that is relevant to the presenting symptom. The hypnotherapist can then ask the patient to keep notes on any dreams that he or she remembers over the next several weeks. Other post-hypnotic suggestions might include the use of creative activities such as painting, writing, or music. For example, if the patient keeps a diary or likes to write, suggestions can be given, such as:

Post-hypnotic suggestions can be given for the patient to have an experience at a later time that will serve to bring about greater insight into a symptom or problem.

> "In the coming weeks, you will notice that you have written something of particular significance toward understanding this problem . . . it will be something that is written automatically . . . so that you notice what you have written . . . it may be a word or a phrase . . . or more . . . but you will recognize its significance . . . when it occurs."

The following case provides an example of direct suggestion, ideomotor signaling, hypnoprojective methods, use of affect, and post-hypnotic suggestion to facilitate insight.

CASE EXAMPLE: TRANSCRIPT OF HRT TO FACILITATE INSIGHT

The patient, Rosa, was a 49-year-old woman who was referred for HRT as an adjunct to an intensive day treatment psychotherapy program, to which she had been admitted due to depression. She was not progressing very well in the program due to a lack of insight into her symptoms. She was able to describe her symptoms of depression, such as feelings of intense sadness, poor sleep, lack of energy, emotional numbness, and feelings of anxiety. However, she was not able to identify any particular issues or specific concerns. She also reported episodes in which she would become very preoccupied and gave the example of driving and missing an exit without realizing it until she had driven some distance.

Rosa's day treatment program provided cognitive–behavioral group counseling, relaxation exercises, creative art therapy, and individual psychotherapy. During the initial consultation for HRT, the EHS was administered and the patient obtained a score of 11, indicating hypnotizability in the high range. The process of a hypnotic relaxation induction was discussed, as was the goal of facilitating insight. The intention of using suggestions for ideomotor signaling was explained to her, and examples of hypnoprojective methods were also discussed. She gave her informed consent and questions were answered before proceeding.

This transcript is provided in two parts. The first part is the initial session, and the second part is the follow-up session, which illustrates the patient's response to post-hypnotic suggestions. As the transcript illustrates, while in a hypnotic state, the patient recalled a very traumatic memory in which her young daughter was killed in a tragic accident. During hypnosis, she realized that these events were so painful that she had put great effort into avoiding thinking about them and had minimized their significance. In the transcript, she is describing these previously avoided events in detail.

Therapist: *Rosa, if you would just go ahead and roll your eyes upwards, just as though you were looking right through your skull . . . and focus your attention there . . .*

Patient: (looks up)

Therapist: *And as you relax . . . concentrate very, very intensely . . . there. Concentrate . . . concentrate . . . more and more . . . concentrate . . . focusing your attention . . . I'd like for you to take a deep, deep breath of air . . . all the air that you can hold in your lungs.*

Patient: (takes deep breath)

Therapist: *Hold . . . hold . . . hold . . . and now as you exhale, letting your eyelids come down, relax. Eyelids closing . . . closing . . . closed. That's right. And as your eyelids close, shut tight, more and more of the feeling of relaxation begins to spread over you . . . arms, neck, head, face, shoulders, relaxing more and more . . . as though you were just sinking down, more and more relaxed, sinking down to the cushions of the chair . . . and notice that, in some way, you've already allowed your breathing to become more comfortable and more relaxed. And hypnosis is a comfortable state of relaxation so* *that with each breath you exhale, going more and more relaxed, deeper and deeper relaxed . . . as though, Rosa, with a part of your mind, you are going to go for a walk today, a very special walk . . . walking down a trail . . . and it's a warm summer day, and you can feel the warmth of the sunshine on your face . . . And there may even be a slightly cool breeze in the air . . . but the most important thing now is to just enjoy, for now, going on this walk . . . and as you walk further along . . . with each step you take . . . passing different trees . . . oak trees and pine trees . . . becoming more and more relaxed . . . that's right, just drifting all the way down . . . In fact, you may even want to take a deep breath of the cool fresh air and relax even more deeply . . . Do you think that'd be alright with you?*

Patient: *Mmmhmmm.*

Therapist: *That's right . . . just enjoying going for this walk today . . . and up ahead there's a small stream of fresh water, a little stream . . . Rosa, the water is cool and fresh, very cold . . . and finding that you may be thirsty . . . so that you take some of the water, as though you had cupped it into your hands and that water is so cool . . . it's so refreshing as you swallow it . . . And the good taste of that fresh water is in your mouth as you swallow it . . . and you feel a little more refreshed and able to go on further . . . and as you concentrate, Rosa, that up ahead there's a cabin . . . and there is something special about this cabin today . . . and it's up ahead. But you're going there and you can consider something important about yourself and about the problems you've had, in that cabin . . . and as you concentrate on taking those steps, I'd like for you with a part of your mind . . . with just a part of your mind . . . focus your unconscious on your left arm and hand . . . so that, Rosa, when I touch your left arm and hand, this arm becomes very light, very weightless. As though, Rosa, there was a large helium-filled balloon attached to your wrist by a string. And this balloon goes up in the air and your arm becomes lighter and lighter and it drifts up all by itself. . . . You're going to feel me touch your wrist, as it just becomes lighter and lighter now, and drifting up higher and higher. And just notice where that hand wants to go and just letting it go wherever it wants to go. . . . That's right; you're doing very, very well. And as I touch this arm again, this feeling passes . . . a heaviness begins to come over the hand . . . and as it drifts back down, toward the chair, becoming more and more relaxed as it touches the chair all the way, twice as relaxed now.*

Patient: (lowers arm and is very relaxed)

Therapist: *Now, Rosa I'd like to begin to ask some questions of your unconscious mind. . . . Rosa, if the answer to a question is "yes," I'd like for you to allow the finger that I touch now to move, this* *finger . . . here, can move . . . And if the answer to a question is "no," letting the answers come from your unconscious . . . letting your fingers move all by themselves . . . I'd like to ask your unconscious mind if it would be alright to go to this cabin and better understand the depression . . . these lapses of memory? That's right . . . just letting your unconscious mind answer . . . that's right.*

Patient: (slightly moves finger on right hand)

Therapist: *That's right . . . a good strong response . . . a strong response all by itself. You're doing very well.*

Patient: ("yes" finger raises and patient breathes more heavily)

Therapist: *So that, Rosa, you've come right to the cabin . . . right on the very steps. . . . And there are several steps that you walk up . . .*

Patient: (sobs, begins to cry)

Therapist: *. . . toward that cabin. And already knowing . . .*

Patient: (sobs) . . . I can't . . .

Therapist: *. . . an important emotion . . . as you reach the cabin . . . And would it be alright to talk about what you're feeling now? What are you feeling?*

Patient: (crying) *I feel afraid.*

Therapist: *The sense of fear. . . . There's something about this cabin . . .*

Patient: (crying)

Therapist: *Would you talk some more about the fear?*

Patient: (crying) *I'm just afraid, I don't want to go in.*

Therapist: *You don't want to go in.*

Patient: (sobs)

Therapist: *Alright . . . so for a moment I'd like for you to just stop right there . . . right there, just outside the cabin . . . and with a part of your mind, you can just stop right there and have a feeling of control . . . you can go into the cabin when you are ready. But perhaps you'll just want to open the door, a little ways . . . But for right now, just stopping . . . just waiting, letting more of a sense of calm come over you . . . and as you are aware of that feeling of fear . . . feeling of fear . . . letting that feeling stay because that's an important . . . important emotion . . . and you may have an image or a thought that begins to come to you . . . so would it be alright to follow that feeling of fear? To see where it leads you, what thoughts come to you . . . ? Would that be alright . . . ?*

Patient: (continues to cry) *I'll try.*

Therapist: *That's right. What are you seeing?*

Patient: (sobs)

Therapist: *What thoughts have come to you?*

Patient: (sobbing) *I see a fire.*

Therapist: *You see a fire?*

Patient: (sobbing more heavily) *Yes.*

Therapist: *Where is the fire?*

Patient: (sobbing) *It's, it's in the house.*

Therapist: *It's in a house.*

Patient: (sobbing) *Oh God . . . My baby's in there and I, they wouldn't get her out.*

Therapist: *Your baby's in there?*

Patient: (sobbing more heavily, shakes head) *I don't wanna go, I don't wanna go.*

Therapist: *It's just as though you were watching it happen.*

Patient: (sobbing and shakes head) *Oh.*

Therapist: *Just observing.*

Patient: (sobbing) *I want to get her out of there and I can't, she's just gone.* (Shudders) *Oh.*

Therapist: *How old are you?*

Patient: (sobbing, tries to speak)

Therapist: *That's right, that's right.*

Patient: (sobbing)

Therapist: *How old is your baby?*

Patient: (sobbing) *She, she's three.*

Therapist: *She was three?*

Patient: (sobbing)

Therapist: *She was three years old?*

Patient: (sobbing) *Yeah.*

Therapist: *And how long ago has this been?*

Patient: (sobbing) *Oh, oh, I don't. It was a long time ago.*

Therapist: *A long time ago? But the feeling is still there, very strong, isn't it?*

Patient: (sobbing) *Oh, why couldn't she get out?*

Therapist: *So your baby is in there and you can't get her out, can you?*

Patient: (sobbing and shakes head) *It's too late.*

Therapist: *It's too late.*

Patient: (sobbing) *It's just too late.* (shudders) *Oh.*

Therapist: *And what happens next, who else is there? Just watching, just observing. Who else is there?*

Patient: *The fire department and they're looking through the house and they can't find her either.*

Therapist: *Yes . . . yes.*

Patient: (sobbing) *And the neighbor. And my husband. And my little boy. And my brother. But they're all out.*

Therapist: *Just your little girl. Everyone else got out?*

Patient: (sobbing) *Yes.*

Therapist: *And can you see these other people around you?*

Patient: *Yes.*

Therapist: *What's happening?*

Patient: *It's just, they're all looking. They're, uh, they're just looking through everything, trying, oh God, they're trying to find her body.* (shudders)

Therapist: *And where do you see your son?*

Patient: *He's,uh—he's at the neighbor's house. His uh . . .*

Therapist: *And where are you?*

Patient: *I'm just coming there.* (shudders) *Oh God, it's so cold.*

Therapist: *It's so cold. What's happening that's cold?*

Patient: *It's, it's, it's cold, there's snow, there's snow everywhere.*

Therapist: *There's snow everywhere today?*

Patient: (sobbing) *Oh, yes. And they won't let me go; they won't let me go try to get her out.*

Therapist: *Is someone holding you?*

Patient: (sobbing) *Yes. And they can't find her, I wanna find her, I wanna get her out of there. But they said, "It's too late. You can't go in there."* (shudders) *Oh.* (starts to breathe heavily and quickly).

Therapist: *That's right. And now, Rosa, finding somehow that you've begun to leave this cabin behind for today.*

Patient: (continues to sob and breathe heavily)

Therapist: *And Rosa, it's as though you've begun to leave the cabin behind and you're back walking away, down this trail, back to a warm summer day. Just letting the waves of comfort and relaxation begin to wash over you, feeling a little more comfortable.*

Patient: (sobbing) *Oh it hurts.*

Therapist: *It hurts . . .*

Patient: (sobbing) *Yes. My heart, it feels like it's just going to burst or something.*

Therapist: *You've held this feeling inside.*

Patient: (sobbing) *Oh, oh.*

Therapist: *Held it inside for too long.*

Patient: (sobbing) *Yeah.*

Therapist: *Somehow you're drawing back to that day. Back to that snowy day.*

Patient: (breathing heavily) *Oh, it's so cold. Oh. Oh.*

Therapist: *And Rosa, you can think about as much of this . . . once you awaken from hypnosis . . . as is important and acceptable for you to consider . . . as much as you can tolerate . . . but you're going to be able to resolve these feelings . . . this feeling of fear . . . this feeling of sadness . . . perhaps other feelings connected to it . . . But you're going to now realize that holding this inward . . . suppressing these feelings . . . has been very harmful to you . . . you're going to be able to talk about and resolve so much of this. And I give you the post-hypnotic suggestion now, Rosa, that you're going to find it easier and easier to express your feelings through paintings . . . through artwork . . . You're going to be able to resolve and express so much of this through your paintings . . . you're going to be able to express and describe and resolve so much of this, that whenever you're in the workshop area and you have the paints and the colors in front of you, you're going to find that you spontaneously begin to paint something very significant, very important to you . . . From your unconscious mind, you're going to be able to make a series of very important paintings . . . and these paintings are going to be so meaningful to you and very valuable to you, that they're going to help you as you resolve all of these feelings in psychotherapy through counseling.*

Patient: (continues to breathe heavily)

Therapist: *That's right; you're doing so very well. You've done very well today. And realizing that you can ponder as much or as little of this consciously as you awaken, as is acceptable to you now . . . as I count from 3 to 1 returning to conscious awareness. 3 . . . 2 . . . and 1.*

Patient: (pauses, slowly opens eyes, still breathing heavily)

Therapist: *You can take some Kleenex beside you there.*

Patient: (takes Kleenex and wipes face)

Therapist: *You had some tears. What are you aware of?*

Patient: (re-orienting herself) *Pardon me?*

Therapist: *What are you aware of?*

Patient: (wipes eyes) *I think, uh, I feel guilty.*

Therapist: *Can you tell me about that?*

Patient: (begins to cry) *That I should have, I think if I was home, if I was there, that wouldn't have happened. But I was in school, I couldn't, I couldn't be home.* (cries)

Therapist: *You've blamed yourself for your daughter's death, haven't you?*

Patient: (crying)

Therapist: *That's right, let those feelings out. Let the tears come out. Let yourself really cry.*

Patient: (crying) *My husband told me that if I had been home being a mother like I'm supposed to, oh God, that wouldn't have happened. But he was home.* (Pauses) *Oh, I don't know.*

Therapist: *You sounded angry.*

Patient: (nods) *I am. I am angry. I'm angry because he was passed out drunk instead of watching the kids the way he was supposed to. And I was angry at my brother because he was with him. And they didn't even try to get them out. He was interested in getting himself out and then he blamed me for them being left in there, and I was just too late, I couldn't, I couldn't get in there. There was just nothing left.*

Therapist: *It was too late?*

Patient: (nods) *The whole house was gone.* (Shudders) *The neighbor, the neighbor got my son out and took him to his house and he had told me, when he got my son into his house, they lived across the road, that he tried to get back into the house himself and tried to get the baby out and he said when he broke the window, everything just came out through and he couldn't get in either.*

Therapist: *Would you talk about this in group therapy today?*

Patient: (nods)

Therapist: *Alright. Let's stop here for today, you've accomplished a lot. Just let yourself kind of wind down a little bit.*

(Session ends)

The next session occurred 2 days later. The patient had attended a creative arts workshop as a part of the day treatment program and brought several of her paintings to the session. The session begins with discussing a painting of a fire with smoke that she painted in response to the posthypnotic suggestion for continued insight.

(Session begins)

Patient: *You told me to go try to go in and work on these things so that they could come out in the paintings and I really . . . after the session with you, I was kind of upset all day long . . . but I felt good that I could kind of understand what was bothering me. . . .*

Therapist: *Uh huh.*

Patient: *But I was—I was really, really uncomfortable with it and I just couldn't seem to let it come up and come out, you know? And I still just had this need to put it out of my mind, I guess, you know. And uh, I didn't want to go into art at all really. And that's kind of unusual, you know—there's nothing in there to be afraid of at all. But I really had an apprehension of going inside, and when I went in I sat down and I was just drawing a blank, I kept thinking, "Well, I don't know what I'm supposed to do," you know, the feelings, how to put them down there, so I said, "Well, I'll just start with a white background." I didn't know what else to do, so I started with that and I just, I started feeling, uh, a lot of anxiety . . . like I was boiling inside, I mean really—I was just kind of shaky all over and I thought, "Boy, you know, I'm really feeling bad here, you know"* (laughs). *I just started with the paint . . . originally I was going to draw the smoke that I hate seeing whenever I first realized what was going on, when I got to the scene, and I don't know, I didn't even know that I had done this until later that night when I went back in to look, to see what I had done. It's like I could see, I could see the fire, I could see what was happening, I could see the fire trucks, and my husband, and my son, and my brother, and the neighbors, and it just all came rushing, all just at one time on me, and I felt like I was going to be sick . . . and then it was just right to here and I left the room. I just, I couldn't deal with sitting there anymore, you know? And uh, I went to my room and I threw up. I threw up and I sat against the wall and I think I cried for 30 minutes. I don't know, I just felt like I was completely drained before I ever stopped crying at all. And it was quite a release, it really was. I felt like maybe I can deal with this thing, really. You know, it hurt; it really, really hurt and I couldn't understand, and I kept with these "why's," you know? Why? I wish it had been me instead of the baby, and all these thoughts just kept running through my mind, running through my mind, and it just wasn't really making a whole lot of sense and I felt sick. I felt really, really sick about it.*

Therapist: *So, that's when you left the art room?*

Patient: *That's when I left the art room, yeah. I was really upset about it.*

Therapist: *You said just a moment ago that you didn't realize what you had drawn.*

Patient: *No, because it was like, boy, I was just going at it, I guess* (laughs). *I was just really going at it and it was like in my mind I was just seeing the actual thing happen, just remembering, I guess, what was happening and I wasn't really seeing what I was putting on that board.*

Therapist: *So it just kind of came out?*

Patient: *I was, yeah, I was just really, really upset about it and I just didn't feel I should stay in there and deal with it because I felt sick and I was afraid that I was going to be sick in there, you know, so I said, "I've gotta get out of this room" . . . and I ended up back in my room.*

Therapist: *As you look back at your picture now, all this down here, what does this represent to you, the red?*

Patient: *When I first looked at it, when I went back inside the art room the other night when I found the courage, I was afraid to look at the painting actually. I was afraid I was going to go back into whatever, you know, state I was in when I left. When I first looked at it, I thought, "Well, it must have been the smoke and the fire," but I don't think so. I think it's just anger. I mean, that hate and that anger that I was feeling that I just could not deal with at all, you know?*

Therapist: *And what emotion does the black bring out to you?*

Patient: *To me, a lot of depression, now. I can kind of see it now, you know, what I was feeling, a lot of depression because I just didn't wish to think about it, I think. You know, I didn't want to bring myself to terms with what had happened. Because I didn't understand it, I didn't understand why it happened. And that's that "why" again, you know? I just couldn't understand why this thing happened and it was just eating at me.*

Therapist: (points to picture) *Under the depression then, it's all this anger.*

Patient: *I think so, yeah. I think it is.*

Therapist: (looking at the bottom of the painting) Tell me about the two people at the bottom.

Patient: *I don't, I don't even remember drawing those in. That's what it was, they were asking me that yesterday in the taping and I didn't remember what I was doing, but the nurse, the girl that was* *in there yesterday, she made a suggestion to me and it really made a lot of sense, I think, because this must have been my husband and myself* (points to the two people in painting) *because I was just so distraught and so upset about this thing happening and not understanding why and I needed to release this thing from me. And we were very far apart, very far apart.*

Therapist: (points to painting) *And this one is crying.*

Patient: *Yeah, I was just really, really upset.*

Therapist: *But no mouth.*

Patient: *I had never talked about it. I've never talked about it.*

Therapist: *Hmm. Let's look at your other paintings.*

The patient was able to continue addressing these issues in her psychotherapy program. Additional HRT sessions focused on teaching self-hypnosis for increased control, relaxation, ego strengthening, and integration. She continued in outpatient psychotherapy, which included cognitive–behavioral therapy, cognitive restructuring, and interpersonal supportive counseling. At a 12-month follow-up, she continued to report excellent progress and no relapse in symptoms of depression.

CHAPTER 19

Ethical Considerations in the Practice of Hypnotic Relaxation Therapy

Careful adherence to appropriate ethical principles is essential for maintaining high standards of professional practice, dealing with difficult situations, and protecting the public (Wall, 1991). This chapter provides a discussion of major ethical considerations and cautions in use of hypnotic relaxation therapy (HRT). This will include a discussion of competence, informed consent, professional judgment, privacy and confidentiality, personal problems and dual relationships, documentation, training, licensure, and recordings of self-hypnosis for patients.

COMPETENCE

Professionals should only provide services for which they have the education, skills, and training to provide competently. Competency refers to the ability to provide services for a specific patient given his or her individual characteristics, including age, gender, ethnicity, national origin, disability, language, and socioeconomic status (American Psychological Association, 2012). Knowledge and sensitivity to the broader multicultural issues should always be considered in formulating treatment plans and in providing the best care for each patient. It is important that the hypnotherapist is aware of and acknowledges his or her limitations and boundaries of competence. One should only provide HRT interventions within the bounds of one's professional license and areas of expertise. If a hypnotherapist lacks the competency to treat a particular problem or patient, he or she should refer the patient to an appropriate service provider with the needed expertise or specialty.

Professionals should only provide services for which they have the education, skills, and training to provide competently.

HRT emphasizes an evidence-based approach and integration of information from research and practice. It is important that hypnotherapists maintain knowledge of current scientific and professional advances to assure competency in the services they provide. Continuing education in the form of workshops, reading, and consultation with colleagues is important in order to keep abreast of current trends and knowledge. HRT has wide applications, and professionals who are providing services in an area that is unfamiliar to them should undertake appropriate consultation and training before providing services in a new area.

It is important for hypnotherapists to maintain knowledge of current scientific and professional advances that are relevant to competency in the services they provide.

PROFESSIONAL JUDGMENTS

Somewhat related to competency is how one determines the basis for his or her professional judgments. HRT is both an art and a science. Each patient is an individual, and it is often the case that professional judgment is required in order to best meet the patient's needs. It is strongly recommended that hypnotherapists rely on scientific knowledge, when it exists, in making professional judgments regarding the appropriateness of HRT and its integration with other methods, referrals, and recommendations.

INFORMED CONSENT

In addition to establishing a good therapeutic relationship, it is necessary to obtain informed consent before providing hypnotherapy services. Informed consent involves providing the patient with sufficient information for him or her to make a decision about services. This may include information about hypnosis and HRT, intended procedures, cost, risks, and anticipated benefits, as well as alternatives to HRT. The practitioner should provide information as accurately as possible and should not, in any way, provide false information or exaggerate anticipated benefits. An accurate perspective of hypnotherapy (e.g. Yapko, 2003) and research evidence should be presented, while myths and misconceptions should be clarified.

Informed consent is an ongoing process, as the nature of services or goals can change during the process of HRT. It is important to initially obtain informed consent in writing and to document that informed consent was appropriately obtained throughout the hypnotherapy process. The therapist should consider the patient's capacity to provide his or her informed consent. This means that the patient should be mentally competent, have sufficient information provided at a level that he or she can understand, not be coerced, and have the legal authority to make his or her own decisions and authorization (Vicol, Bulgaru-Iliescu, Ioan, Astarastoae, 2009).

Informed consent is an ongoing process, as the nature of services or goals can change during the process of HRT.

When HRT is used to aide in addressing previously avoided memories or for forensic purposes, special attention should be given to obtaining informed consent in these areas. Information on state or federal regulations may be discussed, as there have been some cases where testimony obtained under hypnosis has been disregarded in legal settings. In addition, it should be discussed that memory, even when obtained in a hypnotic state, is imperfect and that potential risks can occur. The following wording for obtaining informed consent via a written document is provided as an example:

> Just as there may be risks and hazards in continuing my present condition without treatment, there are also risks and hazards related to the performance of hypnosis and hypnotic relaxation therapy in regard to memory. I realize that risks and hazards may occur in connection with this particular procedure, such as confabulation. My therapist has explained why the use of hypnosis or hypnotic relaxation therapy is recommended in my case. He/she has explained that there are other options available to me should I decline to give my informed consent. My therapist has also provided me with information about the nature of hypnosis and hypnotic relaxation therapy, the myths about it, and my questions about hypnosis and hypnotic relaxation therapy have been answered to my satisfaction.

This detail of informed consent regarding memory is most relevant when forensic considerations or enhanced insight is a focus. In other situations, an ongoing and therapy-specific informed consent process is sufficient.

PRIVACY AND CONFIDENTIALITY

HRT services should be provided in a manner that protects the patient's privacy and confidential information. This includes documentation and the manner in which records are stored. In addition, the patient should be informed of any state or federal limitations to confidentiality. The hypnotherapist should obtain information from the patient that is relevant to treatment and the hypnotherapeutic relationship. If any issues arise that might affect confidentiality, the patient should be informed.

BENEFICENCE

The patient's well-being should be paramount in any recommendations or hypnotherapeutic interventions. The term "beneficence" refers to an attitude of kindness and respectful consideration. The Hippocratic maxim of "first do no harm" is a guiding ethical fundamental of HRT. In addition, where possible, the hypnotherapist should seek to maximize benefits while minimizing possible risks or harm. When used with competence and skill, the risks associated with HRT are very minimal and include such things as possible disappointment or mild distress. However, beneficence directs to always seek and consider options that are in the best interest of the patient.

The patient's well-being should be paramount in any recommendations or hypnotherapeutic interventions.

LICENSURE/PROFESSIONALISM

Each practitioner is bound by the limitations imposed by his or her professional licensure and scope of practice. HRT is a method of treatment, but it is not a profession. It is appropriately used by medical, dental, and mental health professionals within their particular scope of practice. One should not go beyond one's range of professional licensure, and treatment should be confined to those problems that the hypnotherapist is qualified to treat without HRT. Use of hypnotic techniques without adequate knowledge is potentially risky or dangerous (Frauman, Lynn, & Brentar, 1993; Gravitz, Mallet, Munyon, & Gerton, 1982; Sheehan & McConkey, 1993; Wall, 1991).

HRT should only be used for a professional purpose and not for entertainment (American Society for Clinical Hypnosis, 2012). For example, in one case, a psychologist who was well known for her use of hypnosis was invited to present on the use of hypnosis at a hospital auxiliary meeting. Upon entering the room, the psychologist noticed that the room was decorated in cardboard cutouts of moons and hands with eyes painted in the palms. As she reached the podium, the psychologist was surprised to see a large sign over the podium that read "Master Hypnotist!" The psychologist was then asked to provide a demonstration of how to use hypnosis "for fun." In this case, the psychologist refused to provide a demonstration and instead discussed the myths and misconceptions, and provided accurate information on the ways HRT is used in treatment. Maintaining integrity is most important in presenting HRT in a professional manner. To do otherwise risks spreading misinformation and potential harm to the public.

Maintaining integrity is most important in presenting HRT in a professional manner. To do otherwise risks spreading misinformation and potential harm to the public.

RECORDINGS

Recordings of HRT sessions may be made on an individual basis for a particular patient or for use or sale to the general public. When provided to an individual patient, the use of the recording should be explained, frequency of practice discussed, and questions answered. On an individual basis, there is opportunity for follow-up and to address how the recording may be integrated into the overall treatment, such as for the purpose of teaching self-hypnosis.

When electronic recordings are produced for use by the general public, it is important to provide sufficient information and disclaimers for the use of audio tapes, CDs, or other media. The American Society of Clinical Hypnosis (2012) has identified several guidelines for disclaimers in providing recordings to the general public, including:

1. Providing information on the health care professional and his or her qualifications
2. Defining the purpose of the recording and its limits of usefulness

3. Citing any research about how hypnosis supports the use of the recording
4. What will likely happen when listening to the recording
5. How the recording is to be used
6. Answering the question, "What is hypnosis?"
7. Explaining what hypnosis "is not" by clarifying myths and misconceptions
8. Explaining what to do if the recording is not helping
9. Clarifying how to seek more help with the symptom or problem if needed
10. Advising that those patients currently in treatment inform their therapist or physician that they plan to use the recording

The information can be provided in printed materials or as a part of the recording itself. In sum, ethical practice of HRT involves the practitioner functioning within the scope of his or her professional license and in accordance with state and federal regulations. In addition, special competence in HRT is required, as is attention to the qualities associated with the hypnotic state and the hypnotherapeutic relationship. Due to expanding knowledge and research, ethical practice requires ongoing continuing education, keeping up to date on best practices, and integration of research into practice. Attending workshops can be especially useful when they are provided by trained professionals. Leading organizations that provide workshops and professional presentations include the Society for Clinical and Experimental Hypnosis (SCEH); the American Society for Clinical Hypnosis (ASCH); the International Society for Hypnosis (ISH); and the Society for Psychological Hypnosis, Division 30 of the American Psychological Association. Professional membership in a relevant organization is one way to stay connected with advances in the field. SCEH provides workshops and the leading hypnosis journal, the *International Journal for Clinical and Experimental Hypnosis.* ASCH also provides the *American Journal for Clinical Hypnosis,* which publishes useful articles related to professional issues and practice. Also, the British Society for Clinical and Experimental Hypnosis journal, *Contemporary Hypnosis and Integrative Therapy,* is a highly respected resource for current research and practice advances.

Ethics, training, competence, knowledge, and adherence to professional standards of practice are the foundations of HRT.

Practitioners of HRT are encouraged to seek the highest levels of certification and training. There are several boards that provide certification of competence in specialty areas, including: the American Board of Psychological Hypnosis (ABPH), the American Board of Medical Hypnosis (ABMH), the American Board of Dental Hypnosis (ABDH), and the American Board of Hypnosis in Social Work (ABHSW). These boards generally require documentation of training and practice, professional licensure in a relevant area, a written work sample, video demonstration, and passage of an oral examination. Ethics, training, competence, knowledge, and adherence to professional standards of practice are the foundations of HRT.

APPENDIX

*Hypnotherapy and Hypnotic Relaxation Therapy: What You Need to Know**

WHAT TRAINING IS REQUIRED?

The use of HRT is limited to health care providers who have completed training appropriate to their professional mandates. Many professionals receive and refine their training through continuing education workshops.

> Professionals using hypnosis should have taken professional courses in hypnosis under appropriate supervision.

You may find local associations in your state that include psychologists, dentists, medical doctors or nurses, counselors, social workers, and marriage and family therapists with training in hypnotherapy. Your primary care physician may also be an excellent referral source.

A word of caution:

Be wary when using Internet searches, as individuals who are unlicensed lay hypnotists may not have adequate training to diagnose and develop competent treatment plans, or to provide care consistent with professional standards.

> Discuss your concerns with your physician, psychologist, nurse, or health care provider.

Professional Resources

The American Psychological Association (APA), http://www.apa.org/topics/hypnosis/index.aspx

The American Society for Clinical Hypnosis, www.asch.net

The Society for Clinical and Experimental Hypnosis, http://www.sceh.us/

Mind-Body Medicine Research Laboratory, Baylor University, http://www.baylor.edu/psychologyneuroscience/index.php?id=76174

* Download as a full color brochure for distribution from springerpub.com/elkins-brochure

WHAT CAN I EXPECT?

A goal of *Hypnotic Relaxation Therapy* is increased empowerment to help you achieve what you want to accomplish.

> You are in control and can terminate the hypnotic state at any time you wish.

You cannot be hypnotized against your will or be made to do anything against your will.

While HRT involves a process of "letting go" of tension and stress, the goal is increased control of self and symptoms.

You will not spontaneously begin talking or revealing information that you do not wish to provide.

You will be aware of what is going on around you and what suggestions your therapist is providing.

You will be in control of your awareness during HRT.

> While HRT involves a process of "letting go" of tension and stress, the goal is increased control of self and symptoms.

WHAT IS HYPNOTHERAPY OR HYPNOTIC RELAXATION THERAPY?

Hypnotherapy is sometimes referred to as *Hypnotic Relaxation Therapy* (or HRT) because it involves the use of relaxation, mental imagery, and suggestion for a therapeutic purpose.

> The use of relaxation, mental imagery, and suggestion have been used in medicine and healing arts for centuries.

HRT involves learning how to use your mind and thoughts in order to manage emotional distress (e.g., anxiety, stress), unpleasant physical symptoms (e.g., pain, nausea), or to help you change certain habits or behaviors (e.g., smoking, overeating).

HOW WILL I BENEFIT FROM HYPNOTIC RELAXATION THERAPY?

HRT has been demonstrated to have a wide range of benefits, from simply improving symptoms or difficulties, to completely eliminating them.

Most people describe a hypnotic induction as a pleasant experience, during which they feel focused and absorbed in the hypnotic experience.

> Ask your health care provider about his or her training if you have any questions.

Your therapist will structure the suggestions based on your comfort and preference.

What issues tend to respond well to Hypnotic Relaxation Therapy?

Depression

Stress management

Insomnia

Phobias

Sexual problems

Self-esteem

Menopausal symptoms

Sleep problems

Smoking cessation

Weight loss/control

Post-traumatic stress disorder

Chronic pain

Coping with medical procedures

Anxiety disorder

Burn therapy

Cancer side effects

Hot flashes

Irritable bowel syndrome

Headaches

Low back pain

Fibromyalgia

Bruxism

Pain management

In HRT, you are given suggestions to achieve an altered state of awareness in which it is possible to reduce stress, manage pain, or respond to hypnotic suggestions to achieve greater control over behavior or symptoms.

WHAT HAPPENS DURING THE FIRST VISIT FOR HYPNOTIC RELAXATION THERAPY?

Your therapist will likely complete a clinical interview in order to understand the history of your problems, and then develop a treatment plan. He or she will ask about past medical and psychological treatments and determine if there are physical or emotional conditions that would contraindicate the use of HRT.

During the first visit you will be given information on HRT, an initial treatment plan will be developed, and goals of treatment will be discussed.

HOW MANY SESSIONS ARE NEEDED?

Length of hypnotic treatment depends on the severity of the problem and your specific needs. HRT is often used with other psychotherapeutic methods, and usually involves at least five sessions, but may range to twenty or more sessions.

WILL I LEARN SELF-HYPNOSIS?

Your therapist may make tapes or recordings for you to use between sessions or as home practice.

Recordings of sessions are frequently made and you will be encouraged to practice on a daily basis during treatment.

The goal of HRT is to empower the patient, which usually involves teaching how to use hypnotic relaxation methods in a way that increases personal control.

References

Abrahamsen, R., Zachariae, R., & Svensson, P. (2009). Effect of hypnosis on oral function and psychological factors in temporomandibular disorders patients. *Journal of Oral Rehabilitation, 36*, 556–570.

Alladin, A. (2008). *Cognitive hypnotherapy: An integrated approach to the treatment of emotional disorders.* West Sussex, UK: John Wiley & Sons.

Alman, B. (1983). *Self-hypnosis.* San Diego, CA: International Health Publications.

American Psychiatric Association. (1994). *Diagnostic and statistical manual of mental disorders (DSM-IV).* Washington DC: Author.

American Psychiatric Association. (2000). *Diagnostic and statistical manual of mental disorders. (DSM-IV TR).* Washington, DC: Author; Text revision.

American Psychological Association. (2011). In S. J. Knapp (Ed.), *APA handbook of ethics in psychology.* Washington, DC: Author.

American Society for Clinical Hypnosis. (2012). Guidelines for electric recordings of hypnosis for public consumption. Retrieved from http://www.asch.net

Baker, E. L. (1981). A hypnotherapeutic approach to enhance object relatedness in psychotic patients. *International Journal of Clinical and Experimental Hypnosis, 29,* 136–147.

Bandura, A. (1982). Self-efficacy mechanism in human agency. *American Psychologist, 37*(2), 122–147.

Barabasz, A., & Barabasz, M. (1992). Research designs and considerations. In E. Fromm & M. Nash (Eds.), *Contemporary hypnosis research* (pp. 173–200). New York, NY: Guilford Press.

Barabasz, A. F., & McGeorge, C. M. (1978). Biofeedback, mediated biofeedback and hypnosis in peripheral vasodilation training. *American Journal of Clinical Hypnosis, 21*(1), 28–37.

Barabasz, A., & Watkins, J. G. (2005). *Hypnotherapeutic techniques* (2nd ed.). New York, NY: Brunner–Routledge.

Barabasz, M. (1991). Hypnotizability in bulimia. *International Journal of Eating Disorders, 10*(1), 117–120.

Barber, T. X., & Glass, L. B. (1962). Significant factors in hypnotic behavior. *Journal of Abnormal and Social Psychology, 64,* 222–228.

Barlow, D. H. (2002). *Anxiety and its disorders: The nature and treatment of anxiety and panic* (2nd ed.). New York: Guilford Press.

Barnier, A. J., & Council, J. R. (2010). Hypnotizability matters: The what, why and how of measurement. In S. J. Lynn, J. W. Rhue, & I. Kirsch (Eds.), *Handbook of clinical hypnosis* (2nd ed., pp. 47–77). Washington, DC: American Psychological Association.

Bates, B. (1993). Individual differences in response to hypnosis. In J. W. Rhue, S. J. Lynn, & I. Kirsch (Eds.), *Handbook of clinical hypnosis* (pp. 23–54). Washington, DC: American Psychological Association.

Bates, B. L., & Brigham, T. A. (1990). Modifying hypnotizability with the Carleton Skills Training Program: A partial replication and analysis of components. *International Journal of Clinical and Experimental Hypnosis, 38,* 183–195.

Benson, J. K. (1975) *The relaxation response.* New York, NY: William Morrow and Company, Inc.

Berkowitz, B., Ross-Townsend, A., & Kohberger, R. (1979). Hypnotic treatment of smoking: The single-treatment method revisited. *The American Journal of Psychiatry, 136*(1), 83–85.

Biener, L., & Abrams, D. B. (1991). The contemplation ladder: Validation of a measure of readiness to consider smoking cessation. *Health Psychology, 10*(5), 360.

Bliss, E. L. (1983). Multiple personalities, related disorders and hypnosis. *American Journal of Clinical Hypnosis, 26*(2), 114–123.

Bootzin, R. R., Epstein, D. A. N. A., & Wood, J. M. (1991). Stimulus control instructions. In P. J. Hauri (Ed.), *Case studies in insomnia* (pp. 19–28). New York: Plenum Press.

Borkovec, T. D., & Whisman, M. A. (1996). Psychological treatment for generalized anxiety disorder. In M. R. Mavissakalian and R. F. Prien (Eds.), *Long-term treatments of anxiety disorders* (pp. 171–199). Washington, DC: American Psychiatric Press.

Bowers, K. S. (Ed.). (1976). *Hypnosis for the seriously curious.* Monterey, CA: Brooks/Cole Publishing Company.

Bowers, K. S. (1990). Unconscious influences and hypnosis. In J. L. Singer (Ed.), *Repression and disassociation: Implications for personality theory, psychopathology, and health* (pp. 143–179). Chicago: University of Chicago Press.

Bowers, K. S. (1992). Imagination and disassociation in hypnotic responding. *International Journal of Clinical and Experimental Hypnosis, 40,* 253–275.

Bowers, K. S. (1993). The Waterloo–Stanford Group C (WSGC) scale of hypnotic susceptibility: Normative and comparative data. *International Journal of Clinical and Experimental Hypnosis, 41,* 35–46.

Bowers, K. S. (1998). Waterloo–Stanford Group Scale of Hypnotic Susceptibility, Form C: Manual and response booklet. *International Journal of Clinical and Experimental Hypnosis, 46,* 250–268.

Bowers, K. S., & Davidson, T. M. (1991). A neodissociation critique of Spanos's social–psychological model of hypnosis. In S. J. Lynn & J. W. Rhue (Eds.), *Theories of hypnosis* (pp. 105–143). New York: Guilford Press.

Braffman, W., & Kirsch, I. (1999). Imaginative suggestibility and hypnotizability: An empirical analysis. *Journal of Personality and Social Psychology, 77*(3), 578–587.

Brown, D. C., & Hammond, C. D. (2007). Evidence-based clinical hypnosis in obstetrics, labor and delivery and preterm labor. *International Journal of Clinical and Experimental Hypnosis, 55*(3), 355–371.

Bryant, R. A., Creamer, M., O'Donnell, M., Silove, D., & McFarlane, A. C. (2008). A multisite study of initial respiration rate and heart rate as predictors of posttraumatic stress disorder. *Journal of Clinical Psychiatry, 6*(11), 1694–1701.

Butler, L. D., Koopman, C., Neri, E., Giese-Davis, J., Palesh, O., & Thorne-Yocam, K. A. (2009). Effects of supportive-expressive group therapy on pain in women with metastatic breast cancer. *Health Psychology, 28,* 579–587.

Buysse, D. J., Reynolds, C. F., Monk, T. H., Berman S. R., & Kupfer, D. J. (1989). The Pittsburgh Sleep Quality Index: A new instrument for psychiatric practice and research. *Psychiatry Research, 28*(2), 193–213.

Carpenter, J. S. (2001). The Hot Flash Related Daily Interference Scale: A tool for assessing the impact of hot flashes on quality of life following breast cancer. *The Journal of Pain and Symptom Management, 22*(6), 979–989.

Castel, A., Perez, M., Sala, J., Padrol, A., & Rull, M. (2007). Effect of hypnotic suggestion on fibromyalgic pain: Comparison between hypnosis and relaxation. *European Journal of Pain. 11*(4), 463–468.

Chambless, D. L., & Ollendick, T. H. (2001). Empirically supported psychological interventions: Controversies and evidence. *Annual Review of Psychology, 52*(1), 685–716.

Cheek, D. B. (1962). Ideomotor questioning for investigation of subconscious "pain" and target organ vulnerability. *American Journal of Clinical Hypnosis, 5*(1), 30–41.

Cohen, S. B. (1989). Clinical uses of measures of hypnotizability. *American Journal of Clinical Hypnosis, 32,* 4–9.

Cornwell, J., Burrows, G. D., & McMurray, N. (1981). Comparison of single and multiple sessions of hypnosis in the treatment of smoking behavior. *Australian Journal of Clinical & Experimental Hypnosis, 9*(2), 61–76.

Council, J. R. (2002). A historical overview of hypnotizability assessment. *American Journal of Clinical Hypnosis, 44*(3–4), 199–208.

Crasilneck, H. B. (1990). Hypnotic techniques for smoking control and psychogenic impotence. *American Journal of Clinical Hypnosis, 32*(3), 147–153.

Crasilneck, H. B., & Hall, J. A. (1985). *Clinical hypnosis: Principles and applications* (2nd ed.). New York, NY: Grune & Stratton.

Crawford, H., & Barabasz, A. (1993) Phobias and intense fears: Rationale for the use of hypnosis in their treatment. In J. W. Rhue, S. Lynn, & I. Kirsch (Eds.), *Handbook of clinical hypnosis* (pp. 245–298). Washington, DC: American Psychological Association.

Deacon, B. J., & Abramowitz, J. S. (2004). Cognitive and behavioral treatments for anxiety disorders: A review of meta-analytic findings. *Journal of Clinical Psychology, 60*(4), 429–441.

Diagnostic Classification Steering Committee & Thorpy, M. J. (1990). *The international classification of sleep disorders: diagnostic and coding manual.* Rochester, MN: American Sleep Disorder Association.

Dinges, D. F., Whitehouse, W. G., Orne, E. C., Bloom, P. B., Carlin, M. M., Bauer, N. K., et al. (1997). Self-hypnosis training as an adjunctive treatment in the management of pain associated with sickle-cell disease. *International Journal of Clinical and Experimental Hypnosis, 45,* 417–432.

Drangsholt, M., & LeResche, L. (1999). Temporomandibular disorder pain. In I. Crombie, P. Croft, S. Linton, I. LeResche, & M. Korff (Eds.), *Epidemiology of pain* (pp. 203–233). Seattle, WA: IASP Press.

Elkins, G. R., Cheung, A., Marcus, J., Palamara, L., & Rajab, H. (2004). Hypnosis to reduce pain in cancer survivors with advanced disease: A prospective study. *Journal of Cancer Integrative Medicine, 2*(4), 167–172.

Elkins, G. R., Fisher, W. I., & Johnson, A. K. (2012). Clinical hypnosis in the treatment of postmenopausal hot flashes: A randomized controlled trial. *Menopause,* Oct 22 [Epub ahead of print] PMID: 23096250.

Elkins, G. R., Jensen, M. P., & Patterson, D. R. (2007). Hypnotherapy for the management of chronic pain. *International Journal of Clinical and Experimental Hypnosis, 55*(3), 275–287.

Elkins, G. R., Johnson, A. K., & Fisher, W. I. (2012). Cognitive hypnotherapy for pain management. *The American Journal of Clinical Hypnosis, 54*(4), 294–310.

Elkins, G., Marcus, J., Bates, J., Rajab, M. H., & Cook, T. (2006). Intensive hypnotherapy for smoking cessation: A prospective study. *International Journal of Clinical and Experimental Hypnosis, 54*(3), 303–315.

Elkins, G.R., Marcus, J., & Rascoe, T. (2003). *Development of a new scale to measure hypnotizability in clinical research.* Paper presented at the 44th Annual Meeting of the American Society of Clinical Hypnosis, Arlington, VA.

Elkins, G., Marcus, J., Stearns, V., Perfect, M., Rajab, M. H., Ruud, C., et al. (2008). Randomized trial of a hypnosis intervention for treatment of hot flashes among breast cancer survivors. *Journal of Clinical Oncology, 26*(31), 5022–5026.

Elkins, G., Marcus, J., Stearns, V., & Rajab, M. H. (2007). Pilot evaluation of hypnosis for the treatment of hot flashes in breast cancer survivors. *Psychooncology, 16*(5), 487–492.

Elkins, G., White, J., Patel, P., Marcus, J., Perfect, M. M., & Montgomery, G. H. (2006). Hypnosis to manage anxiety and pain associated with colonoscopy for colorectal cancer screening: Case studies and possible benefits. *International Journal of Clinical and Experimental Hypnosis, 54*(4), 416–431.

Engvist, B., Biorklund, C., Engman, M., & Jakobsson, J. (1997). Preoperative hypnosis reduces postoperative vomiting after surgery of the breasts: A prospective, randomized and blinded study. *Acta Anaesthesiologica Scandinavica, 41*(8), 1028–1032.

Epstein, S. (1973). The self-concept revisited, or a theory of a theory. *American Psychologist, 28*, 404–416.

Epstein, S. (1990). Cognitive–experiential self-theory. In L. Pervin (Ed.), *Handbook of personality: Theory and research* (pp. 165–192). New York: Guilford Press.

Epstein, S. (1994). Integration of the cognitive and the psychodynamic unconscious. *American Psychologist, 49*(8), 709–724.

Epstein, S. (2003). Cognitive–experiential self-theory of personality. In I. B. Weiner (Ed.), *Handbook of psychology* (pp. 159–184). Hoboken, NJ: John Wiley & Sons, Inc.

Epstein, S., & Pacini, R. (1999). Some basic issues regarding dual-process theories from the perspective of cognitive–experiential self-theory. In S. Chaiken & Y. Trope (Eds.), *Dual-process theories in social psychology* (pp. 462–482). New York, NY: The Guilford Press.

Erickson, M. H. (1977a). Control of physiological functions by hypnosis. *American Journal of Clinical Hypnosis, 20*(1), 8–19.

Erickson, M. H. (1977b). Hypnotic approaches to therapy. *American Journal of Clinical Hypnosis, 20*(1), 20–35.

Erickson, M. H., Rossi, E. L., & Rossi, S. I. (1976). *Hypnotic realities: The induction of clinical hypnosis and forms of indirect suggestion.* New York, NY: Irvington Publishers, Inc.

Everett, J., Patterson, D., Burns, G., Montgomery, B., & Heinbach, D. (1993). Adjunctive interventions for burn pain control: Comparison of hypnosis and Adavan: the 1993 clinical research award. *Journal of Burn Care and Rehabilitation, 14*, 676–683.

Fedoroff, I. C., & Taylor, S. (2001). Psychological and pharmacological treatments of social phobia: A meta-analysis. *Journal of Clinical Psychopharmacology, 21*(3), 311–324.

Feske, U., & Chambless, D. L. (1995). Cognitive behavioral versus exposure only treatment for social phobia: A meta-analysis. *Behavior Therapy, 26*(4), 695–720.

Fiore, M. C., Bailey, W. C., Cohen, S. J, Dorfman, S. F., Goldstein, M. G., Gritz, E. R., & Wewers, M. E. (2000). *Treating tobacco use and dependence: A clinical practice guideline.* Rockville, MD: Agency for Health Care Policy and Research, Public Health Service.

Foenander, G., Burrows, G. D., Gerschman, J., & Horne, D. J. (1980). Phobic behavior and hypnotic susceptibility. *Australian Journal of Clinical & Experimental Hypnosis. 8*(1), 41–46.

Forrest, D. (1999). *Hypnotism: A history.* London: Penguin.

Frankel, F. H. (1976). *Hypnosis: Trance as a coping mechanism.* New York: Plenum.

Frankel, F. H., & Orne, M. T. (1976). Hypnotizability and phobic behavior. *Archives of General Psychiatry, 33*(10), 1259.

Frauman, D., Lynn, S., & Brentar, J. (1993). Prevention and therapeutic management of "negative effects" in hypnotherapy. In J. Rhue, S. Lvnn, & I. Kirsch (Eds.), *Handbook of clinical hypnosis* (pp. 95–120). Washington, DC: American Psychological Association.

Frischholz, E. J., Braun, B. G., Sachs, R. G., & Schwartz, D. R. (1991). Construct validity of the Dissociative Experiences Scale (DES): I. The relationship between DES and other self-report measures of DES. *Dissociation: Progress in the Dissociative Disorders, 4,* 185–188.

Frischholz, E. J., Spiegel, H., Tryon, W. W., & Fisher, S. (1981). The relationship between the hypnotic induction profile and the Stanford Hypnotic Susceptibility Scale, Form C: Revisited. *American Journal of Clinical Hypnosis, 24,* 98–105.

Frischholz, E. J., Tryon, W. W., Fisher, S., Maruffi, B.L., Vellios, A. T., & Spiegel, H. (1980). The relationship between the hypnotic induction profile and the Stanford Hypnotic Susceptibility Scale, Form C: A replication. *American Journal of Clinical Hypnosis, 22,* 185–196.

Fromm, E., & Nash, M. R. (1992). *Contemporary hypnosis research.* New York: Guilford Press.

Galovski, T. E., & Blanchard, E. B. (1998). Treatment of irritable bowel syndrome with hypnotherapy. *Appied Psychophysiological Biofeedback, 23*(4), 219–232.

Gay, M. C., Philippot, P., & Luminet, O. (2002). Differential effectiveness of psychological interventions for reducing osteoarthritis pain: A comparison of hypnosis and relaxation. *The European Journal of Pain, 6,* 1–16.

Gerschman, J. A., Burrows, G. D., & Reade, P. C. (1987). Hypnotizability and dental phobic disorders. *International Journal of Psychosomatics. 34*(4), 42–47.

Gerschman, J. A., Burrows, G. D., Reade, P. C. & Foenander, G. (1979). Hypnotizability and the treatment of dental phobic illness. In G. D. Burrows and D. R. Collison (Eds.), *Hypnosis 1979,* pp. 33-39 Amsterdam: Elsevier/ North Holland Biomedical Press.

Gould, R. A., Otto, M. W., Pollack, M. H., & Yap, L. (1997). Cognitive behavioral and pharmacological treatment of generalized anxiety disorder: A preliminary meta-analysis. *Behavior Therapy, 28*(2), 285–305.

Gravitz, M. A., & Gravitz, R. F. (1977). The collected writings of Milton H. Erickson: A complete bibliography 1929–1977. *American Journal of Clinical Hypnosis, 20,* 84–94.

Gravitz, M., Mallet, J., Munyon, P., & Gerton, M. (1982). Ethical considerations in the professional applications of hypnosis. In M. Rosenbaum (Ed.), *Ethics and values in psychotherapy: A guidebook* (pp. 297–312). New York, NY: Free Press.

Green, J. P., & Lynn, S. J. (2000). Hypnosis and suggestion-based approaches to smoking cessation: An examination of the evidence. *International Journal of Clinical and Experimental Hypnosis, 48*(2), 195–224.

Gruzelier, J. H. (2006). Frontal functions, connectivity and neural efficiency underpinning hypnosis and hypnotic susceptibility. *Contemporary Hypnosis, 23*(1), 15–32.

Haanen, H. C., Hoenderdos, H. T., Van Romude, L. K., Hop, W. C, Mallee, C., Terwiel, J. P., & Hekster, G. B. (1991). Controlled trial of hypnotherapy in the treatment of refractory fibromyalgia. *Journal of Rheumatology, 18*(1), 72–75.

Haley, J. (1973). *Uncommon therapy: The psychiatric techniques of Milton H. Erickson, M.D.* New York, NY: W. W. Norton & Company, Inc.

Hammond, D. C. (1983). *Myths about Erickson and Ericksonian hypnosis.* Paper presented at the Annual Meeting of the American Society of Clinical Hypnosis, Dallas, TX.

Hammond, D.C. (1990). *Handbook of hypnotic suggestions and metaphors.* New York, NY: W. W. Norton & Company, Inc.

Hartland, J. (1965). The value of "ego-strengthening" procedures prior to direct symptom-removal under hypnosis. *American Journal of Clinical Hypnosis, 8*(2), 89–93.

Hawkins, R. M. F. (2001). A systematic meta-review of hypnosis as an empirically supported treatment for pain. *Pain reviews, 8*(2), 47–73.

Heatherton, T. F., Kozlowski, L. T., Fecker, R. C., & Fagerström, K. O. (1991). Measuring nicotine dependence: A review of the Fagerström Tolerance Nicotine Questionnaire. *British Journal of Addiction, 86,* 1119–1127.

Hilgard, E. R. (1965). *Hypnotic susceptibility.* New York, NY: Harcourt, Brace & Jovanovich.

Hilgard, E. R. (1973). A neodissociation interpretation of pain reduction in hypnosis. *Psychological Review, 80,* 391–398.

Hilgard, E. R. (1974). Toward a neo-dissociation theory: Multiple cognitive controls in human functioning. *Perspectives in Biology and Medicine, 17,* 301–316.

Hilgard, E. R. (1977). *Divided consciousness: Multiple controls in human thought and action.* New York, NY: John Wiley and Sons.

Hilgard, E. R. (1979). The Stanford hypnotic arm levitation induction and test (shalit): A six-minute hypnotic induction and measurement scale. *International Journal of Clinical and Experimental Hypnosis, 27*(2), 111–124.

Hilgard, E. R. (1981a). The eye roll sign and other scores of the hypnotic induction profile (HIP) as related to the Stanford Hypnotic Susceptibility Scale, Form C (SHSS: C): A critical discussion of a study by Frischholz and others. *American Journal of Clinical Hypnosis, 24,* 89–97.

Hilgard, E. R. (1981b). Further discussion of the HIP and the Stanford Form C: A reply to a reply by Frischholz, Spiegel, Tryon, and Fisher. *American Journal of Clinical Hypnosis, 24,* 106–108.

Hilgard, E. R. (1986). *Divided consciousness. Multiple controls in human thought and action* (rev. ed.). New York, NY: John Wiley and Sons.

Hilgard, E. R. (1991). A neodissociation interpretation of hypnosis. In S. J. Lynn, & J. W. Rhue (Eds.), *Theories of hypnosis: Current models and perspectives* (pp. 83–104). New York: Guilford Press.

Hilgard, E. R., Crawford, H. J., & Wert, A. (1979). The Stanford Hypnotic Arm Levitation Induction and Test (SHALIT): A six-minute hypnotic induction and measurement scale. *International Journal of Clinical and Experimental Hypnosis,* 27, 111–124.

Hilgard, E. R., & Hilgard, J. R. (1975). *Hypnosis in the relief of pain.* Los Altos, CA: William Kaufmann.

Hilgard, J. R., & Hilgard, E. R. (1979). Assessing hypnotic responsiveness in a clinical setting: A multi-item clinical scale and its advantages over single-item scales. *International Journal of Clinical and Experimental Hypnosis, 27,* 134–150.

Hilgard, E. R., & Hilgard, J. R. (1983). *Hypnosis in the relief of pain* (2nd ed.). Los Altos, CA: William Kaufmann.

Holroyd, J. (1980). Hypnosis treatment for smoking: An evaluative review. *International Journal of Clinical and Experimental Hypnosis, 28*(4), 341–357.

Hull, C. L. (1933). *Hypnosis and suggestibility: An experimental approach.* New York, NY: Appleton-Century.

Hylands-White, N., & Derbyshire, S.W.G. (2007). Modifying pain perception: Is it better to be hypnotizable or feel that you are hypnotized? *Contemporary Hypnosis, 24*(4), 143–153.

Hyman, G. J., Stanley, R. O., Burrows, G. D., & Horne, D. J. (1986). Treatment effectiveness of hypnosis and behavior therapy in smoking cessation: A methodological refinement. *Addictive Behaviors, 11*(4), 355–365.

Javel, A. F. (1980). One-session hypnotherapy for smoking: A controlled study. *Psychological Reports, 46*(3), 895–899.

Jensen, M. P., Barber, J., Romano, J. M., Molton, I. R., Raichle, K., & Osborne, T. L. (2009). A comparison of self-hypnosis versus progressive muscle relaxation in patients with multiple sclerosis and chronic back pain. *International Journal of Clinical and Experimental Hypnosis, 57,* 198–221.

Jensen, M. P., Abresch, R. T., Carter, G. T., & McDonald, C. M. (2005). Chronic pain in persons with neuromuscular disease. *Archives of physical medicine and rehabilitation, 86*(6), 1155–1163.

Jensen, M. P., Alschuler, K. N., Smith, A. E., Verrall, A. M., Goetz, M. C., & Molton, I. R. (2011). Pain and fatigue in persons with post-polio syndrome: Independent effects on functioning. *Archives of Physical Medicine and Rehabilitation, 92*(11), 1796–1801.

John, R., Hollander, B., & Perry, C. (1983). Hypnotizability and phobic behavior: Further supporting data. *Journal of abnormal psychology, 92*(3), 390.

Johnson, D. L., & Karkut, R. T. (1994). Performance by gender in a stop-smoking program combining hypnosis and aversion. *Psychological Reports, 75,* 851–857.

Jones, E. (1955). *The life and work of Sigmund Freud* (Vol.2). New York, NY: Basic Books.

Jones, E. (1959). *Free associations: Memories of a psycho-analyst.* London: Hogarth Press.

Jones, H., Cooper, P., Miller, V., Brooks, N., & Whorwell, P. J. (2006). Treatment of non-cardiac chest pain: A controlled trial of hypnotherapy. *Gut, 55*(10), 1403–1408.

Kelly, S. F. (1984). Measured hypnotic response and phobic behavior: A brief communication. *International Journal of Clinical and Experimental Hypnosis, 32*(1), 1–5.

Kessler, R. C., Berglund, P., Demler, O., Jin, R., Merikangas, K. R., & Walters, E. E. (2005). Lifetime prevalence and age-of-onset distributions of DSM-IV disorders in the National Comorbidity Survey Replication. *Archives of General Psychiatry, 62*(6), 593.

Kessler, R. C., Chiu, W. T., Demler, O., & Walters, E. E. (2005). Prevalence, severity, and comorbidity of 12-month DSM-IV disorders in the National Comorbidity Survey Replication. *Archives of General Psychiatry, 62*(6), 617.

Kiecolt-Glaser, J. K., Marucha, P. T., Atkinson, C., & Glaser, R. (2001). Hypnosis as a modulator of cellular immune dysregulation during acute stress. *Journal of Consulting and Clinical Psychology, 69*(4), 674–682.

Kihlstrom, J. F. (1985). Hypnosis. *Annual Review in Psychology, 36*, 385–418.

Kihlstrom, J. F. (1990). The psychological unconscious. In L. Pervin (Ed.), *Handbook of personality: Theory and research* (pp. 445–464).New York, NY: Guilford Press.

Kihlstrom, J. F. (2008). The domain of hypnosis, revisited. In M. R. Nash, & A. J. Barnier (Eds.), *The Oxford Handbook of Clinical Hypnosis* (pp. 21–52). Oxford, UK: Oxford University Press.

Kirsch, I. (1985). Response expectancy as a determinant of experience and behavior. *American Psychologist, 40*, 1189–1202.

Kirsch, I. (1990). *Changing expectations: A key to effective psychotherapy.* Pacific Grove, CA: Brooks/Cole.

Kirsch, I. (1991). The social learning theory of hypnosis: Current models and perspectives. In S. J. Lynn, & J. W. Rhue (Eds.), *Theories of hypnosis: Current models and perspectives* (pp. 439–465). New York: Guilford Press.

Kirsch, I. (1999). Setting the record straight (again). *American Journal of Clinical Hypnosis, 41*, 226–230.

Kirsch, I. (2005). The flexible observer: A neodissociation theory. *Contemporary Hypnosis, 22*(3), 152–153.

Kirsch, I., & Lynn, S. J. (1998). Dissociation theories of hypnosis. *Psychological Bulletin, 123*(1), 100–115.

Kirsch, I., & Lynn, S. J. (1999). Automaticity in clinical psychology. *American Psychologist, 54*(7), 504–515.

Kirsch, I., Silva, C. E., Carone, J. E., Johnston, D. J. & Simon, B. (1989). The surreptitious observation design: An experimental paradigm for distinguishing artifact from essence in hypnosis. *Journal of Abnormal Psychology, 98*(2), 132–136.

Kopp, S. (1971). *Guru: Metaphors from a psychotherapist.* Palo Alto, CA: Science and Behavior Books.

Kosslyn, S. M., Thompson, W. L., Costantini-Ferrando, M. F., Alpert, N. M., & Spiegel, D. (2000). Hypnotic visual illusion alters color processing in the brain. *American Journal of Psychiatry, 157*, 1279–1284.

Lang, E. V., Benotsch, E. G., Fick, L. J., Lutgendorf, S., Berbaum, M. L., Berbaum, K. S., Spiegel, D. (2000). Adjunctive non-pharmacological analgesia for invasive medical procedures: A randomized trial. *The Lancet, 355*(9214), 1486–1490.

Lankton, S., & Lankton, C. (1983). *The answer within: A clinical framework of Ericksonian hypnotherapy.* New York, NY: Brunner Mazel Publishers, Inc.

Lynn, S. J. (1997). Automaticity and hypnosis: A sociocognitive account. *International Journal of Clinical and Experimental Hypnosis, 45*, 239–250.

Lynn, S. J. (2000). Hypnosis as an empirically supported clinical intervention: The state of the evidence and a look to the future. *International Journal of Clinical and Experimental Hypnosis, 48*(2), 239–259.

Lynn, S. J., Kirsch, I., & Rhue, J. W. (Eds.). (1996). *A casebook of clinical hypnosis.* Washington, DC: American Psychological Association.

MacHovec, F. J. (1975). The Cult of Asklipios. *The American Journal of Clinical Hypnosis, 22*, 85–90.

McCauley, J. D., Thelen, M. H., Frank, R. G., Willard, R. R., & Callen, K. E. (1983). Hypnosis compared to relaxation in the outpatient management of chronic low back pain. *Archives of Physical Medicine and Rehabilitation, 64*(11), 548–552.

McConkey, K. M. (1984). Clinical hypnosis: Differential impact on volitional and non-volitional disorders. *Canadian Journal of Psychology, 25,* 79.

McConkey, K. M., & Perry, C. (2002). Benjamin Franklin and mesmerism, revisited. *Journal of Clinical and Experimental Hypnosis, 50*(4), 320–331.

Melzack, R. (1975). The McGill Pain Questionnaire: Major properties and scoring methods. *Pain, 1*(3), 277–299.

Montgomery, G. H., David, D., Winkel, G., Silverstein, J. H., & Bovbierg, D. H. (2002). The effectiveness of adjunctive hypnosis with surgical patients: A meta-analysis. *Anesthesia and Analgesia, 94*(6), 1639–1645.

Montgomery, G. H., DuHamel, K. N., & Redd, W. H. (2000). A meta-analysis of hypnotically induced analgesia: How effective is hypnosis? *International Journal of Clinical Hypnosis, 48*(2), 138–153.

Morgan, A. H., Johnson, D. L., & Hilgard, E. R. (1974). The stability of hypnotic susceptibility: A longitudinal study. *International Journal of Clinical and Experimental Hypnosis, 22,* 249–257.

Morgan, A. H., & Hilgard, J. R. (1978 Oct–1979 Jan). The Stanford Hypnotic Clinical Scale for Children (SHCS:Child). *American Journal of Clinical Hypnosis, 21*(2–3), 148–169.

Morgan, A. H., & Hilgard, J. R. (1978–1979a). The Stanford Hypnotic Clinical Scale for Adults (SHCS:Adult). *American Journal of Clinical Hypnosis, 21,* 134–147.

Morin, C.M. (1993). *Insomnia: Psychological assessment and management.* New York: Guilford.

Musês, A. M., & Young, C. (Eds.). (1972). *Consciousness and reality: The human pivot point.* New York, NY: E. P. Dutton & Co.

Nash, M. (1987). What, if anything, is regressed about hypnotic age regression? A review of the empirical literature. *Psychological Bulletin, 102*(1), 42–52.

Nash, M. R. (1988). Hypnosis as a window on regression. *Bulletin of the Menninger Clinic, 52*, 383–403.

Neron, S., & Stephenson, R. (2007). Effectiveness of hypnotherapy with cancer patients' trajectory: Emesis, acute pain, and analgesia and anxiolysis in procedures. *International Journal of Clinical and Experimental Hypnosis, 55*(3), 336–354.

Nestoriuc, Y., Martin, A., Rief, W., & Andrasik, F. (2008). Biofeedback treatment for headache disorders: A comprehensive efficacy review. *Applied Psychophysiology and Biofeedback 33*(3), 125–140.

Neufeld, V., & Lynn, S. J. (1988). A single-session group self-hypnosis smoking cessation treatment: A brief communication. *International Journal of Clinical and Experimental Hypnosis, 36*(2), 75–79.

Niaura, R., & Abrams, D. B. (2002). Smoking cessation: Progress, priorities, and prospectus. *Journal of Consulting and Clinical Psychology, 70*(3), 494.

Olness, K., MacDonald, J. T., & Uden, D. L. (1987). Comparison of self-hypnosis and propranolol in the treatment of juvenile classic migraine. *Pediatrics, 79*(4), 593–597.

Orne, M. T. (1959). The nature of hypnosis: Artifact and essence. *Journal of Abnormal and Social Psychology, 58*, 277–299.

Orne, M. T., Hilgard, E. R., Spiegel, H., Speigel, D., Crawford, H. J., Evans, F. J., et al. (1979). The relationship between the hypnotic induction profile and the Stanford Hypnotic Susceptibility Scales, Forms A and C. *International Journal of Clinical and Experimental Hypnosis, 27*(2), 85–102.

Palsson, O. S., Turner, M. J., & Whitehead, W. E. (2006). Hypnosis home treatment for irritable bowel syndrome: A pilot study. *International Journal of Clinical and Experimental Hypnosis, 54*(1), 85–99.

Patterson, D. R., & Jensen, M. P. (2003). Hypnosis and clinical pain. *Psychological Bulletin, 129*(4), 495–521.

Patterson, D. R., & Ptacek, J. T. (1997). Baseline pain as a moderator of hypnotic analgesia for burn injury treatment. *Journal of Consulting and Clinical Psychology, 65*, 60–67.

Pederson, L. L., Scrimgeour, W. G., & Lefcoe, N. M. (1975). Comparison of hypnosis plus counseling, counseling alone, and hypnosis alone in a community service smoking withdrawal program. *Journal of Consulting and Clinical Psychology, 43*(6), 920.

Perry, C., Nadon, R., & Button, J. (1992). The measurement of hypnotic ability. In E. Fromm & M. R. Nash (Eds.), *Contemporary Hypnosis Research* (pp. 459–490). New York, NY: Guilford Press.

Pettinati, H. M., Horne, R. L., & Staats, J. M. (1985). Hypnotizability in patients with anorexia nervosa and bulimia. *Archives of General Psychiatry, 42*(10), 1014–1016.

Piccione, C., Hilgard, E. R., Zimbardo, & P.G. (1989). On the degree of stability of measured hypnotizability over a 25-year period. *Journal of Personality and Social Psychology, 56*(2), 289–295.

Prior, A., Colgan, S. M., & Whorwell, P. J. (1990). Changes in rectal sensitivity after hypnotherapy in patients with irritable bowel syndroms. *GUT: An International Journal of Gastroenterology and Hepatology, 31*(8), 896–898.

Prochaska, J. O., & DiClemente, C. C. (1983). Stages and processes of self-change of smoking: Toward an integrative model of change. *Journal of Consulting and Clinical Psychology, 51*(3), 390.

Rabkin, S. W., Boyko, E., Shane, F., & Kaufert, J. (1984). A randomized trial comparing smoking cessation programs utilizing behavior modification, health education or hypnosis. *Addictive Behaviors, 9*(2), 157–173.

Rainville, P., Hofbauer, R. K., Bushnell, M. C., Duncan, G. H., & Price, D. D. (2002). Hypnosis modulates activity in brain structures involved in the regulation of consciousness. *Journal of Cognitive Neuroscience, 14,* 887–901.

Rucklidge, J. J., & Saunders, D. (2002). The efficacy of hypnosis in the treatment of pruritus in people with HIV/AIDS: A time-series analysis. *International Journal of Clinical and Experimental Hypnosis, 50*(2), 149–169.

Schoenberger, N. E., Kirsch, I., Gearan, P., Montgomery, G. H., & Pastyrnak, S. L. (1997). Hypnotic enhancement of a cognitive behavioral treatment for public speaking anxiety. *Behavior Therapy, 28,* 127–140.

Sheehan, P. W., & McConkey, K. M. (1993). Forensic hypnosis: The application of ethical guidelines. In J. Rhue, S. J. Lynn, & I. Kirsch (Eds.), *Handbook of clinical hypnosis* (pp. 719–738). Washington, DC: American Psychological Association.

Shenefelt, P. D. (2000). Hypnosis in dermatology. *Archives of Dermatology, 136*(3), 393–399.

Shor, R. E., & Orne, E. C. (1962). *Harvard group scale of hypnotic susceptibility.* Palo Alto, CA: Consulting Psychology Press.

Spanos, N., & Hewitt, E. C. (1980). The hidden observer in hypnotic analgesia: Discovery or experimental creation. *Journal of Personality and Social Psychology, 39*(6), 1201–1214.

Spanos, N. P., Mondoux, T. J., & Burgess, C. A. (1995). Comparison of multi-component hypnotic and non-hypnotic treatments for smoking. *Contemporary Hypnosis, 12*(1), 12–19.

Spanos, N. P., Radtke, H. L., Hodgins, D. C., Bertrand, L. D., Stam, H. J., & Dubreuil, D. L. (1983). The Carleton University responsiveness to suggestion scale: Stability, reliability, and relationships with expectancy and hypnotic experiences. *Psychological Reports, 53,* 555–563.

Spanos, N. P., Sims, A., de Faye, B., Mondoux, T. J., & Gabora, N. J. (1992–1993). A comparison of hypnotic and nonhypnotic treatments for smoking. *Imagination, Cognition and Personality, 12*(1), 23–43.

Spanos, N. P., Stenstrom, R. J., & Johnson, J. C. (1988). Hypnosis, placebo, and suggestion in the treatmet of warts. *Psychosomatic Medicine, 50,* 245–260.

Spanos, N. P., Williams, V., & Gwynne, M. L. (1990). Effects of hypnotic, placebo, and salicylic acid treatments on wart regression. *Psychosomatic Medicine, 52*(1), 109–114.

Spiegel, D., & Bloom, J. R. (1983). Group therapy and hypnosis reduce metastatic breast carcinoma pain. *Psychosomatic Medicine, 45,* 333–339.

Spiegel, D., Frischholz, E. J., Fleiss, J. L., & Spiegel, H. (1993). Predictors of smoking abstinence following a single-session restructuring intervention with self-hypnosis. *American Journal of Psychiatry, 150,* 1090–1090.

Spiegel, D., Hunt, T. H., & Dondershine, H. E. (1988). Dissociation and hypnotizability in posttraumatic stress disorder. *American Journal of Psychiatry, 145,* 301–305.

Spiegel, D., Tryon, W. W., Frischholz, E. J., & Spiegel, H. (1982). Hilgard's illusion. *Archives of General Psychiatry, 39,* 972–974.

Spiegel, H. (1970). A single-treatment method to stop smoking using ancillary self-hypnosis. *International Journal of Clinical and Experimental Hypnosis, 18*(4), 235–250.

Spiegel, H., Greenleaf, M., & Spiegel, D. (2000). Hypnosis. In: Sadock B., Sadock V. (Eds.) *Comprehensive Textbook of Psychiatry,* 7th ed. (pp. 2128–2145). Philadelphia: Lippincott, Williams, & Wilkins.

Spiegel, H., Greenleaf, M., & Speigel, D. (2000). Hypnosis. In: Sadock, B. J., Sadock, V. A. (Eds.) *Kaplan & Sadock's Comprehensive Textbook of Psychiatry.* Vol. 2. 7th ed. Philadelphia, PA: Lippincott, Williams, & Wilkins.

Spiegel, H. & Spiegel, D. (1978). *Trance and treatment: Clinical uses of hypnosis.* New York, NY: Basic Books.

Spielman, A. J., Saskin, P., & Thorpy, M. J. (1987). Treatment of chronic insomnia by restriction of time in bed. *Sleep: Journal of Sleep Research & Sleep Medicine, 10*(1), 45–56.

Spinhoven, P., & Linssen, A. C. G. (1989). Education and self-hypnosis in the management of low back pain: A component analysis. *British Journal of Clinical Psychology, 28,* 145–153.

Stanton, H. E. (1978). A one-session hypnotic approach to modifying smoking behavior. *International Journal of Clinical and Experimental Hypnosis, 26*(1), 22–29.

Sternbach, R. A. (1968). *Pain. A psychophysiological analysis.* New York: Academic Press.

Stutman, R. & Bliss E. (1985). Post-traumatic stress disorder, hypnotizability and imagery. *American Journal of Psychiatry, 142*(6), 741–743.

Szechtman, H., Woody, E., Bowers, K. S. & Nahmias, C. (1998). Where the imaginal appears real: A positron emission tomography study of auditory hallucinations. *Proceedings of the National Academy of Sciences of the United States, 95*(4), 1956–1960.

Vicol, M. C., Bulgaru-Iliescu, D., Ioan, B., & Astarastoae, V. (2009). The drug-addict: Patient or prisoner?. *Romanian Journal of Legal Medicine. 17,* 309–312.

Wall, T. W. (1991). Ethics: The royal road to legitimacy. *American Journal of Clinical Hypnosis, 34*(2), 73–78.

Walsh, J. K., & Schweitzer, P. K. (1999). Ten-year trends in the pharmacological treatment of insomnia. *Sleep: Journal of Sleep Research & Sleep Medicine, 22,* 371–375.

Watkins, J. G. (1971). The affect bridge: A hypnoanalytic technique. *The International Journal of Clinical and Experimental Hypnosis, 19*(1), 21–27.

Weitzenhoffer, A. M., & Hilgard, E. R. (1959). *Stanford Hypnotic Susceptibility Scale: Forms A and B.* Palo Alto, CA: Consulting Psychologists Press.

Weitzanhoffer, A. M. & Hilgard, E. R. (1962). *Stanford Hypnotic Susceptibility Scale: Form C.* Palo Alto, CA: Consulting Psychologists Press.

Weitzenhoffer, A. M. & Hilgard, E .R. (1963). *Stanford Profile Scales of Hypnotic Susceptibility, Forms I and II.* Palo Alto, CA: Consulting Psychologists Press.

Weitzenhoffer, A. M. & Sjoberg, B. M. (1961). Suggestibility with and without an induction of hypnosis. *Journal of Mental and Nervous Diseases, 132*, 204–220.

Weston, D., & Morrison, K. (2001). A multidimensional meta-analysis of treatments for depression, panic, and generalized anxiety disorder: An empirical examination of the status of empirically supported therapies. *Journal of Consulting and Clinical Psychology, 69*, 875–899.

White, R. W. (1941). An analysis of motivation in hypnosis. *Journal of General Psychology, 24,* 145–162.

Wickless, C., & Kirsch, I. (1989). Effects of verbal and experiential expectancy manipulations on hypnotic susceptibility. *Journal of Personality and Social Psychology,* 57(5), 762–768.

Williams, J. M., & Hall, D. W. (1988). Use of single session hypnosis for smoking cessation. *Addictive behaviors, 13*(2), 205–208.

Winocur, E., Gavish, A., Emodi-Perlman A., Halachmi, M., & Eli, I. (2002). Hypnorelaxation as treatment for myofascial pain disorder: A comparative study. *Oral Surgery, Oral Medicine, Oral Pathology and Endontics, 93*(4), 425–434.

Woody, E. Z., & Sadler, P. (2008). Dissociation theories of hypnosis. In S. J. Lynn, & A. J. Barnier (Eds.), *The Oxford Handbook of Clinical Hypnosis* (pp. 81–110). Oxford: Oxford University Press.

Yapko, M. D. (2003). *Trancework: An introduction to the practice of clinical hypnosis.* New York, NY: Brunner-Routledge.

Index

Abreactions, trance management and, 206–207
Acrophobia, 126
Adaptive dissociation, 21–22
  concept of, 23–24
  and hypnotic response, 24
Affect bridge technique, 209–210
Alcohol consumption and antihistamines, 198
Alerting
  in first HRT session, 65
  and hypnotizability assessment, 118
  in second HRT session, 74–75
  suggestions for, 42
Alteration in pain sensation, 152–153
American Psychological Association (APA), 3, 227
American Society for Clinical Hypnosis (ASCH), 3, 225, 227
Animal magnetism, 1
Antihistamines, 198
Anxiety management
  assessment and case conceptualization, 184
  case example, dental anxiety, 188–193
  conscious/rational versus unconscious/experiential processing of threat, 184
  hypnotic relaxation and cognitive–behavioral therapy, 185
  hypnotic suggestions for, 185–188
  hypnotizability and, 184–185
  insomnia and, 196
Arm heaviness/arm immobility
  EHS, 105–107
  induction, 113–114
  scoring inquiry, 121
Arm lightness/arm levitation
  EHS, 107
  induction, 45–46, 114–115
  scoring inquiry, 122
Arm-lowering induction, 46
Atonia, 197
Authority problems, 128

Barber Suggestibility Scale, 104
Behavioral treatments, for insomnia, 198
Beneficence, 223
Benzodiazepine receptor agonists, 197
Bernheim, Hippolyte, 2
Braid, James, 2
Breathing-focus induction, 43–44
Breuer, Josef, 2
Bulimia, diagnosing patients with, 101

Carleton University Responsivity to Suggestion Scale, 104
Case conceptualization and treatment planning of anxiety problems, 184
  case of Linda, 52–55
  diagnosis, 51

Case conceptualization (*Continued*)
  HRT, discussion of, 52
  hypnotic experience and ability, 51
  management plan, 52
  mental status examination, 51
  presenting problems, 47–48
    experiential representations, 50–51
    history of, 49
    physical factors, 49
    psychological factors, 49–50
    social environment, 50
    timeline and key events, 49
  strengths and weaknesses, 52
  summary statement and goals, 51
Charcot, Jean Martin, 2
Chronic insomnia, 195
Clinical research and hypnotherapy, integration of, 4–6
Cognitive-Experiential Self Theory (CEST), 18
Cognitive restructuring, 186
Cognitive unconscious, 18
Cognitive–behavioral therapy (CBT)
  hypnotic relaxation and, 185
Coin-drop induction, 44–45
Comfort, 63
Communication, therapeutic, 10–11
Competence, 221–222
Confidential information, protecting patient's privacy and, 223
Conscious and unconscious minds, 17–19, 59
Contemplation Ladder, 163
Coping skills, developing, 14, 88–89

Deepening
  and dissociation, 64, 174
  relaxation, 186
  suggestions, 38–39
  trance, mental imagery for relaxation, 63
Defense against psychopathology, 129
Defiance versus resistance, 126
Delta sleep, 197
Delta waves, 197
Dental anxiety, case example, 188–193
Depression, 196
Direct versus permissive suggestions, 34
Dissociated control theory, 23
Dissociation
  adaptive, 21–22, 23–24
  from cravings, 166
  and deepening, 174
  deepening and, 64
  mental imagery and, 39–40, 74, 107, 115, 123
  from pain experience, 151–152
  therapeutic, 10, 21
Dissociative identity disorder (DID), 100
Dissociative theories, of hypnotic response, 22–23
Dual-process theory of personality, 17–18

Eating disorders and hypnotizability, 101
Ego-strengthening suggestions, 143–146
Elkins Hypnotizability Scale (EHS), 10, 51, 99, 148
  administration protocol for, 111
  constructs of
    arm heaviness, 105–107
    arm lightness, 107
    mental imagery and dissociation, 107
    positive hallucination, 107–108
    post-hypnotic amnesia, 108
    rose-scent olfactory hallucination, 107
  development of, 102, 104–105
  and EHS: C, 110–111
  psychometric properties of, 108–111
  scoring summary, 119
Emotional distress, 149
Emotional relaxation, 24
Erickson, Milton, 4
Ericksonian Hypnosis, 4
Esdaile, James, 2
Eszopiclone, 198
Ethical considerations
  beneficence, 223
  competence, 221–222
  in hypnotic relaxation therapy practice, 221–225

informed consent, 222–223
licensure/professionalism, 224
privacy and confidentiality, 223
professional judgments, 222
recordings of HRT sessions, 224–225
Expectancy
creating positive, 32
effects of, 20–21
Experiential/unconscious system
information processing, 91–92
and insight, 205–206
language of, 36–37
and rational/conscious system, 19
threat, 184
Eye closure, 38
Eye-focus induction, 42–43

Fading of the generalized reality orientation (GRO), suggestion for, 38
Fagerstrom Test of Nicotine Dependency, 163
Finger movements, 140
Formal metaphors, 142
issues of codependency, 142–143
Franklin Commission, 1–2
Freud, Sigmund, 2, 17–18

General ego-strengthening suggestions, 143
Generalized reality orientation (GRO) fading, suggestion for, 38
Goals, in HRT, 11–12, 40

Hand-warming exercises, 80
Harvard Group Scale of Hypnotic Susceptibility, Form A (HGSHS: A), 103
Hilgard, Ernest, 3
Hot Flash Daily Diary, 172
Hot Flash Daily Interference Scale, 170
Hot flashes
case example, 175–181
evidence for HRT for, 169–170
general treatment guidelines, 170–171
hypnotic suggestions for
individualization of, 171
treatment, 173–175
recording, 172–173
Hull, Clark L., 3
Hypnoanalgesia, for pain management, 154–155
Hypnoprojective methods, 208–209
Hypnosis
Erickson's publications on, 4
history of, 1
recognized, 5
rise of scientific study of, 3–4
in treatment of mental health conditions, 6
use of, 2–3, 5
Hypnosis Research Project, 3
Hypnotherapeutic relationship, 27–28
Hypnotherapy
and clinical research, integration of, 4–6
practice of, 15
Hypnotic depth, 105
Hypnotic experience and ability, 51
Hypnotic induction
alerting, 42
arm-levitation induction, 45–46
arm-lowering induction, 46
breathing-focus induction, 43–44
coin-drop induction, 44–45
deepening suggestions, 38–39
eye closure, 38
eye-focus induction, 42–43
fading of the generalized reality orientation (GRO), 38
in first session
alerting, 65
comfort, 63
deepening and dissociation, 64
eye focus induction, 62–63
mental imagery
for reducing anxiety and headache, 64
for relaxation and deepening trance, 63–64
post-hypnotic suggestions, 65
reinforcement, 64

Hypnotic induction (*Continued*)
relaxation, 63
setting the overall session goal, 63
focusing of attention, 37
in fourth session, 95–96
inadequate preparation for, 127
and individualization, 46
initial suggestions for relaxation, 37–38
mental imagery and dissociation, 39–40
post-hypnotic suggestions, 41–42
refining the process of, and interventions, 137–146
ego-strengthening suggestions, 143–146
formal metaphors, issues of codependency, 142–143
hypnotic phenomena, use of, 138–139
ideomotor responses, use of, 140–141
targeting hypnotic suggestions, 139
therapeutic metaphors, use of, 141–142
trance management, 139–140
variation in voice quality and intensity, 137–138
verbal and nonverbal hypnotic suggestions, 138
reinforcement of response, 40–41
in second session
alerting, 74–75
deepening suggestions, 73
encouraging fading of the generalized reality orientation, 72–73
focusing of attention, 72
initial suggestions for relaxation, 72
mental imagery and dissociation, 74
post-hypnotic suggestion, 74
reinforcement of response, 74
setting the overall session goal, 73
setting the overall goal, 40
structure of, 13, 37–42
in third session, 82–83
Hypnotic Induction Profile (HIP), 103–104
Hypnotic interventions, early historical events in development of, 2–3
Hypnotic phenomena, 32–34
use of, 138–139
Hypnotic relaxation-based interventions
in cancer-related pain, 5
for mental imagery and symptom reduction, 5
for pain relief, 6
in treatment of gastroenterological disorders, 6
Hypnotic relaxation induction
and cognitive–behavioral therapy, 185
for improving sleep, 200–203
and suggestions, 5
Hypnotic relaxation therapy (HRT). *See also* Pain management
adaptive dissociation, 21–22
concept of, 23–24
becoming skilled clinician in, 15
benefits, 228
case conceptualization review, 52
conscious and unconscious minds, 17–19
daily practice, at home, 9
dissociative theories, of hypnotic response, 22–23
effectiveness
for chronic pain, 155–159
directing toward a specific goal, 11–12
within positive therapeutic relationship, 8–9
empowering the patient, 9
ethical considerations in practice of, 221–225
to facilitating insight, 205–220
case example, 210–220
during first visit, 230
goal of, 228
hypnotherapy and, 227–230
hypnotic inductions and suggestions
methods for, 12–13
structure and individualization of, 13–14

hypnotic state, 22–24
hypnotizability, individual differences in, 9–10
for insomnia, 200
integration of, 87
with cognitive–behavioral interventions, 12
conscious and unconscious information processing, 91–92
coping skills, developing, 88–89
insight, developing, 89–91
relapse prevention, 91
symptom reduction, 87–88
length of hypnotic treatment, 230
presenting problems, 48
principles of, 7–15
professional resources, 227
recordings of, sessions, 224–225
self-hypnosis, learning, 230
for smoking cessation. *See* Smoking cessation
social/cognitive factors, 20–21
structure of first session, 57–66
dealing with myths and misconceptions, 58–60
hypnotic induction, 62–65. *See also* Hypnotic induction, in first session
post-hypnotic inquiry, 65–66
preparatory talk, 61–62
providing CD recording, at end of session, 66
rating of symptoms, 61
setting the treatment session goal, 60–61
for treatment of patient's presenting issue, 57–58
structure of fourth session
communicating session goals and approaches, 94–95
homework assignment and scheduling, at end of session, 97
hypnotic relaxation induction, 95–96
identifying integration methods, 94
post-hypnotic inquiry, 97
rating symptom of focus, 94
reviewing the patient's experience and progress, 92–93
setting the session goal, 93–94
structure of second session, 67–68
gathering information for individualization, 69–71
homework assignment and scheduling, at end of session, 76
individualized hypnotic induction, 72–75. *See also* Hypnotic induction, in second session
post-hypnotic inquiry, 75
rating of symptoms, 71
review of patient's progress with open-ended questions, 68–69
setting the session goal, 71
structure of third session, 78
gather information for individualization, 79
homework assignment and scheduling, at end of session, 85–86
hypnotic induction, 82–83
patient practice of self-hypnosis with minimal prompts, 83–84
post-hypnotic inquiry, 84–85
review patient's progress with hypnotic relaxation, 78
self-hypnosis, review steps and instructions for, 80–82
setting the session goal, 79–80
summarizing, 25
theoretical basis for, 17–25
therapeutic communication, involving, 10–11
therapeutic relaxation, 24–25
training through continuing education workshops, 227
uses of
bio-psycho-social formulation in treatment planning, 12
coping skills development, 14
facilitating insight, 14
relapse prevention, 14
symptom relief, 14

Hypnotic state, 10, 22
concept of adaptive dissociation, 23–24
dissociative theories of hypnotic response, 22–23
process of letting go, 11
Hypnotic suggestion, 4. *See also specific suggestions*
for anxiety management, 185
cognitive restructuring, 186
deepening relaxation, 186
mindfulness suggestions, 187
post-hypnotic suggestion, 187–188
visualization and exposure therapy, 186–187
formulation of, 28–29
for hot flashes
deepening hypnotic state and dissociation from, 174
individualization of, 171
mental imagery and suggestions for coolness, 173–174
positive imagery for future, 175
post-hypnotic suggestions, 174–175
relaxation, 173
self-hypnosis, 175
treatment, 173–175
individualization of, 13–14, 33
law of concentrated attention, 28
law of dominant affect, 29
law of reversed effect, 28–29
methods for, 12–13
for smoking cessation
comfort, 165
commitment, 165–166
dissociation from cravings, 166
positive imagery for benefits of, 167
post-hypnotic suggestions, 166
relaxation, 165
self-hypnosis, 166–167
targeting, for desired effect, 139
as three-step process, 29–30
verbal and nonverbal, 138
Hypnotic techniques, for treating pain, 150
Hypnotism, 2
Hypnotizability
and anxiety, 184–185
clinical research, 101–102
defined, 99
determination of resistance versus hypnotic ability, 100
diagnosis, 100–101
and eating disorders, 101
Elkins Hypnotizability Scale (EHS), 99, 148
administration protocol for, 111
constructs of, 105–108
development of, 102, 104–105
psychometric properties of, 108–111
scoring summary, 119
individual differences in, 9–10
induction, 112–118
alerting, 118
arm heaviness/immobilization, 113–114
arm levitation, 114–115
imagery involvement/dissociation, 115–116
positive hallucination, 116–118
post-hypnotic amnesia, 118
overview of scales, 102–104
patient assessment for pain management, 148
patient with experience of hypnotic relaxation, 101
and phobias, 101
post-hypnotic inquiry and scoring form, 119–124
reasons for assessing patient's hypnotic ability, 99–100
and resistance, 130–131
treatment planning, 100

Ideomotor responses
to facilitating insight, 207–208
use of, 140–141
Implication of response suggestion, 34
Indirect suggestions, 34–36
advantage and disadvantage of, 34
examples

implication of response, 34
questions as suggestions, 35
suggesting all possible responses, 35
suggestions that are truisms, 35
use of past experiences, 35–36
and permissive suggestions, 131–132
Individualization
gathering information for, in HRT, 69–71, 79–80
hypnotic inductions and, 46
of hypnotic suggestion, 13–14, 33
for hot flashes, 171
Informed consent, 222–223
Insight
affect bridge technique, 209–210
developing, 89–91
experiential system and, 205–206
HRT to facilitating, 205–220
case example, 210–220
hypnoprojective methods, 208–209
ideomotor responses to facilitating, 207–208
post-hypnotic suggestion, 210
trance management and abreactions, 206–207
Insomnia
assessment, 196
behavioral treatments for, 198
case example, 203–204
definition of, 195–196
HRT for, 200
hypnotic relaxation induction for improving sleep, 200–203
medications for, 197–198
sleep hygiene, 198
recommendations, 199
sleep restriction therapy, 199–200
sleep stages and age, 196–197
stimulus control instructions, 198–199
for improving sleep, 199
International Society of Hypnosis, 3

Janet, Pierre, 3

"Kinder and gentler" unconscious, 18

Laboratory of Hypnosis Research, 3
Law of concentrated attention, 28
Law of dominant affect, 29
Law of reversed effect, 28–29
Leading and pacing, process of, 30–31
Learned insomnia. *See* Primary insomnia
Licensure/professionalism, 224
Liebeault, Ambroise-Auguste, 2
Mental imagery
and dissociation, 39–40, 74
EHS, 107
induction, 115–116
scoring inquiry, 123
for reducing anxiety and headache, 64
for relaxation and deepening trance, 63–64
and suggestions for coolness, 173–174
and symptom reduction, 5
Mental status examination, 51
Mesmer, Franz Anton, 1
Mesmerism, 1–2
Metaphors, therapeutic, 141–142
Mind-Body Medicine Research Laboratory, 169, 227
Mind–body interventions, 5
Mindfulness suggestions, 187
Monoideism, 2
Motivation, 21
Muscular relaxation, 24, 25, 30
Myths and misconceptions, HRT dealing with, 58–60

"Neodissociation" theory, of hypnotic responding, 23
Nonbenzodiazepines, 197–198
Nonverbal and verbal hypnotic suggestions, 138

Orne, Martin, 3

Pacing
and leading, 30–31
suggestions for relaxation, 30

Pain management
alteration in pain sensation, 152–153
case example, transcript of HRT with chronic pain patient, 155–159
dissociation from pain experience, 151–152
hypnoanalgesia for, 154–155
hypnotic relaxation therapy (HRT) for, 147
hypnotic techniques for, 150
patient assessment for, 148
biopsychosocial factors, 148–149
emotional distress, 149
goals, 150
hypnotizability, 148
perception of pain, 149
suffering, 149, 153–154
post-hypnotic suggestions for, 155
questions to asking about pain description, 150
relaxation and pain reduction, 151
self-hypnosis suggestions for coping with pain, 154
Parasomnias, 197
Permissive suggestions
versus direct suggestions, 34
versus indirect suggestions, 131–132
Personality, dual-process theory of, 17–18
Phobias and hypnotizability, 101
Physical and emotional relaxation, 14, 24, 39, 88, 151, 230
Pittsburg Sleep Quality Index, 169
Positive hallucination
EHS, 107–108
induction, 116–118
scoring inquiry, 124
Positively worded suggestions, 31
Positron emission tomography (PET) scan, 22
Post-hypnotic amnesia
EHS, 108
induction, 118
scoring inquiry, 120
Post-hypnotic inquiry, HRT
first session in, 65–66
fourth session in, 97
and scoring form, 119–124
second session in, 75
third session in, 84–85
Post-hypnotic suggestions, 41–42, 65, 74
for anxiety, 187–188
facilitating insight, 210
for hot flashes, 174–175
for pain management, 155
and self-efficacy, 145
for smoking cessation, 166
Post-menopausal and hot flash symptoms, 169–181
Post-traumatic stress disorder (PTSD), 100–101
insomnia and, 196
treatment of, 140
Preparatory talk, 61–62
Presenting problems
case conceptualization and treatment planning, 47–55
history of, 49
identifying, and determining goals for HRT, 47–48
physical factors, 49
psychological factors, 49–50
social environment, 50
timeline and key events, 49
within unconscious/experiential system, 50–51
Primary gain, 128–129
Primary insomnia, 195–196
Privacy and confidentiality, 223
Professional judgments, 222
Professionalism/licensure, 224
Psychoanalysis, theories of, 2–3
Psychopathology, defense against, 129
Psychophysiological insomnia. *See* Primary insomnia

Questions
to asking about pain description, 150
as suggestions, 35

Rapid eye movement (REM) sleep, 197
Rational/conscious system
  and experiential/unconscious system, 19
  information processing, 91–92
  threat, 184
Recordings of HRT sessions, 224–225
Reinforcement, 31–32, 64
  of response, 40–41, 74
Relapse prevention, 14, 91
Relaxation, 63
  for hot flashes, 173
  pacing suggestions for, 30
  and pain reduction, 151
  physical and emotional, 14, 24, 39, 88, 151, 230
  response, 24
  for smoking cessation, 165
  therapeutic, 24–25
Research, in hypnotherapy applications, 101–102
Resistance
  authority problems, 128
  avoidance of confrontation, 129–130
  dealing with, 125
  defense against psychopathology, 129
  versus defiance, 126
  failure to adequately establishing rapport, 127
  fear of failure, 127
  fear of loss of control, 127
  hypnotizability and, 130–131
  inadequate preparation for hypnotic induction, 127
  inappropriate technique, 128
  induction for, 133–135
  management of, 130–131
  permissive and indirect suggestions, 131–132
  primary and secondary gain, 128–129
  sources of, 126
Response, implication of, 34
Rose-scent olfactory hallucination
  EHS, 107
  scoring inquiry, 124
Secondary gain, 129
Secondary insomnia, 196
Self-efficacy, concept of, 144–145
Self-hypnosis, 5, 8, 9, 14, 41–42, 77–78
  coping skills, developing, 88–89
  hypnotic induction following, 82–83
  instructions, 80–82
  learning, 230
  practicing with minimal prompts, 83–84
  for reduction of hot flashes, 170, 175
  review steps for, 80
  for smoking cessation, 164, 166–167
  suggestions for coping with pain, 154
6 D's, of chronic pain assessment, 148
Sleep difficulties, 196. *See also* Insomnia
Sleep hygiene, 198
  recommendations, 199
Sleep spindles, 197
Sleep stages and age, 196–197
Sleep window, 200
Smoking cessation
  assessment for, 162–163
  case example, 167–168
  general guidelines for HRT for, 163–164
  hypnotic suggestions for, 165–167
Social-psychological components, of HRT, 20–21
Society for Clinical and Experimental Hypnosis (SCEH), 3, 225, 227
Society for Psychological Hypnosis (SPH), 3, 225
Stanford Hypnotic Arm Levitation and Induction Test, 104
Stanford Hypnotic Clinical Scale, 103
Stanford Hypnotic Susceptibility Scale, Form C (SHSS: C), 102–103
Stanford Hypnotic Susceptibility Scale, Forms A and B (SHSS: A, B), 102
Stanford Hypnotic Susceptibility Scales (SHSS), 3–4
Sternbach's 6 D's, of chronic pain assessment, 148

Stimulus control instructions, 198–199
for improving sleep, 199
Suffering, pain and, 149, 153–154
Suggestions. *See also* Hypnotic suggestion; Hypnotic induction
for alerting, 42
creating positive expectancy, 32
deepening suggestions, 38–39
direct versus permissive suggestions, 34
ego-strengthening suggestions, 143–146
general, 33, 143
for generalized reality orientation (GRO) fading, 38
for glove analgesia, 32
for hypnoanalgesia, 154–155
for ideomotor response, 141, 207
indirect suggestions, 34–36
mindfulness suggestions, 187
pacing and leading suggestions, 30–31
permissive and indirect suggestions, 131–132
for physical and emotional relaxation, 88
positively worded suggestions, 31
post-hypnotic suggestions, 41–42
for relaxation, 30, 37–38
self-hypnosis suggestions for coping with pain, 154
for symptom alteration, 88
unconscious/experiential system processes, 36–37
verbal and nonverbal hypnotic suggestions, 138
Symptom reduction, 87–88

Therapeutic metaphors, use of, 141–142
Therapeutic relaxation, 24–25
Touch, use of, 138
Trance logic, 36
Trance management, 139–140
and abreactions, 206–207
Trance/hypnotic state, 10, 21
reinforcement and, 31–32
Truisms, 35, 141–142
Trust, 8

Unconscious minds, 59. *See also* Experiential/unconscious system
conceptualizations of, 17–18
and conscious minds, 17–19
presenting problems within, 50–51

Verbal and nonverbal hypnotic suggestions, 138
Visualization and exposure therapy, 186–187
Voice quality and intensity, variation in, 137–138

Waterloo–Stanford Group Scale of Hypnotic Susceptibility, 103
Weitzenhoffer, Andre, 3

Zaleplon, 197–198
Zolpidem, 197–198

www.ingramcontent.com/pod-product-compliance
Ingram Content Group UK Ltd.
Pitfield, Milton Keynes, MK11 3LW, UK
UKHW021845100926
8556IPUK00019B/1055

9 780826 199393